Directing for Community Theatre

Directing for Community Theatre is a primer for the amateur director working in community theatre. With an emphasis on preparedness, this book gives the amateur director the tools and techniques needed to effectively work on a community theatre production. Covering play analysis, blocking, staging, communication, and working with actors, designers, and other theatre personnel, this how-to book is designed to have the community theatre director up and running quickly, with full knowledge of how to direct a show. The book also contains sample forms and guidelines, including acting analysis, character analysis, rehearsal schedule, audition form, prop list, and blocking plans. *Directing for Community Theatre* is written for the community theatre participant who is interested, or already cast, in the role of the director.

Daniel L. Patterson is Professor Emeritus of Keene State College in New Hampshire, where he taught for 40 years and directed over 40 productions. He received two Kennedy Center medallions for his work with the Kennedy Center American College Theatre Festival. He is an MFA graduate of the University of Texas in Austin (1975) and was one of the co-founders of the TheatreWorks company in Colorado Springs in 1975. He has acted in 18 of Shakespeare's plays in various companies around the country. Professor Patterson also worked with the Association for Theatre in Higher Education where he served as a director and an actor in their new play development program.

Directing for Community Theatre

Daniel L. Patterson

Routledge
Taylor & Francis Group
NEW YORK AND LONDON

Designed cover image: *Dracula* by Bram Stoker. Photo © Jeremy Robarge.
Projection designer: Jeremy Robarge. Scenic designer: Tiffany (Dalian) Abatino

First published 2023
by Routledge
605 Third Avenue, New York, NY 10158

and by Routledge
4 Park Square, Milton Park, Abingdon, Oxon, OX14 4RN

Routledge is an imprint of the Taylor & Francis Group, an informa business

© 2023 Daniel L. Patterson

The right of Daniel L. Patterson to be identified as author of this work has been asserted in accordance with sections 77 and 78 of the Copyright, Designs and Patents Act 1988.

All rights reserved. No part of this book may be reprinted or reproduced or utilised in any form or by any electronic, mechanical, or other means, now known or hereafter invented, including photocopying and recording, or in any information storage or retrieval system, without permission in writing from the publishers.

Trademark notice: Product or corporate names may be trademarks or registered trademarks, and are used only for identification and explanation without intent to infringe.

Library of Congress Cataloging-in-Publication Data
Names: Patterson, Daniel L., author.
Title: Directing for community theatre / Daniel L. Patterson.
Description: New York, NY : Routledge, 2023. | Includes bibliographical references.
Identifiers: LCCN 2022056580 (print) | LCCN 2022056581 (ebook) |
ISBN 9781032418841 (hardback) | ISBN 9781032418834 (paperback) |
ISBN 9781003360216 (ebook)
Subjects: LCSH: Amateur theater—Production and direction—Handbooks, manuals, etc. | Community theater.
Classification: LCC PN3156 .P38 2023 (print) | LCC PN3156 (ebook) |
DDC 792.01—dc23/eng/20230209
LC record available at https://lccn.loc.gov/2022056580
LC ebook record available at https://lccn.loc.gov/2022056581

ISBN: 978-1-032-41884-1 (hbk)
ISBN: 978-1-032-41883-4 (pbk)
ISBN: 978-1-003-36021-6 (ebk)

DOI: 10.4324/9781003360216

Typeset in Times New Roman
by codeMantra

Dedication

To the love of my life and the best literary and dramatic critic I know: my wife, Cheryl Perry.

To my advisor and mentor at San Jacinto Jr. College in Pasadena, Texas (1968–70): Jerry Rollins Powell, who taught me to behave realistically in the imaginary circumstances of the play.

To my advisor and mentor at the Theatre Department of the University of Texas at Austin (1970–75): Dr. Francis Hodge, who taught me about Dramatic Action and Picturization, which opened all the rest of the doors in Wonderland.

Contents

1	Introduction	1
2	Obsession	5
3	Blocking Notes	7
4	Stages of Rehearsal	10
5	A Directing Primer	21
6	Play Analysis	28
7	Production Organization	52
8	Directors and Design	65
9	The Visual Tools	79
10	Acting Exercises	95
11	Playwrighting	101
12	Memorization	107
13	Ethics and Behavior	111
14	Diversity	119
15	The Stage Manager	122
	Appendix 1: Sample of an Analysis of Given Circumstances	127
	Appendix 2: Sample of an Analysis of Idea	132
	Appendix 3: Sample of a Character Analysis	136
	Appendix 4: Sample of an Analysis of Dialogue	144
	Appendix 5: A Sample Dramatic Action Analysis	150

Appendix 6: Sample of a Character–Scene Chart	153
Appendix 7: Samples of Rehearsal Schedules	154
Appendix 8: Sample Audition Forms	158
Appendix 9: A Sample Prop List for *Dracula* by Steven Dietz	163
Appendix 10: Sample Character Sketches	168
Appendix 11: Sample Photocall Lists	171
Appendix 12: Sample Sound Concept Themes and Bridges	173
Appendix 13: A Sample Sound Concept	180
Appendix 14: A Sample Blocking Groundplan	182
Appendix 15: A Sample Blocking Script	184
Appendix 16: A Sample Master Movement Plan	186
Appendix 17: A Sample Groundplan	187
Appendix 18: The Designer's Homework	189
Index	*193*

1 Introduction

I have spent forty plus years acting, directing, and teaching Acting and Directing. I have directed for educational theatre, and community theatre. I have not directed professionally, and so cannot speak knowledgeably about professional directing. I certainly can, however, speak to directing on the amateur level. I have also worked extensively in community theatre as an actor, which has given me many close-up experiences watching others direct. I majored in Directing and studied with one of the major academic influences on directing (Dr. Francis Hodge). I taught directing for forty years and have directed so many shows that I have literally lost count. I feel that I have something to say about the techniques and skills necessary to direct. It is mostly from watching so many inexperienced directors fumbling around trying to figure out what to do and making the same rudimentary mistakes over and over, that I decided to write this book.

I have been very lucky to study with some real geniuses in the theatre. I found a real mentor in Jerry Rollins Powell while attending a Junior College in Texas. He gave me much needed experience and wouldn't accept crap from me. He once stopped me during rehearsal one day and said "That thing you're doing? Stop it." I said, "I'm acting." He said, "Yes that."

At the University of Texas at Austin, I was mentored in Directing by an amazing gentleman in the person of Dr. Francis Hodge. James Moll was my acting mentor and was the one who cast me over and over again. If you learn by doing, he was the one who gave me the opportunity to do so. Dr. Paul Reinhardt was a genius costume designer, as was Dr. John Rothgeb (who was a former student of the legendary scene painter, Jo Mielziner) in scenic design, and Dr. Webster Smalley who taught playwriting. I even learned about lighting design from Dr. David Nancarrow. It was an amazing faculty and I count myself lucky to have been placed among them. I wasn't required to take all the design courses but did anyway, because Dr. Hodge preached that a good director should know a little about everything. I also owe a big debt of thanks to Dr. John Brokaw, who taught me an appreciation for theatre history. I don't think he knew it at the time, because I was such a lousy student (his class was at 8am and I was always in rehearsal late the night before). He taught me that it's not always necessary to know an answer *as long as you know a good source in which to find it.*

It is my profound belief that, no matter at what level one is directing, the same painstaking preparation is required. There is no substitute for preparation. Directors who seem ill-prepared are not necessarily lazy, they are likely just unaware how to prepare. One simply cannot just read the play five times and then show up on the first day of auditions ready to direct.

A director must have a vision for a production. That doesn't mean that one will see the entire thing completely conceived, but one needs to begin imagining it visually and aurally when one reads it. When I directed *Camille* by Alexandre Dumas, several scenes came alive for me. The first was the duel between Gaston and the Baron. This was not a scene that was described either in the book or the play, but simply reported after the fact. In my mind, I saw a bare stage against a sky background with figures in stark silhouette and, perhaps the shadow of a tree to indicate a clearing in the woods. The music that I envisioned was from the soundtrack of Stanley Kubrick's film *Barry Lyndon*, on which Handel's *Sarabande* was played entirely on tympani. I envisioned the characters separated into two groups, the duelists and their seconds. The formal duel ensued with two figures back-to-back, pacing off ten steps, turning and firing. One falls. The offstage gunshots were very loud. This image stayed with me for days. It was one of the first clear images I had of the play. Another scene was after Marguerite Gautier (Camille) dies and Gaston goes to her grave with a letter Camille wrote to him just before she died. As he reads, he sinks to the ground with one hand on top of her gravestone. Marguerite appears on the other side of the gravestone and speaks the letter aloud. As she reaches the end, she places her hand down on top of his. Here is the last moment as I described it in my version of the script:

> "I have nothing to leave you except the knowledge that my love for you will be eternal. (*Margueritte has come near Armand and, on the last word, she reaches out and puts her hand over his on the headstone.*) Marguerite." (*Armand, weeping, bends to place the camelias on her grave as the lights fade.*)

It was shamelessly romantic and that is the feeling I wanted from the play. That is what I mean about having a vision. There must be something that reaches out and grabs you when you first read the play that compels you to want to direct it. In my forty plus years of directing, I always got to choose my own material, and I always chose material that I had emotional reactions to. I directed *Noises Off* by Michael Frayn and another one entitled *Inspecting Carol* by Daniel Sullivan because they made me laugh uncontrollably. Another one was called *Those That Play the Clowns* by Michael Stewart, about the players in *Hamlet*. In each instance I could not stop laughing as I read them. Since I was in bed with my wife at the time, I was keeping her from falling asleep and ended up having to relate the entire story to her in the wee small hours. It never failed to get us both laughing. It doesn't always happen like that, but more often than not, it will. It gets your creative juices flowing.

Of course, one doesn't always get to choose one's material. Circumstances arise in which directors are assigned to a project by the leaders of the group. In those cases, one must decide if there is sufficient merit in the material to keep one stimulated. In many cases, turning down the project will mean that one may not be selected the next time a project comes up. In any case, I am adamant about a director needing to find some kind of creative inspiration in the material. If a play is well written, there will be indications of the playwright's passion in it. That alone is often enough to get the juices flowing. If the material is not one's "cup of tea", then it may be prudent to take a pass. However, my feeling is that almost anything can be stimulating to work on with the exercise of one's imagination.

Another example of a vision came to me when I directed Arthur Miller's *After the Fall*. I always felt that the audience needed to understand the context of the play a little more from the beginning. I imagined the stage lit only upstage where we see a group of hospital personnel standing around a gurney and dressed as for surgery. The sound of a heart monitor beeps rhythmically, then suddenly flatlines into a single tone. The tone continues for a beat and then becomes the sound of a single child's clear tenor singing the same note which then becomes a religious choral piece. Quentin leaves the upstage group and comes downstage to a single spot, where he begins to speak to the audience. At the end of the play, we return to the same image upstage with Quentin speaking downstage. The tone begins again in flatline. As Quentin moves up to embrace his new life with his new wife, Holga, the ghosts of his past begin to fade and the rhythmic "beep" of the heart monitor returns. Presenting the play with this framework implies that Quentin had "died" and now he has returned to life. So, the entire play is Quentin trying to decide between living and dying. This is not described by Miller but was entirely my invention and I had a sound designer who understood perfectly what I wanted. The meshing of the "flatline" tone with the child's tenor was seamless. In all modesty, it was an incredibly moving moment. In this vision, the entire play takes place while Quentin is "between" life and death, struggling to find a reason to continue living.

The methods in this book for preparation are painstaking, detailed, and involve a lot of work. The more you do, the better prepared you will be when it comes to meetings with designers, and casting and rehearsing the play. I was listening to a pro football player discussing a famous quarterback that he had worked with. He kept stressing that the thing that differentiated this quarterback from everyone else was the amount of time he spent preparing. Of course, this quarterback was making upwards of twenty million a year.

If I were making that kind of money, I'd be able to spend all my time rigorously preparing as well, having nothing else to do. I've heard the same things said about Meryl Streep (again, she makes millions a year).

"Having nothing else to do". This might be the thing that sets the professionals apart from the amateurs. In the amateur world we work in, we all have other jobs that require our time, energy, and attention. This applies to everyone in your cast as well. Keep it in mind. We all have other things that require our attention. Taking the time to work in a concentrated way on a play is not always an easy thing for us to do. *For everyone involved in the production of a play in community theatre, there must be some sacrifice of time.* One reason I prefer community theatre over professional theatre is that the people involved are there solely because they *love it* and for no other reason. Very few if any are being paid and they all have other lives that need to be put on hold for a time. What a sacrifice that is! It truly is an immense sacrifice that cannot be understated. Why do we do it? There has been some conjecture that this desire and need to tell stories and share other people's lives and cultures is as much a part of our basic life make-up as the need for food and shelter and love.

Bibliography

Brockett, Oscar G., Robert J. Ball, and Andrew Carlson. *The Essential Theatre*, 11th ed. Boston, MA: Cengage Learning, 2016.

Brockett, Oscar Gross. *The Theatre: An Introduction*, 4th ed. Fort Worth, TX: Holt, Rinehart & Winston, 1979.

Brook, Peter. *The Empty Space*. New York: Atheneum Publishers, 1968.

Cohen, Leah Hager. *The Stuff of Dreams: Behind the Scenes of an American Community Theatre*. New York: Penguin Putnam, 2001. (*One of the best overviews of Community Theatre history and philosophy that I have ever read.*)

Downs, William Missouri. *The Art of Theatre: Then and Now*, 4th ed. Boston, MA: Cengage Learning, 2017.

Whiting, Frank M. *An Introduction to the Theatre*. New York: Harper & Brothers, 1961.

2 Obsession

More than a few books on theatre remark on the single-mindedness of theatre people in both professional and amateur venues. There is even a myth that one of the larger and more well-respected actor-training programs in this country tells incoming students that "Acting is a disease and we want to see if you have it". While that may be a little extreme, there is certainly more than just a nugget of truth here. Most of us are truly obsessed with this creative thing we do. It's very easy to let this little "pretending" game we do get under our skin. I recently polled a number of my colleagues about what motivated them to go into theatre. Among the answers I received were an astonishing number of replies that indicated that most of these people could not imagine having gone into any other field.

Jay Leno remarked on a talk-show (not his own) recently that he practiced stand-up comedy every day. He couldn't imagine anyone saying that this was something they wanted to do *only* a couple of times a week. Even at the height of his popularity and success, he goes out to perform in comedy clubs, he estimates, "about 300 days of the year". The implication here is that this thing we do amounts to nothing less than an obsession. It is something that we need to do and we can't imagine life without it.

I wonder if this isn't also a more primal urge. Perhaps there is something in us (although admittedly perhaps not all of us) that must tell stories, get involved in fantasy worlds, and use our imaginations and our creative impulses. Perhaps it is a need as basic to us as food and shelter and love. Have I said that before? Yes! Think about it. For some of us, it is a *primal* need.

Does this seem a bit unhealthy? Certainly, the example given above of the "disease" concept implies something that is not necessarily desirable or healthy. Who wants to have a disease that they can't cure? Is it unhealthy? Is the need for food unhealthy? Or shelter? Or love? Of course, we must all guard against the unhealthy version of "obsession" where one let's every other aspect of life go in order to feed the addiction. I recently read a joke: "Give a person tickets to the theatre and they'll be entertained for an evening. Teach a person to *do* theatre and they'll be poor for a lifetime." Fortunately, most of us who do community theatre are not in the "addict"

DOI: 10.4324/9781003360216-2

category and do what we do simply for the fun and social stimulation of the practice. We must thank our lucky stars that the "high" we get from doing theatre does not take over our lives. It is ultimately rewarding, but not destructive.

Leah Hager Cohen, in her excellent book about Community Theatre *The Stuff of Dreams*, profiles a number of people working in community theatre for whom the idea of doing theatre is something that they gleefully run off to after a long hard day at their "normal" jobs. These are people who will take time off from their jobs as "tech week" approaches for a community theatre production so that they can devote enough time to the job to get it done properly. And virtually none of the many thousands of workers in community theatre across this country are paid at all, and even those who are paid receive a tiny pittance.

The answer is obviously that we do this kind of work because we love it. We gain something from it that makes us feel better about ourselves and perhaps understand better our place in the world. And we find it rewarding that we can share this understanding with our audiences. Even those who are highly paid for doing this kind of thing are often heard to comment, "Oh, I would do this for nothing, who doesn't like being paid to do something that you love?" Easy for them to say. But I, personally, find my "pay" in the creative and artistic high of making others laugh or cry at the foibles and adventures of the imaginary people in the imaginary world that we create on the stage.

3 Blocking Notes

I want to bring this up early because it is about the "physicalization" of an action. The great acting teacher, Constantin Stanislavski, developed something he called "the method of physical action", which has been somewhat erroneously foreshortened to "The Method". The important thing to remember is that the expression of action and even emotion was, to Stanisavski, a physical thing and if you could find that physicality, you could find a character and reach an audience.

Blocking is the movement of actors around the stage for the purposes of illustrating the action both for the actor and for the audience. That is why a basic understanding of action is necessary. Action is what the characters are *doing* to, for, or at other characters in order to attain their goals. Action involves a type of forcing to be enacted on another character. When I throw an action at another character, that character receives the action, reacts to it, and responds by throwing an action back at me. This is the basic nature of conflict and is often referred to as "reciprocation". An action may involve many internals for a character, but it is not truly an action until it becomes externalized. I can "be angry with you", but that, in itself, is not an action. I must manifest that anger in a specific way. In a larger sense, keep the audience in mind here, as well. How do they know that you are angry with the other character unless you can give them something to hear or see that gives them a sense of that feeling. It is always far too easy to confuse action with emotion. Almost any description of an action that describes a "state of being" is not describing an action. It describes the motivation for an action. I can "be in love with you", but the action is when I "speak to you tenderly" or "caress your cheek". The lines of dialogue always give the clues.

Different actions create different movements. Movement basically conforms to a repulsion/attraction scenario. An action is very broadly either forward, away, or stationary. Each of these basic compositional concepts assumes different meanings and foci when animated with gesture and facial expression as well as vocal expression. The result is literally hundreds of variations of physicality for each line of the play.

DOI: 10.4324/9781003360216-3

Should there be movement on each line? Not necessarily, because stillness is also important, although stillness is also animated by facial expression. The question is when to use motion and when to use stillness.

Can there be movement without speaking? Absolutely. In our day and age, we have become much more visually oriented than past generations. Many modern movies are almost exclusively visual in illustration and contain very little dialogue. The stage is more of a balance between the visual and the aural. But much meaning can be communicated to an audience by simple stage business without the need for a lot of talking. There have been plays written that are "plays without dialogue", although these are more experimental in nature and tend to be very short. Nevertheless, it is important to keep in mind that "pictures are often worth a thousand words".

Blocking is the director's vision of the physical forces at work with each line. Use your instincts. If the character's action is "teasing" or "bullying" or "stalling" or "avoiding", she will move differently for each. "Teasing" conjures a kind of indirect movement. "Bullying" conjures a kind of direct attack. "Stalling" conjures a stasis or even a backwards movement. "Avoidance" definitely conjures an "away" kind of movement. Generally speaking, all movement conforms to the concept of "forward", "backward", and "standing still".

The difference between actor instincts and directorial instincts is merely that, instead of focusing on only one character, the director must focus on all characters.

This could be why directing is a good course of study for actors. It begins to make one aware of the interplay of actions physically between two or more characters. One suddenly begins to think about how one wants the other actor to react to what is being done to them instead of just concentrating on what one is doing.

Many people say there is a dichotomy here. If one is thinking about the other characters, then one is not "in character" or "in the moment". I disagree because I think that characters are *always* interested in the effect of what they are doing on others, the same way we as people are. Sometimes it's conscious, sometimes its subconscious. Either way it doesn't hurt to think about it and its *essential* for the director to think about it.

Blocking will be explored more in Chapter 4: Stages of Rehearsal (see Appendix 14, 15, 16).

Bibliography

Barton, Robert. *Acting Onstage and Off*, 6th ed. Belmont, CA: Wadsworth Publishing, 2011.
Benedetti, Richard. *The Actor at Work*. Englewood Cliffs, NJ: Prentice-Hall, 1981.
Brockett, Oscar Gross. *The Theatre: An Introduction*, 4th ed. New York: Holt, Rinehart & Winston, 1979.

Brook, Peter. *The Empty Space.* New York: Atheneum Publishers, 1968.
Carter, Conrad, A. J. Bradbury, and W. R. B. Howard. *The Production and Staging of Plays.* New York: Arc Books, 1963.
Clurman, Harold. *On Directing.* New York: Macmillan, 1972.
Cole, Toby, and Helen Krich Chinoy, eds. *Directors on Directing*, 2nd rev. ed., Indianapolis, IN: Bobbs-Merrill, 1963.
Cole, Toby, and Helen Krich Chinoy. *Directing the Play.* Indianapolis, IN: Bobbs-Merrill, 1953.
Dean, Alexander, and Lawrence Carra, *Fundamentals of Play Directing*, 5th ed. Long Grove, IL: Waveland Press, 2009.
Dietrich, John E., *Play Direction*, 2nd ed. Englewood Cliffs, NJ: Prentice-Hall, 1983.
Dolman, John Jr., and Richard K. Knaub. *The Art of Play Production.* New York: Harper & Rowe, 1973.
Guskin, Harold, and Kevin Kline. *How to Stop Acting*, 1st ed. Farrar, Straus & Giroux, 2003.
Hagen, Uta, and Frankel Haskel. *Respect For Acting.* New York: Macmillan, 1973.
Hodge, Francis and Michael McLain. *Play Directing: Analysis, Communication, and Style*, 7th ed. New York: Routledge, 2009.
Lessac, Arthur. *The Use and Training of the Human Body.* Pondicherry, India: Lessac Research, 1978.
McGaw, Charles. *Acting Is Believing.* New York: Holt, Rinehart, & Winston, 1980.
Seivers, W. David, Harry E. Stiver, Jr., and Stanley Kahan. *Directing for the Theatre.* Dubuque, IA: Wm C. Brown Company, 1974.

4   Stages of Rehearsal

A production must grow throughout the rehearsal period (just as the characterizations of the actors). There is a learning curve that can't be skipped. There is no such thing as "instant theatre (or acting)". One of the most common mistakes of young and inexperienced artists is trying to rush things. There is a tendency to want immediate results and instant gratification (a trend that is simply a reflection of our "fast-food" society). As a result, actors try to "act" too soon. And directors push them in that direction. They begin to paste superficial attitudes, gestures, faces, etc. on their characters from the first reading on. Of course, most seasoned artists have realized that this is a very bad way to work. A personality is constantly growing and always in flux. It has taken a person the number of years they are to become the person that they are today. They will probably be even a bit different tomorrow, and certainly a lot different in several years. It takes years to grow a "real" personality. When we are trying to create, why do we not understand that it will take a little time? Impatience? Probably. Stress? Time pressure? I don't think I have been involved in a single production where everyone didn't think they could have used just one more week of rehearsal by the time the play opened. I used to feel that approximately forty hours of rehearsal was a good average. When one is working three nights a week for three hours at a time, that gives me roughly four to five weeks before beginning tech and dress rehearsals. In the educational world, six weeks of rehearsal was typical. Community theatre is roughly the same. I have a friend who likes to take twelve weeks to rehearse, which seems to me to be a bit long. The Moscow Art Theatre under Stanislavski liked to work on a piece for up to a year! None of us have that kind of luxury or stamina. Still, one should have a little patience. One should not try to jump in full bore. One should allow the production to grow.

First Reading

First reading should be just that, a reading. Often called a "table read". It is natural to want to experiment with voices and inflections, pauses and punctuation at the first rehearsal. That's fine. Never be afraid to experiment. But don't worry about trying to "act". The build of emotion, the ebb and flow of conflict, and the rhythm and timing of the play will not happen all at once. It shouldn't. If it does, I would be extremely suspicious. Besides, if all of that is present at the first reading, then you have nowhere to go. The best thing that a director ever said to me was when, as a young actor fresh out of high-school I began to "act" at the first reading of a play I had been cast in in college. This director just looked at me and said, "stop that". I was, of course, confused and asked him what he wanted me to stop. He said, "That thing you're doing." I told him that I was trying to "act". He said "Yes, that. Stop it." He went on: "Just read it, try to sound like you are having a normal conversation." (I was fresh from doing a "classical" piece in High School, and was doing my best "classical" voice.) It was an immediate shock to me. It was also an immediate wake-up call. I had not really been acting up to that point, I had simply been doing "voices".

The first reading of a play is for the purpose of hearing it read by all of the people who will be actually playing all of the parts. Its function is mostly to "hear" the play for the first time. It is also a time to firm up rehearsal schedules, fill out forms, and take care of a lot of the minutiae of business that accompanies the first meeting of all of the people involved in the production. It is also usually excruciating for the inexperienced director because there is virtually nothing happening the way he or she envisioned it. The image that always enters my mind is the wonderful scene from the movie "*All That Jazz*" by and about Bob Fosse. The scene is the first reading of the new musical that he is directing. At some point after the actors begin reading, all of the ambient sound of the room fades away and we hear only the nervous shuffling of the director as he stubs out and lights a new cigarette, repositions his chair, takes deep breaths, and finally snaps a pencil in half behind his back and lets the pieces fall to the floor. We see past his head all of the actors reading and laughing and having a great time. The director is obviously not. But he keeps up a public smile.

Now that, of course, is a bit extreme. Any director worth his salt is not going to be expecting a lot from the first rehearsal. In fact, there are many directors who skip this stage altogether and jump into the first blocking rehearsal. That's a bad idea because you need that first "table read" to get everyone familiar with the language and pronunciations and meanings of words, etc.

But the point is that the actor should not really be trying to "push" the character forward at this rehearsal. The first few weeks of rehearsal should be devoted to trying to "find" the character. The character should begin to appear in layers as new discoveries are made at rehearsal. Each rehearsal provides a series of new discoveries and revelations which add yet another layer of understanding for the actor. In this way, the character is built up gradually in many layers over the weeks of rehearsal. The important thing for the actor to understand is that it *will* happen. One does not have to *force* it to happen. If the play is well written, the character is there. The playwright has provided a lot of clues and the actor will be discovering these as well as seeing the insights of the other actors about their characters and the relationships between them.

The active force at work here is almost outside of your control. If you simply lay back and "let" things come through, most of the time they will.

The best example that I can give of this (and one of the first times that I noticed the principle at work), was a show I was acting in called *The House of Blue Leaves* by John Guare. I was playing Artie Shaughnessy. I was trying to work on my new-found discovery: the principle of not pushing, of letting the character come out on its own. At one point, mid-way through rehearsals, the director came to me and said: "I really have been enjoying the work that you are doing with the dialect for this character." I was not aware that I had been doing any sort of dialect. By not imposing my will on the development of the character and the script, I had unconsciously allowed the natural rhythms of the dialogue to go to work on their own. The playwright had written the play with an ear toward the subtle phrasings and rhythms of the "Brooklyn" manner of speaking. By not forcing it, I had allowed it to happen. At another point in the rehearsals, the director also praised me for my "concentration" and "active listening". Again, I had been simply trying to listen with the character's ear and think with the character's mind, leaving my own ego out of it. As a result, all of my reactions were coming to me naturally, springing from the character, rather than from the me.

Blocking

The first rehearsals after the reading stage (which can range from one to several rehearsals), usually involve getting the actors on their feet and beginning to flesh out the physicalization of the play. Physicalization is a term used here in lieu of the old "illustration". Many theatre people shy away from the word "illustration" because it carries implications of superficiality with it. That's fine, because superficiality is exactly what should be avoided. Physicalization means that the impulse to *move* in the fleshing out of a play should spring from within the characters as actors are involved in trying to understand and "illustrate" the conflicts springing from the circumstances of the play. Several acting books that I have read call this "organic blocking" and it really is the best term. Any movement by a character must come from somewhere within the character. Blocking that is simply "traffic management" for the purpose of creating "attractive compositions" is usually less than useless and will not "feel" right to an actor or a director. I believe that there are always going to be times on the stage where "traffic management" is necessary, but most productions try to keep these moments down to a minimum. In other words, each movement performed by an actor on the stage needs to have a meaning and a motivation. That is what "blocking" is for.

Another way to think of blocking is as a means of communicating to the audience. One of the really good rules for the theatre that I have heard is that "an audience cannot read your mind; you must find some way to let them know what is going on".

This is, of course, a direct contradiction of the ideal that, in the illusion of the play, nothing exists for the actor/character except the circumstances of the world of the play. I disagree. An actor needs to be aware of the dual reality of the stage. There is the reality of the world of the play, and there is the reality of the world of the stage. This is what prevents any actor from becoming so immersed in a character that he loses sight of his own personality. I do not think that this is at all possible, and even if it were it would be extremely detrimental to a production. The audience is part of the experience and they cannot and will not be denied. One needs to be as totally in character as possible, and yet still be able to find where the light is on the stage and where the props are in the pockets. It is impossible to deny this dual awareness.

There are several types of blocking rehearsal. The first is the rehearsal in which the director blocks the play. This usually happens because the director has sat down and, over a period of time, thought out the series of physical images that he or she feels best illustrate the story and the conflicts of the play. A good director tries to be the actor in these private sessions, constantly looking for meaning and motivation in the physicalization of the play. When this director gives blocking, it is usually because he or she has a strong reason to support each movement. It becomes the actors' job to discern what the director has in mind. The second type of blocking rehearsal, which takes more time but which is more "organic" is the type of rehearsal in which the director encourages the actor to explore the movement potentials in each scene. The blocking for each scene is thus "improvised" and, through a long series of rehearsals, is usually distilled down to the "best" choices. The actor and director have to work very closely in this manner and usually the final result is a successful blending of the creative abilities of both. This is not to say that the first method cannot achieve such a blending, but it is simply done in turns: first, the director; then, the actor. This first method is favored by directors who are laboring under time constrictions (four to five weeks of rehearsal, for instance.) and/or who are working with inexperienced actors. It allows the director to give the show a rough shape, which communicates to the actor all of the thought process he or she has put into the play up to that point. This then becomes the jumping off point for exploration and experimentation. The initial blocking usually changes significantly before opening night as the actors' input is blended into the directors' vision. The biggest drawback to the "improvisational" approach to blocking is that a lot of time is spent searching for the right path to the illustration of the action. It's fine if you have the time to spend doing that (a nice, luxurious eight weeks to rehearse), but most productions I have been involved with are under extreme time pressures and that casual approach is just not efficient.

Both techniques are equally valid and are only limited by two potentially damaging factors: lack of preparation on the part of the director, and/or lack of imagination on the part of the actor. If either of these factors is present, the process will suffer.

Blocking rehearsals are the time for exploring the physicality of the character and the play. It provides time for experimentation and exploration. It allows the actor yet more time in which to build the layers of characterization.

Working

The next stage of rehearsals is the working rehearsals or detail stage. After the initial blocking in which the show begins to find a rough shape physically, the rehearsals then begin to focus more minutely on each scene and each moment. These rehearsals take longer and begin to focus on the moment-by-moment details that flesh out scenes even more. When I'm directing, I like to call these "work-throughs". Thoughtful directors will try to estimate how much time it will take to rehearse each scene and then call only the actors who are needed for these scenes. It is not always easy to anticipate how long it will take to work on something though, and that is why these rehearsals often take longer than anticipated. This frequently means that you will be called for a rehearsal at a certain time and end up having to wait as the previous scene is running long. As an actor, one should not get upset or frustrated with these waits. You can use the time to go over lines, discuss interpretation with other cast, even do some vocal or physical warm-ups. (Note: Actors should always come to each rehearsal mentally and physically prepared to rehearse. Do not waste others' time by not being prepared. It is one of the worst faux-pas of the theatre.)

A general rule of thumb for directors is that it usually takes about a minute for each page of dialogue. Of course, this will vary with the brevity or denseness of the dialogue. But one does not schedule a rehearsal for that amount of time because it will obviously take more time to work on a page than it does to perform it. My rule of thumb is to allow more time than I think is necessary. That way, if I run short, the only one whose time is wasted is mine, not the actors. If I run long, then I've tried to allow for that. There will always be times when you will run long, it is not something that can be rigidly controlled. But since you are working with actors who are generally volunteering their time (in community theatre), you can avoid a lot of ill will by trying to accurately judge the amount of time needed and not keep actors waiting, or worse, not even getting to them at all in that rehearsal period.

The work-through stage is obviously one of the most productive times as there is time to really explore, experiment, question, and evolve. Obviously more layers of perception and understanding as well as physicalization are discovered. The characters begin to become deeper and more three-dimensional. The actors will still have the script in their hand at this time and so there should be no distractions to mental concentration (though many actors are by now trying to learn lines and may be fumbling). It is perhaps ideal for them to not be trying to memorize lines during this stage, because they need to be able to focus on characterization. Near the end of the "work-through" stage is the more appropriate time to work lines. I am often asked if I want lines off right after the first rehearsal (though I have only met one or two actors who were really capable of doing that). I maintain that you need to have a certain amount of time with the text in your hand. The actual physical appearance of the pages and the words can be a help in jogging the memory for both blocking and lines during this period. I think the danger of learning lines too early (aside from the tendency to set things in stone once the script is gone) is that there are lots of clues that need to be learned from the way the play is written. Unless you have a photographic memory, once the script is out of your hand you do not have references to the stage directions, or even the punctuation.

There is a school of thought concerning Shakespeare that the punctuation used in the First Folio (which is perhaps the closest thing we have to Shakespeare's actual written script) contains many clues to the actual interpretation of the lines. If you pay close attention to reading the lines using the punctuation written by the playwright, you will find that there is a "sound" that the writer is trying to express. This is often thought of as the musical notation of the play. Any writer for the stage with any talent "hears" the dialogue in addition to mentally "seeing" it on the page. The sound that the writer hears is expressed by the words and *just as importantly*, the punctuation. A period means a finish, a comma means a pause, an ellipsis (...) can mean an unfinished thought or sometimes a line that is cut off by another character. Underlined or italicized words are generally meant to have an emphasis. Stage directions such as "(*weakly*)" obviously provide clues as to the interpretation of the line. If you pay close attention to this "music" it will provide many clues to understanding. It is very important to try to stay very close to the text as written for a while in rehearsals before departing from the playwright's intentions and adding your own pauses and emphasis. A director that I respected a lot once told us: "You have to earn your pauses." A very good way of saying that one does not just throw in dramatic pauses arbitrarily, but uses them only when they count the most. Of course, that same principle applies to anything.

Any technique that is overused has a lulling effect so that the audience becomes used to it and it loses effectiveness. I once sat through a Greek play which had the actors yelling through the entire performance in what was supposed to be grief and passion. It got so monotonous that I almost fell asleep. It would have been so much more effective if the yelling had been saved for those moments when the characters just truly couldn't contain themselves anymore. Save the dramatic pause for the moment when it will truly do the most good. The same applies to climactic composition: when the actors get very close. It should be saved for the moments when the characters are truly compelled to come together. If the characters are constantly blocked very close together, the device loses its effectiveness at the end of the scene when the lovers, for example, truly do actually come together.

Memorization

This stage of rehearsals is the most necessary, but the most excruciating. Virtually nothing can happen during this stage of rehearsal concerning character development. The play cannot progress to a new plateau of richness until this stage is past. While the actors are learning their lines, the only things going through their minds will be, of necessity, "what is my next line". Nuance is gone, character is gone. Everything hangs in limbo, waiting for the actors to emerge from the other side of darkness into the light. There is no sense getting tense about this stage, *it is a necessary evil*. One tries to get past it as quickly as possible, but one doesn't try to rush it. One just has to have patience and hang in there. It is vitally important to have someone "watch book" during these rehearsals. This means that someone must follow closely along in the script and give the actors prompts when they call for them. My general rule is not to give a line unless someone calls for it by saying "line" or "cue". I tell my actors that simply looking expectantly toward the stage manager (SM) is not sufficient. You must call for it. There is no shame to be attached to it. There is no competition (except perhaps with yourself). A prompt needs to be given in a *clear, loud voice and generally all that is needed is the first three words of the line*. If more is needed, then the actor can call for "more". It really becomes a judgement call and requires a good stage manager to know when to give cues that the actors do not call for. Obviously if three lines of dialogue are skipped, then there is a need to stop and go back. If someone is truly lost and helpless and doesn't even know it is their line that is missing, then the SM should give the cue. SMs should be careful not to give a cue when the actor is simply indulging in a dramatic pause, either. As actors, these are the things that you can and should expect. It is your right. Do not expect prompting to continue beyond the date that the director sets as the absolute cut-off deadline. This is generally because you should not need it and because the stage manager is generally beginning to get busy with technical details at a certain point and simply cannot afford the time to "watch book" anymore. A lot of this depends on which level of theatre you are working. Community theatres generally do not have the resources to have more than one stage manager, so there is no one "watching book" past a certain point anyway. College theatres vary, but generally the same is true. Often an assistant stage manager can be assigned to watch book when the main SM is busy working on technical cues. Most of the "professionals" that I have worked with had their lines off by the deadline and so simply did not need to be prompted. (The term "professional" is a misleading one. I have worked with some "professionals" who were not worthy of the title and some "amateurs" who could give lessons in professional behavior.)

One common mistake among inexperienced theatre companies is not to allow enough rehearsal time beyond the memorization stage of rehearsals. These companies set the "lines-off" deadline so close to opening night that many times there are actors who are very shaky with their lines on opening night. We have all heard these horror stories so I will not labor the point here. Suffice it to say that, once the lines are down cold, the actors should have at least another week of rehearsals to truly enjoy the freedom they have won. The script is gone from their hands, freeing up the body for gestures. The mind can once again return to thinking character thoughts rather than actor thoughts. Progress can once again continue.

Memorization will be addressed in more detail in Chapter 12.

Polishing

This is the stage of rehearsals after memorization when the actor is most gloriously free. Having released themselves of the bonds of the script and the technical stress of needing to learn the lines, now the actor can really begin to make the words (and the world) his/her own. That is really what you are trying to do now. Once the lines are second nature and actors don't have to actively think about them, then the words belong to them. They can make them their own. Now is the greatest step for reaching the next creative plateau. All of the work done up to this time has been preparation for this moment when one can really be free to play with the character. If many new ideas and discoveries do not flow from this stage, then something is very wrong. This is where things begin to become fun again. And believe me, you need it after the excruciating agony of the memorization period. This period of rehearsal sees a few more layers added to the production. This is also a set-up for the next, fairly difficult period of rehearsals: technical rehearsals.

Technical Rehearsals

There is no point in trying to pretend that tech rehearsals are for the actors. Initial tech rehearsals should and must be for the technicians. The actors have usually been working on developing the play into performance by now for several weeks (much shorter in summer stock). The lighting people, sound people, special effects people, props people, and set people have only these few tech rehearsals to get their jobs down so that the show can run smoothly. Actors must have patience here. The only thing that should be happening during these rehearsals is establishing the smooth running of the technical details. This is often difficult for actors because they have just reached a level of freedom where they really want to take off with the play. But they can't because there are now other artists that need the practice. I have worked in theatre companies where most of the tech was rehearsed separately from the actor rehearsals so that the meshing of actors and tech went very smoothly during these rehearsals. But often there is no substitute for having the actor there to establish things like the split-second timing that is so often necessary for technical cues. "Tech" should not be thought of as a necessary evil. It is just as much a part of the process of bringing the creative whole into being as the work of the actors. Good tech work can enhance a play so much that often actors will make new discoveries about the play and their characters based on such simple things as the interplay of light and shadow around them. Of course, one tries to introduce new things into the rehearsal process with the same care and timing that one uses to bring a character along. Props should be introduced to the actors in full right after the scripts are out of their hands. Before that they really cannot handle *all* of the props. Each new element introduced into the production as the designs become part of the play should be a new stimulus for the actor, rather than a burden. If the tech is becoming a burden, then perhaps it is time to pare down.

Dress Rehearsals

By this time, those few rehearsals designated as "dress rehearsals" will be a blending of all of the design and technical elements with the efforts of the actors. I still think of putting on my costume for the first time as "getting into the skin of the character". If at all possible, actors should be allowed/encouraged to wear appropriate footwear, rehearsal skirts, cloaks, etc. as soon as possible when rehearsals begin. This is especially true if the costumes will be restrictive in unusual ways such as corsets, long skirts, sandals, etc. Conversely, a bad costume can put a complete monkey wrench into things. I have been lucky, in my career, to have talented and sensitive costume designers who put me into really spectacular "skins" for my characters. Only once, when I was playing Tybalt in *Romeo and Juliet*, did I have a problem.

The design was wonderfully rendered by the designer, only the body she drew it on was more of a superhero body than I possessed. It looked great on Superman, but on me it resembled nothing so much as a large black trash bag pulled over my head with armholes. In addition, the tights I was to wear were given leopard spots on a beige background. Fortunately, the designer saw the folly of this immediately when I stepped onstage. I was quickly given a whole new costume designed more for my body type than for Arnold Schwarzenegger. The funny thing is that, by this time, the poster for the play had been designed on which my character appeared as the "Superman" physique in the leopard leotard and the dashing black tunic. We all had a laugh at this and I often wondered if audiences were looking for "that character" to show up.

Performance

Theoretically, rehearsals end when the play goes into performance. In a lot of professional situations, the director leaves the production very soon after it opens and the maintenance of the show falls into the hands of the stage manager. But in the amateur theatre, the director is still there, giving notes. Should they give notes after the show has opened? There is a lot of difference of opinion on this, but many times actors still need help with business that isn't working well, and so the director is still valuable for guiding the show through its development even as it progresses to closing night. A show can still improve after it opens. But one must be very careful not to intrude too much at this stage. Remember that the actors are still discovering things and developing even in performance. They have, hopefully, reached an awareness of what works and what doesn't and are fully capable of making adjustments on their own. Many times, the director begins to feel a bit left out by this stage, and that is good. The thing that you have helped to bring to life is now living on its own and doesn't need you to be constantly holding its hand and jump-starting its heart.

The progression of the director through the stages of rehearsal is that of being completely embroiled in the inner working of the play to gradually stepping back out of it and assuming the role of the audience watching it for the first time, to finally letting it go to be what it will be on its own. The director's job is essentially to eventually make himself or herself superfluous.

Bibliography

Brockett, Oscar G., Robert J. Ball, and Andrew Carlson. *The Essential Theatre*, 11th ed. Boston, MA: Cengage Learning, 2016.

Brockett, Oscar Gross. *The Theatre: An Introduction*, 4th ed. New York: Holt, Rinehart & Winston, 1979.

Carter, Conrad, A. J. Bradbury, and W. R. B. Howard. *The Production and Staging of Plays*. New York: Arc Books, 1963.

Clurman, Harold. *On Directing*. New York: Macmillan, 1972.

Cole, Toby, and Helen Krich Chinoy, *Directing the Play*. Indianapolis, IN: Bobbs-Merrill, 1953.

Dean, Alexander, and Lawrence Carra, *Fundamentals of Play Directing*, 5th ed. Long Grove, IL: Waveland Press, 2009.

Dietrich, John E., *Play Direction*, 2nd ed. Englewood Cliffs, NJ: Prentice-Hall, 1983.

Dolman, John Jr., and Richard K. Knaub. *The Art of Play Production*. New York: Harper & Rowe, 1973.

Hodge, Francis and Michael McLain. *Play Directing: Analysis, Communication, and Style*, 7th ed. New York: Routledge, 2009.

Seivers, W. David, Harry E. Stiver, Jr., and Stanley Kahan. *Directing for the Theatre*. Dubuque, IA: Wm C. Brown Company, 1974.

Vardac, A Nicholas. *Stage to Screen: Theatrical Method from Garrick to Griffith*. Cambridge, MA: Harvard University Press, 1949.

Whiting, Frank M. *An Introduction to the Theatre*. New York: Harper, 1961.

5 A Directing Primer

After the stage manager, the director needs to be the second most organized person on the production staff. The director has the artistic responsibility for the entire production. The director interprets how the playwright's script will be presented, coordinates the work of the designers and actors, and shapes the performance that the audience experiences. The director must be deeply inside the play and able to help the actors with motivation and guidance, and then, at a certain point, be able to step outside the play and begin looking at it as the audience.

Giving direction involves four basic, different functions: *guidance*, or telling performers how to get someplace (i.e.: blocking); *instruction*, or showing how to do something (i.e.; how one bows to a king, how one does a pratfall, how to grab someone by the hair, etc.); *explanation*, or telling what something means (i.e.: words in the script that the actors don't understand, etc.); *inspiration*, or helping people to find motivation.

The duties of the director may be roughly broken down as follows:

Selecting the script. Ideally a director would like to work only on material that they value as theatrically vital, emotionally and intellectually moving, has an important message for the audience, and reveals some truth about human experience that may help to make the world a better one. In the professional world, the producer or the Board of Producers often choose the play. In community and college theatre, however, choice of material is often the province of the director. Director proposals will often include information such as story summaries, cast breakdown and potential casting flexibility, scope of the play such as number of sets, period in which the play is set, etc., as well as possible budgetary estimates and rationale for choosing the play relating to the mission of the theatre, etc.

Choosing the key collaborators. Directors need a team of artists who will design the scenery, costumes, lighting, sound, props; who will conduct the musicians and coach the singers; who will choreograph dances and stage fights; and who will do key research and provide materials for analytical study. A larger community theatre often has people accustomed to these roles who cheerfully contribute their time and talents. Smaller groups may find that there is much doubling up of this work. In my first real outing in the world of community theatre, I directed *The Baltimore Waltz* by Paula Vogel. I found myself designing the set, the slide projections, the sound design, and the lights, as well as finding most of the props. Fortunately, the actors found their own costumes. Due to staffing problems, I also found myself running the lights and sound and projections for the show as well as functioning as the stage manager. At the time, I was used to a fairly large college theatre organization which had separate people specified for each of those jobs. Needless to say, I was completely exhausted. Of course, my biggest problem had been that I did not try to find others to help me. I was too proud and thought I could do it all myself. That was stupid. One needs collaborators in order to produce quality theatre.

An artistic production team needs to have a common vision and way of working. The director, of course, provides the inspiration for such a vision. The director must *conceptualize* or see the play in his mind's eye, the same way that one visualizes a novel while reading it. This requires "dramatic imagination". This is often called the "director's vision" and forms the basis for the unique interpretation of a script that will make each production of that script different from the last one or the next one.

Directors and designers should then go through a series of "Design Conferences" in which the visualization of the play becomes a set of blueprints for the elements that will appear on the stage:

- The first conference is one in which the director explains his/her vision.
- The second conference is one in which the designers explain their ideas about how to present the vision. This is the "rough sketch" stage.
- The third conference is one in which the designs have begun to be more completely realized. This involves presentation of rendering and models.
- The final conference is one in which the designs are approved.
- An additional conference may be necessary after the technical director has "costed" the designs and determined that changes are needed in order for the designs to be built within the productions budget.

A good director needs to have some education in how to research and analyze scripts. In addition, directors should study design and acting so that they will be able to talk with designers and actors in their common language.

Casting the roles. If the audience doesn't believe in the characters, the whole show fails, no matter how beautifully it is designed or written. The audience experiences most of the play through the actors. Each role requires particular skills and attributes and the director must find actors who possess them.

Realizing the production. Rehearsals begin in which the show is blocked and the production begins to evolve. In addition, periodic checks must be made with the designers to ensure that all are progressing toward the same final vision. These checks are usually done in weekly "production meetings".

The director's rehearsal work consists of:

Staging the play. Moving the actors around on the set and deciding on their movement patterns which is effectively illustrating the action in a visual way, and is called "blocking" (see Chapter 3). Directors often pre-plan blocking by writing out their visualization of it in their script and then spending the early rehearsals giving blocking. Other directors tend to go with a less pre-planned approach in which the blocking is "improvised" by the actors at each rehearsal until the patterns of the movement begin to fix themselves. This approach, while being more "organic" in a sense, also takes more time. Amateur theatre typically takes 6 to 8 weeks to rehearse a play, while professional theatre rarely goes beyond three weeks and often less. The difference is that professionals basically commit all of their working time to rehearsing, while amateurs generally have jobs to think about and so their time to devote to rehearsals is often limited to evenings and weekends.

Coaching the actors. Each actor works in a unique way and the director must have flexible working methods. A good director is also sensitive to the eccentricities of each performer and needs to learn how to deal with them sensitively. One person responds well to coaching, while another may prefer to be left alone for a while. One person may want to discuss things until they gel in his or her mind, while another person may prefer to just "do" and not talk a lot. Most people respond well to positive reinforcement, which many directors forget about as they are often only concentrating on the things that *aren't* working in a production as opposed to those things that *are*. Human beings need to be patted on the back once in a while and it is an astute director that remembers this. Egos are fragile things and directors often find themselves figuring out how to handle people with kindness, sensitivity, firmness, directness, and honesty. A good director must *earn* the respect of the cast not *expect* it. Once that respect is lost, one almost never gets it back.

Structuring the dynamics of a production. A production needs to flow smoothly from beginning to end and along the way go through a series of ups and downs of intensity, thought and emotion. These are the rhythms and tempos of a production composing the "dynamic" of the show. I personally prefer to call it the "flow". A production almost never achieves the proper "flow" until the actors have become confident with their lines and the technical staff are able to run the show without errors. Always remember that the technical rehearsals for a show are the time when the technical staff are learning to do their jobs. It takes time and a lot of starting and stopping for this to happen and they are being asked to achieve technical perfection in about a week, where the actors have had four or five. *Don't sell them short. Technical rehearsals (at least the first few) are not for the actors, they are for the crew.*

Standing in for the audience. Directors try to imagine how the audience will see, feel, and hear a production. Directors try to anticipate the audience's response to the production. If the audience finds the play too slow, or doesn't believe or feel empathy for the characters, or if they become confused by the staging, then the director has failed. *However, since no two people experience things in exactly the same way, it is impossible to make everyone happy unless one descends to the lowest common denominator, taking no risks and provoking no challenges. This is also deadly theatre.* My wife is the most devastating critic I know because she will quite frequently say to me, after we've seen a show (not necessarily one of mine), "Well, I didn't like anybody in that". She is often referring to the characters, and not the actors, but she will be equally frank about the acting if pressed. *It is a good thing to note that an audience is looking for someone to like and if they don't find them, you've lost them. This is not necessarily the fault of the director, it may be a shortcoming of the play, but it still holds true.* Another truth to keep in mind is that audiences are looking for "out of body" experiences. They want to become emotionally involved with the characters and the story. It is called "catharsis" or "willing suspension of disbelief". I asked my dad once what he liked when he went to see a movie or a play and he answered, "I like to laugh". Well, who doesn't? But then why do we ever do plays that are sad or serious or make us cry? Because we, as humans, find a cathartic release in a good cry! People do like to cry! As long as they can step out of it a bit later and say to themselves "Well thank god that was only pretend"!

Orchestrating the final rehearsals. The final phase of the director's work includes the dress rehearsals. This is when the actors get to work on the set, under lights and in costume. It is also the time the technical crew has actually had time to practice their jobs. The crew usually have a very few rehearsals to get their job right, while the actors have had weeks. At dress rehearsals, one is hoping to see things finally being drawn together and everything working as a unified whole. It is vitally important for a production to achieve its "flow" at this time. The director is responsible for coordinating this effort, but may also find that he or she is becoming redundant or unnecessary as things begin to come together. It is actually a bit of a luxury to be able to just sit and watch a show as the audience will see it. Of course, one is still making notes but one is by now not stopping the rehearsals to correct things. Notes will be given later.

Being the spiritual leader. Leading a large group of extremely talented yet temperamental artists and craftspeople is the director's charge throughout all of this work. From the first conference to opening night, a director must earn the respect of all of the people involved and know exactly when to push and when to pull, when to be there and when to back off, when to nudge and when to kick. I must confess that I still have difficulty watching a performance of one of my own shows. I find myself flinching and making little noises whenever something doesn't go the way I wanted it to. This, of course, is very disruptive for the audience sitting near me. But one must ultimately learn when to let go.

Is the director a creative artist? Or merely a conduit for the playwright's work? The problem with directors who consider themselves to be the ultimate creative artist is that, too often, their own voice drowns out the playwright's voice. Directors who see themselves as merely servants of the playwright are, too often, afraid to find new and dynamic ways to illustrate the playwright's work. Both are bad directors. The best directors are those who aren't afraid to be creative and yet hold the *essence* of the playwright's work sacred. Both are needed. The story rules. But the story can often be illuminated in ways the playwright hasn't even thought of. One important note here is that, if I desire to change the playwright's work in any way that I feel is usurping their creative energy, I will do my utmost to contact the playwright to discuss it and ask permission. I have been turned down several times. I once wrote to Paula Vogel when I was directing *The Baltimore Waltz* to let her know that we had decided to stage it in the round. She was very interested in how it would work that way and we carried on a nice correspondence about it. Another instance I have heard of is the one of Samuel Becket's *Endgame*, which a noted professional theatre decided to set in a post-apocalyptic subway station. The story goes that Beckett threw a tantrum and revoked his permission for them to do the play. *Never assume.* I had heard of another occasion when a theatre company desired to do a production of Arthur Miller's *All My Sons* set during the Vietnam war. Mr. Miller was apparently very nice and considerate but let them know that he could not support such a change. They didn't do it.

A Brief History

From about 450 bc to 350 bc, the playwrights of ancient Athens supervised rehearsals of their own plays. In fact, the playwright functioned as the "director" in this manner for 2,000 years. By the Elizabethan age, even Shakespeare supervised the staging of his own plays.

In the 17th and 18th centuries, decisions on how to do a play moved out of the playwright's hands. Because it became obvious that the public would pay to see a "star", leading actors founded their own theatre companies and assumed the status of "actor–manager". For the next 200 years, theatre was directed by the actor–managers. Actor–managers directed productions to suit their own egos and plays were often rewritten to give them the best lines. Plays were also often staged with the lead actor taking the front and center position on the stage and rarely yielding it. Toward the end of the 19th century, another major change took place: The Duke of Saxe-Meiningen, who was the absolute ruler of the German Duchy of Saxe-Meiningen, began to produce theatre in his town using tax revenues and local talent. He was neither a playwright nor an actor but assumed control of all elements of the production. In essence, he became the first director. The emphasis in these productions was on the unification of the efforts of all of the artists into one cohesive, creative whole. It had essentially never been done before. In 1847, The Duke of Saxe-Meiningen took his theatrical troupe on tour in Europe and created a sensation. No one had ever seen stories told onstage in a way that made the story the major element. Each part strove to make the whole greater. Many major European theatre companies began to copy this method. Among them were the French (André Antoine and the Théâtre Libre) and the Russians (Stanislavski and the Moscow Art Theatre). One of the revolutionary concepts of this new style of theatre was the idea of realism in acting in which actors actually turned and spoke to each other as in real life. Before this, the "norm" had been to face front and "declaim" with great vocal dexterity and oratory. In fact, if an audience liked the way a particular piece was performed, the actor might repeat it. As actors were often "sponsored" by rich patrons, entire passages of the play might be performed exclusively in the direction of the box in which the "patron" sat. The work of The Russians and French became the pattern for our modern sense of the director, particularly the influence of Stanislavski.

The rise of the theory of "determinism" in the fledgling field of Psychology may have led to the emergence of "realism" as an artistic movement, which also led to the development of psychological realism in the theatre. The theory of determinism states that man's behavior is the result of the events of his past experiences. What he *does* has been *determined* by what he has experienced in his past. This study of a person's past was determined to be best done by someone *other* than the person himself; someone outside of his life who could see it with an objective eye. Stanislavski may have been additionally influenced by the work of Pavlov and his work in "conditioned response". Stanislavski may have seen the correlation between triggering responses in an audience by the use of physical mimicry to those of the dogs who were conditioned to become hungry at the ringing of a bell. He developed what he called the "Method of Physical Action" which has been much interpreted and misunderstood in modern times and erroneously shortened to "The Method" by so-called students of Stanislavski who placed much more emphasis on the concept of "emotional memory" in which it is said that one may call up an emotion by remembering a moment in one's own life where something similar had occurred. I believe that Stanislavski was much more interested in trying to call up an emotion by re-creating the physical attributes of the emotion. Although any student of Stanislavski can't help but get the impression that even he was not completely satisfied with his results, and seems to have completely discounted "emotional memory" in his later writings.

Note: The information in this chapter is drawn from my experience teaching a course entitled "Introduction to Theatre" and was compiled from a variety of sources, including: *The Art of Theatre: Then and Now* by William Missouri Downs; *Another Opening, Another Show* by Tom Markus and Linda Sarver; *An Introduction to the Theatre* by Frank M. Whiting; *Theatrical Design and Production* by J. Michael Gillette; *History of the Theatre* by Oscar G. Brockett; and *The Theatre: An Introduction* by Oscar G. Brockett.

Bibliography

Brockett, Oscar G., Robert J. Ball, and Andrew Carlson. *The Essential Theatre*, 11th ed. Boston, MA: Cengage Learning, 2016.

Brockett, Oscar G., *History of the Theatre*, 10th ed. Boston, MA: Pearson, 2007.

Brockett, Oscar Gross. *The Theatre: An Introduction*, 4th ed. New York: Holt, Rinehart & Winston, 1979.

Carter, Conrad, A. J. Bradbury, & W. R. B. Howard. *The Production and Staging of Plays*. New York: Arc Books, 1963.

Cole, Toby, and Helen Krich Chinoy, eds., *Directors on Directing*, 2nd rev. ed. Indianapolis, IN: Bobbs-Merrill, 1963.

Cole, Toby, and Helen Krich Chinoy, *Directing the Play*. Indianapolis, IN: Bobbs-Merrill, 1953.

Dean, Alexander, and Lawrence Carra, *Fundamentals of Play Directing*, 5th ed. Long Grove, IL: Waveland Press, 2009.

Dietrich, John E., *Play Direction*, 2nd ed. Englewood Cliffs, NJ: Prentice-Hall, 1983.

Dolman, John Jr., and Richard K. Knaub. *The Art of Play Production*. New York: Harper & Rowe, 1973.

Downs, William Missouri. *The Art of Theatre: Then and Now*, 4th ed. Boston, MA: Cengage Learning, 2017.

Hodge, Francis, and Michael McLain. *Play Directing: Analysis, Communication, and Style*, 7th ed. New York: Routledge, 2009.

Seivers, W. David, Harry E. Stiver, Jr., and Stanley Kahan. *Directing for the Theatre*. Dubuque, IA: Wm C. Brown, 1974.

Vardac, A. Nicholas. *Stage to Screen: Theatrical Method from Garrick to Griffith*. Cambridge, MA: Harvard University Press, 1949.

Whiting, Frank M. *An Introduction to the Theatre*. New York: Harper & Brothers, 1961.

6 Play Analysis

The "Prep"

I studied Directing at the University of Texas at Austin under Dr. Francis Hodge, who was my mentor. His book, *Play Directing: Analysis, Communication, and Style*, was a huge influence on me and I use the concepts of that book all the time. I found the play analysis section did not offer specific methods for executing the analysis. As a result, I created my own methodology. *Note*: these are labor intensive and will take some time to complete. This method is very intuitive in nature and requires a creative state of mind. Try to approach the techniques in as neutral a frame of mind as possible because your mood, good or bad, can influence the outcome of certain sections. The things that one person might find in the analysis may be different from those of others. In many ways, it depends on the person and their creative state of mind at the time.

Hodge called his workbook a "Preparation" for directors. We tended to call it "The Prep". Why prep? Because it is terrifying to go into your first week of rehearsals without knowing what you are doing. You face all those actors and designers, terrified that you don't know what to do. It is so much more comforting to go into meetings and rehearsals with some concrete thoughts and ideas about the play.

By the time you have completed this prep, you will have read the play many times, each time with a different focus. If nothing else, you will know the play backwards and forwards. This work is not designed to limit your creativity but to stimulate it and put you at the best possible starting point to begin rehearsals.

Step One: Read the Play

Read the play? Well, duh! If you hadn't read the play, you wouldn't have decided to do it in the first place. But did you really read it closely? The director needs to start out the entire process by being the central authority on the play, next, of course, to the playwright. But sometimes I even wonder about them. I was in a show where we had the playwright in attendance at rehearsals and she kept giving me line-reading notes. I finally said, "But he wouldn't say it like that" and she was amazed that I thought I knew the character better than her. Perhaps we just had different visions about the play, but she saw it as an almost superficial comedy while I saw some very dark, serious overtones to the characters that deepened them quite a bit, and made the play both comic and tragic in tone. In the end she saw that there was more in her play than she originally thought and we compromised. Another primary example of playwrights not always knowing exactly what they have created occurred to me during a production of *Inherit the Wind* by Jerome Lawrence and Robert E. Lee. The playwrights had taken most of the dialogue directly from the court transcript of the famous "Scopes Monkey Trials", which considered the debate about whether it is appropriate to teach evolution in schools. As a result, the play is very compelling but doesn't answer a fundamental question about point of view. If we believe, as we are taught, that the main character in a play is the one who undergoes the largest story arc (in other words the one who changes the most by the end), then we see in this play that neither of the main characters makes any significant change of mind or heart by the end. Who then, is the major character? I began to notice that it is the people of the town, who comprise the audience in the courtroom, who make the biggest shift in attitude. They are challenged in their mindless support of the William Jennings Bryant anti-evolution arguments and, by the end of the play, are seen to seriously question their own attitudes. This is evidenced by the jury's penalty for the defendant which comes down in the amount of one dollar. While they are saying that Scopes was guilty for teaching evolution in the classroom, they are also saying that the whole matter is trivial. I don't think the playwrights were even cognizant of this.

Step Two: Prepare the Script

I propose that you read the play with a different objective each time (as detailed in Chapter 6, Play Analysis). An excellent way to get inside the dialogue and language of the play is to *completely retype the script* on your computer. This will give you an electronic copy that is easy to edit, add notes, change font size for easier reading, etc. It doesn't matter if you type slowly or badly. In fact, the slower the better because then you can really pay attention to all the words and the order in which they come.

Is this time consuming? Yes, it is! But when you are preparing yourself to direct a play, you cannot get in the habit of taking shortcuts. It takes time to do these things and it is time well spent. Trust me on that one. You will need to begin preparing for your production many months ahead of rehearsal. It cannot be sped up if you want to be thorough.

Why should the director be the authority on the script? Well, obviously, because everyone will be looking to you for ideas and guidance. It is also important to note that these roles may change and that *is a good thing*. While you start out as the expert on the play, you hope that the actors will eventually surpass you. That means they are learning and trying things and developing and extending their sensitivities to the play and the production.

In fact, you might say that the director's job is to make him- or herself superfluous by the time you reach opening night. In other words, you will need to learn to be able to let go and let others take the lead. Imagine if everyone depended on you to get through the play every night. No no no no. You don't want that.

Retyping the script can also give you a clean script to work with. I had a teacher who said that one of the first things you should do is to go through your script with a black magic marker and cross out all the stage directions. As you all know, there is a big difference between stage directions that are simply blocking recorded by the stage manager of the original production, and stage directions that are actually written by the playwright. For instance: "Crosses R to L of the couch" was probably not written by the playwright; but "Loudly and angrily" probably was. Learn to tell the difference and decide which ones you really need. It should also be said that the "acting versions" of the script sometimes also contain a diagram of the set at the back. Again, this is from the original production and should not concern your production at all.

With a clean copy of the script, you can focus on the things that are important to your production. You can even insert your own stage directions if you are of a mind to visualize the play physically on paper. This is not a bad idea. If you do block your play on paper like this, you will have a very good starting point for working with the actors and can sometimes work more quickly. *Never be afraid to let these blocking ideas change as you go.* Actors often come up with different and better ideas as things develop, and so you will need to be adaptable. One of the worst traits of a bad director is to be so in love with your own ideas that you can't let go when doing so will help the show.

Regarding copyrights, it is frowned upon to make copies of your cleaned script to hand out to the actors, because the publishing companies want to sell copies of the script that you are licensing. But distributing the "clean" copy that you have created not only gives everyone the same script, it gives them a version that is free of blocking notes and is easier to write in. Much confusion can be avoided if everyone has the same script. Find out if you can do that by contacting the publisher. They might agree if you go ahead and purchase their scripts even though you are planning to use yours. That way they are not being cheated out of any money.

Another advantage to using your cleaned scripts is that everyone will have the same page numbers. I cannot tell you how much chaos can ensue if everyone has different page numbers. Even if you cannot distribute your own version of the script, you can get on the same page as the actors by putting their script page numbers in the margin of your script.

I prefer to print one script page per single-sided sheet rather than duplexing the scripts. I know it saves paper to duplex, but it is useful to have that blank facing page to make notes. *Use pencil* when making notes in order to be able to erase things if needed (and it will be needed).

A word about the stage manager at this point. It would be extremely advantageous to have a good stage manager for your endeavor. The problem is, on the amateur level, that even if you can get someone to do it, they usually don't know what the responsibilities of the stage manager are. One of the big responsibilities of the stage manager, traditionally, is script management. In other words, making sure everyone has the same script and gets the current changes in time to be able to assimilate them. I was in a show where the director decided to make script cuts during rehearsal about a week after rehearsals started. Since not everyone was at that rehearsal and there was no real stage manager, this meant that we all pretty much had different scripts. This, coupled with the fact that the director kept assigning roles to different people based on who was present at rehearsals, there was a lot of confusion and wasted time as no one had the same script, no one knew which roles they were actually playing, and all of the page numbers were different, so it was extremely difficult to find where we were in the rehearsal. I kept thinking that the whole show could have been done much more quickly and efficiently with some rudimentary script management. I will attempt to comment about the stage manager more as we progress. A good stage manager will make your life so much easier. A bad one will not be much use as you will end up doing that job too (see Chapter 15).

Step Three: The Facts (See Appendix 1)

Where to begin an analysis of the play? Let's start with the facts as we can deduce them from the play.

Environmental Facts

Geographic Location

Where does the play take place? Is there anything specific given about the location of the play? Are we in Norway? Denmark? St. Louis? New York? Is there anything particularly important about this place? Could the play, in fact, be in any large city? Or any small town? Or any country in the world. Why are we specifically thinking that one particular geographic location has significance to the world of the play? That's a very good way of thinking about this section, by the way – we're trying to define the "World" of the play. Another good question to ask is: "Whose place is this?" In *Hedda Gabler* by Henrik Ibsen, for example, is it important that we are in Hedda's father's house that they have had to borrow a lot of money to buy? Is it Hedda's place? Or is it, in fact, actually owned by the man who lent them the money, Judge Brack? How does Hedda feel about that? The answers will go a long way toward understanding some of her actions.

Time

The year, season, and time of day, etc. may be set out quite specifically by the playwright. They may be ignored completely. Your task is to figure out whether these facts are important in some way. A playwright may be simply assuming that the play takes place in "the present day". Is that the year that it was written or might the playwright want you to actually set the play in your "present" day? There is significance in how you answer that question. Are there climate concerns? I did a play that was set on an expedition to the South Pole. We discovered that the elements were such a factor in that play that one's survival depended on how one dressed when one got up in the morning. A small cut in that environment was much more dangerous than in a temperate climate. One character dies of gangrene from such a cut. The climate became practically another character.

There may also be spans of time in a play. Scene one may be at night, while scene two is the next morning. Act I may be in the Fall, while Act II is in the Spring. What are the spans of time in the play and how are they important to the story? *Romeo and Juliet* takes place over a span of several weeks, but the *impression* is that only a few days have passed. What are the clues? It is the impression that events are moving very quickly that contributes mightily to the overall sense of the speed of the play. It feels as if things are moving so fast that they are quickly getting beyond anyone's control. There is an overwhelming sense that, if things could just slow down, they could be dealt with rationally and sensibly. But they aren't. One clue is in the friar's line "Wisely and slow, they stumble that run fast" which becomes foreshadowing.

Economic Environment

What is the relative state of wealth or poverty of the characters? Is that important? What is even more important is how the characters feel about their relative states of wealth or poverty. Are they happy where they are? Do they desperately desire more? Are these motivating factors behind their behavior?

Political Environment

There are two basic ways of thinking about the political environment:

1. *Formal.* What is the form of governance under which the characters live and how important is it to them personally? What are their attitudes toward the politics with which they must deal?
2. *Informal.* This can be thought of as the "Power" environment. It may or may not have anything to do with the formal political environment. Who is in control of their lives? Who has the power? Who doesn't? Who wants more of it? How much control do the characters have over their own lives? How important is that to them? How does this environment change, if at all? *The Lion in Winter* by James Goldman is all about power and who has it and who will get it and how far will they go to achieve it.

Social Environment

What are the forms of social institution under which the characters live? How are they connected socially? What is considered proper and improper in their social world? Are there class differences? One play might deal exclusively with the complex social hierarchy of the family structure, while another might deal with the social structure of a set of young students all rooming together in one apartment during the sixties (*Moonchildren* by Michael Weller). *Hedda Gabler* by Henrik Ibsen deals with a society in which a woman who leaves her husband and children is an outcast and faces prospects little better than prostitution. Think about what keeps Romeo and Juliet from just eloping and starting over in another country. Things weren't so simple in their world.

Religious Environment

One may think of this category in two essential ways:

1. *Formal.* What religious institutions have significance to the characters? *Agnes of God* by John Pielmeier is obviously and excruciatingly Catholic in nature, as is *Doubt* by John Patrick Shanley. Some plays will not specify the formal environment in which case one must theorize what importance it has on the story.
2. *Informal.* This involves the basic morality of the character. No matter their religious beliefs, what are their beliefs when it comes to the question of right and wrong? What is right and what is wrong? Where do they draw the line? How far will they go to get what they want? This environment is often the more important one in terms of understanding the behavior of the characters.

Summary

By the time you have finished examining the play in the light of all of these categories and questions, you will probably have reached some conclusions about the factors that define the world in which the characters live. You will have a much better understanding of what makes them behave the way they do. Now, try to draw a few simple conclusions about the environment of the world of the play. Which things seem to have more importance than the others? Which things have been discounted as factors and which have risen to the top as motivating factors? One thing to keep in mind is that it is quite possible that the *lack* of something may be as significant as its presence. Beware of the words "Does not apply". Make sure you have considered things carefully before deciding they aren't important.

Previous Action

This is information that you may have already begun to glean from the previous section as to what, exactly, is unique about the world of this particular play. When thinking about what you want your audience to understand, one important thing to consider is what events have taken place involving the characters, *before* the play has actually begun. This is sometimes called "exposition" or "back story". At one time, this information was presented to the audience at the beginning of the play in order to bring them up to speed as to the events of the play which then begin to happen in "real" time. As writing has become more sophisticated, playwrights have learned that it is more realistic to dole this information out in smaller doses throughout the play. The worst example, though, is the crucial piece of information that the audience has been missing, which is revealed just at the end, making everything make sense. A lot of old mysteries are dealt with in this manner, giving a very melodramatic conclusion. As the old lady's locket is opened in the last scene, revealing that the victim was, in actuality, *her daughter*! Or that the handbag in which Earnest was found as a child was actually the handbag of …. Well, you get it. As a comic device it is much more successful than as a serious one. Read *The Real Inspector Hound* by Tom Stoppard for an absolutely hilarious revelation of exposition by the housekeeper who answers the phone at the beginning and proceeds to tell us everything we need to know before hanging up on a "wrong number".

One way to approach this is to skim through the play, underlining each thing that refers to something that has happened *before the play begins.* Make a list of them, organizing them in the order that they occurred. Then step back, look at your list, and try to draw conclusions about how important all of the previous action is to understanding the play. What things are absolutely crucial for the audience to understand in order for them to see the events of the play with clarity? One trick that playwrights often use is to repeat things that are considered crucial. If the audience doesn't get something the first time, they probably will the second or even the third time it is repeated. Not everyone does this so it is not a hard and fast rule, but it can be a clue.

Polar Attitudes

Who wins? Who loses? It has been said that the changes that a character makes from the beginning to the end of the play help to define the meaning of the play and the nature of the character. So, ask yourself "Who changes?" And then, "Who changes the most?" Do any characters seem set up to possibly make a major decision or discovery which then forces them to change their attitudes by the time the play is over? One of the best examples is Mr. Scrooge from *A Christmas Carol* by Charles Dickens. No one can dispute that he has undergone a huge change of spirit by the end of the play. You could even say that the events of the play specifically work to make him change. This pretty clearly defines him as the major character of the play.

I once worked on a play called *Inherit the Wind* by Jerome Lawrence and Robert E. Lee, which is a dramatization of the events of the Scopes "monkey trial" in the early part of the century. It is taken from the transcripts of the trial involving Clarence Darrow for the defense and William Jennings Bryant for the prosecution. Each man is given a very specific attitude toward the controversy concerning the legality and morality of teaching evolution in the public schools. Darrow is for it, Bryant is against. By the end of the play, each side has taken their best shot at convincing the jury of their side of the question. The thing that struck me about this play is that, by the end, neither man has been swayed to back down and accept the other's argument. The jury, which seems to have started out staunchly on the side of Mr. Bryant, finds the defendant guilty in the end, but penalizes him to the tune of only one dollar. So, nothing has really changed. But wait! The onlookers at the trial; the people of the town, have been asked to question things that they never had to question before. Most of them have gone from staunch Bryant supporters to allowing the arguments of Mr. Darrow to challenge their beliefs. The crowd has the biggest polar shift! Does that make them, by our definition, the major character of the play? Well, one begins to think about how this piece will be staged as a result.

Spine

The spine is the central action around which all other actions revolve as they interconnect. All the characters will relate to the spine in some way. It may be too early to decide these things, and you may certainly keep them simmering in the stew of ideas in your mind. It is not crucial to make definite decisions on everything right now. But you want to begin asking the questions and seeking the answers.

So now, can you sum up the action of the play in a single sentence? Bear in mind that if you reach a definition at this point, it becomes a "working hypothesis" and certainly may change as you make further discoveries and decisions throughout the production process. *Always be open to the idea that it is all right for you to change your mind.* (For example: "This is a play about a woman who wants power over the men in her life and ultimately fails because she underestimates them and overestimates herself" – *Hedda Gabler*.)

Does this seem like a lot of work? You bet! And you've just scratched the surface. There is a lot more and it's all designed to get your head as deeply into the play as is possible. As you gain experience, you can skip steps, but you really need to put the time and effort into this comprehensive study of the play so that you are prepared to talk about it intelligently with all the other members of your creative team. It's worth spending the time with the play early, so that you aren't just "making it up as you go" when the time comes to discuss design and begin rehearsals.

Step Four: Dialogue (See Appendix 4)

Playwrights often make choices about the attitudes and meanings of the play as well as the nuances of character through the use of particular words and phrases. This comprises the flavor and tone of a play, much as poets do. They are, after all, play*wrights*. The words and images they use are carefully crafted. Let's begin by assuming that, by the time a play has reached production and performance as well as publication, it has probably been rewritten a number of times. This means that every word has been considered in some detail and focus. Therefore, an examination of the way words and phrases are used will give you insights into the attitudes and emotions of the play as well as, perhaps, the playwright. The exercises here are very much intuitive. *You will be riding what is known as a "stream of consciousness" and making choices not with the analytical part of your brain, but with the intuitive, almost subconscious part. Don't stop to ask yourself why you were drawn to something, just let it happen and ask questions later.*

Word Choice

Skim the play rapidly, pausing only when a word sticks in your mind as unusual, interesting, particularly expressive, or even just repeated a lot. Use a pencil to lightly underline things as you go that can then be pulled out and put into a list. In making my list of words, I often try to put them all on one page in different columns, so that I can see them all together. If you can't go through the entire play at one sitting, don't spend any time analyzing what you've done until you have done the entire script. Examine the list and see whether they lead you to draw some conclusions. Write your conclusions out. An example of one that I did for Arthur Miller's *After the Fall* can be seen in Appendix #4.

Note: I have found that I am often influenced by the mood that I am in when I sit down to do this. If I am in a dark mood, I am drawn to dark things. If I am in a sad mood, I will be drawn to sad things. Try to maintain a neutrality of mood. The only other way around this is to repeat the exercise at a different time and see if your results are somehow different.

Phrase Choice

Do the same "skimming, scanning, and listing" exercise, paying attention to word groupings, or phrases. Again, write your conclusions. Do your conclusions from different sections seem to support each other?

Pauses or Silence

Do the same exercise for the use of pauses. Often pauses can be indicated by a stage direction "pause" or "long pause", etc. Harold Pinter may have been the first playwright to begin to use the word "silence" in his scripts. How long is a silence? How long is a pause? A famous director called plays "interrupted silence". Sometimes pauses are indicated by dashes or three or four dots, although these have most often been used to designate when a line is interrupted or cut off by the next line. It may not be as easy to make a meaningful list in this case but one can certainly get an idea how the dialogue is punctuated by a playwright. It has been postulated that George Bernard Shaw tried to indicate small pauses by putting more space between words and even indicating when a word was to be drawn out by putting space between the letters of a word. Some of Shaw's more faithfully reproduced scripts illustrate that this was, indeed, the case. It is even a theory of mine that sometimes playwrights indicate the length of a particular movement on the stage with the duration of the speech. I know that many playwrights actually hear their dialogue as they are writing and it cannot help but influence them in their thinking that the length of a speech may correlate with the length of a movement: "It takes me this long to cross the stage to reach her because it takes the entire speech for me to do it." This, alas, is an unproven theory. Also ask yourself if different characters use pauses differently.

Images or Metaphors

Repeat the exercise and note any words or word groupings that seem particularly poetic. Many writers try to create visual images through the use of words and phrases. Is there a sense that much is being said using few, very selective words? Are there a lot of descriptive phrases? I have found Miller and Williams to be particularly poetic in their use of language. Conversely, are there vulgarities and crudities of language present? How are these used? Is it particular to any one character or group of characters? Studying Shakespeare's use of language has been developed into a literary science all its own.

Unusual Characteristics

Repeat the exercise one last time to list choices the playwright has made in terms of slang, vulgarities, unusual words or phrases, contractions, dialects, inverted wordings, unusual sounds, colloquialisms, etc. What is the overall effect of the use of these language tricks? Are they character driven? Is it an attempt to capture the sound and idioms of a particular place or time period?

Step Five: Dramatic Action (See Appendix 5)

Dramatic action is the forces of conflict at work between character's desires and intentions. It comes with the knowledge that characters are "goal oriented" and are constantly seeking to fulfill an intention, a desire. Every single thing that a character does is aimed at getting something from another character. *This is the single most important concept for actors and directors.* When I learned about dramatic action in directing class, I immediately understood how I could make it work as an actor and began to use it at the very next rehearsal I attended. It was that clear and immediate for me. None of my acting classes to that point had made such an impact on my understanding of the nature of the dynamics between characters. It makes one's acting "active", to put it simply. Quite simply stated: if an actor focuses on this factor, it immediately gives them something active to pursue at every moment on the stage. Almost more importantly, it focuses one on the *other*, which tends to take the major focus off of themselves (the most common mistake of inexperienced actors). If an actor is constantly reminding him or herself: "In this scene, I am trying to convince _____ that I love her" (or some other action verb), it gives them something to strive for, something to do, something active to pursue. A concept that hit home to me is also that action involves a kind of "forcing" (Use the force, Dan!). In other words, I am actively trying to get someone else to do something and I'm not doing it in a passive manner, I'm doing it in a "forceful" manner. The things that my character wants aren't things that he just "kinda, sorta" wants. They are things that he feels he can't live without: "If I can't win her love, there's no use going on." Action, then, is not just a description of what I want, but how badly I want it.

Plays are broken into acts and scenes but can also be broken into "action units". In essence, every time the action changes, a new action unit is begun. These units are not so clearly delineated and one must be careful when breaking the play down into these segments. There is also a concept in drama called the "French Scene" which says that every time a character enters or leaves a scene, a new scene has begun. I would amend this to say that these scenes are more significant if one qualifies the breakdown to indicate when "major" characters enter or leave. For instance, when the butler enters to tell Jack that his dinner is served, it doesn't really significantly change the action of the scene. The new information brought by the butler can be significant enough to change the action, but usually such information only serves to postpone the action.

In analyzing the action of a play, the most significant question is: "What is happening in this scene?" or "How do the actions of a scene progress and change by the end of the scene". In other words, a scene may contain a number of alterations of action as the characters try out ploys that don't work and shift to other ploys. It can be extremely helpful to try to identify those moments when the action shifts. A play that embodies the principles of shifting ploys and strategies from moment to moment is *The Lion in Winter* by James Goldman. I highly recommend it as a study play.

One should also be aware that actions may involve emotions, but actions aren't emotions. Usually, actions evoke emotions but they cannot be described using emotional descriptors. My character may "feel" sad in a particular scene, but his action is most likely not "sad" to another character. It doesn't work as an action verb. Actors and directors should certainly not ignore emotions but they need to first understand the actions that lead to them.

There are also action verbs that simply describe activity. I can "be angry" with another character, but, again, the action isn't to "anger" them. There is a big distinction between what a character "feels" and what he or she "does". If you have to describe an action with words that express a "state of being", then you may have missed the "action".

I have also learned that it doesn't matter how many words it takes to describe an action, as long as you can describe it. In fact, using qualifying words sometimes help to express the nuances of an action.

The most important thing to grasp for each "unit" of action is *"Who is doing what to whom and how is it reciprocated?"*. It is important to note that action, though it may be precipitated by one character, usually results in a *re*-action by another character: "I do something to you, and as a result, you do something back to me."

Unit Divisions

Divide the play into units. Remember that a unit is delineated by a distinct change in the action. Provide each unit with a descriptor such as: "A does this to B and B does this back to A." The action ends in one of three ways: one character achieves his/her goal; the action is postponed by another character; or the action is postponed as one of the characters leaves.

One technique for doing this is to draw a line across the entire page of script to divide the dialogue into units. Notes in the margin can indicate what you believe is the principal action of that unit – "Wants to see if she still loves him", "She leads him on to see if she can trap him".

These ideas concerning action should most certainly be discussed with the actors in rehearsal: "What do you think your character is trying to do in this scene?"

I am often asked if an action can repeat. The textbook answer is no, but I disagree. I believe actions can and do repeat, but very so often they are repeated with increased emphasis, or with shadings of intention. I can "refute" someone's arguments "forcefully" or I can do so "gently" or "angrily" or "sarcastically". I have always allowed qualifiers to help describe actions as I believe that it is necessary to see the "tone" of a character or scene.

Note for actors: In a very simple and stripped-down way, I have found that, in auditions, I will illustrate actions by physically moving toward my scene partner on each of my lines. Often this gets me so within their sphere that they are forced to move away. Then I pursue further. If they don't move away, I will begin to circle them so that they begin to feel awkward. This doesn't always work, especially if my character is not the aggressive one in the scene, but I have found that it at least begins to give us a sense of back and forth with the *other* rather than just standing there waiting for something to happen. That is what I mean by the concept of "forcing". There is an implied "force" behind the idea of action. It needs to be illustrated physically as well as vocally. When actors become aware of this, it "activates" them.

The single most important thing is to help the actor understand the action. Another wrinkle in understanding action is the idea that one may postpone the pursuit of an objective when insurmountable obstacles occur; but when that happens one will probably just wait until a later time and then return to the active pursuit of the objective when circumstances have changed slightly. Is this a "new" action? Or is it simply a return to a previous one? In this way one can see that actions can repeat, though they may not repeat back-to-back.

Any discussion of acting must include "super objective". It is probably the single most important concept for actors to understand. Stanislavski is credited with using the term for the first time. Harold Clurman called it "the spine", which is another really superb way to look at it. Simply stated, it is the goal for which the character strives throughout the entire play and either does or does not gain by the end. This is one of the most central principles in acting. An actor needs to discover the "spine" of his/her character. All of the actions that character performs in the course of the story of the play are designed to move him/her toward the ultimate goal or "super objective". While these goals may involve tangible, material gain, most often they involve broad emotional concepts. Hedda Gabler's super objective is to gain "Power and revenge over the men who have manipulated my life". Quentin, in Arthur Miller's *After the Fall* desires: "Release from the guilt and self-doubt which tortures me and makes me incapable of loving anyone including myself." These are highly emotional goals and involve psychological motivations that drive the characters to do the things they do.

One subtlety that I believe often gets lost when discussing the concept of super objective is that of intensity. What is the "or else" involved in any character's super objective – "If I don't achieve my goal, what are the consequences for me?" My belief is that the answer to this question must always be extreme and intense, often involving life and death. Characters don't simply want things in a trivial way because they think it would be "kinda nice". On the contrary, they want things because they cannot conceive of life without them. "If I cannot achieve my desire, my life will be over", puts a nice edge of intensity on the playing of actions. This concept applies to comedy as well as drama. If Corrie Bratter in *Barefoot in the Park* cannot reconcile the incompatibilities with her husband, then she will have failed and her marriage will end in divorce and her life will essentially be a waste and a failure. Of course, we the audience, know this is not true, but *Corrie does not*! That is one of the things that help make comedies funny. The characters in comedy must be as committed to their actions and their objectives as those in tragedy.

As the super objective must always be a presence in the character's mind and heart (as well as the actor's), so too must the scene objective be an immediate presence. In fact, the scene objective is probably a much more immediate presence for the actor than the super objective. Why? Because it is specific enough that it is always at the forefront of one's mind in every scene. It provides one with the intellectual and emotional springboard to launch one into a scene with clarity and intensity. The scene objective must be a goal that will move the character toward the achievement of the super objective. Yet it must be unique to the scene being played. "In this scene, I want to convince Hedda that I can be a dangerous man and that she'd better take me seriously" (Judge Brack). The scene objective must be something that is not accomplished too easily, and it must be something that can be won and lost. If an objective is accomplished too easily, then there is no tension in the scene. If my scene objective is something that one might not achieve, that one might fail to accomplish, then it makes the outcome doubtful, which heightens dramatic tension. Of course, the objective may be something that the character actually does fail to achieve. Not every objective is achieved. These little defeats serve to heighten tension as well as sharpen the character's resolve to pursue more intensely the super objective. They can also be seen as "tactics": "I will try to accomplish this by doing that. If that fails, I will still try to accomplish this but I will change my tactics and try something else. If that fails, I will try something else." This cycle obviously continues until the objective is either won or lost or the action is postponed for some reason (a prime example of this kind of "gamesmanship" approach to action tactics may be found in *The Lion in Winter* by James Goldman, or in *Who's Afraid of Virginia Woolf?* by Edward Albee; possibly two of the clearest and easiest to follow examples of the give and take of dramatic action ever written).

A trick I use during rehearsals to keep my objectives before me at all times is to write my scene objective at the top of each page of the script. Then I am constantly reminding myself of my goal every time I look down at my script. I find this helps me to sharpen my mind and senses in each moment of playing.

I'm not sure if this belongs in this section, but it is on my mind. In addition to the idea of "life and death" intensity in acting is *the concept of "the first time"*. It constantly amazes me in working with actors how often they want to take the easy way out rather than seeing that the more difficult and challenging way is the one that will make the most interesting and dynamic dramatic choices. I quite frequently will stop an actor and ask them: "Is this argument that you are having with your wife something that you have had before." It is surprising to me that so many actors will answer, "Oh, yes, this is just one of many battles we've had on this subject". I will invariably then try to steer the actor toward making the choice that the characters have not, in fact, ever actually confronted each other before in this way. They may have thought the thoughts but not said the words. They may have wanted to have the confrontation, but never did. This, then, *is the first time*.

Almost every choice made by actors on the stage will be more interesting, dynamic, and intense if the answer to my question is always: "This is happening for the first time, it has never happened before." I am not in the habit of making hard and fast rules for the theatre because I find that for every rule there is an exception, as in life. But here I have very rarely found this to be wrong. The vitality of every situation in almost every play can be found by understanding that these characters are saying and doing everything that they do for the very first time. That every scene in every play has a uniqueness that makes it vital and fresh. That every choice will have much more spice if the question is always: "What's new here? What is happening that has never happened before?" I can almost guarantee this will work.

Of course, as we all know, saying it and playing it are often two very different things. An understanding of something does not lead to automatic clarity of technique. The actor is still faced with the very important task of finding the most appropriate way to physicalize the action, to let the audience in on the interior process, to find ways to illustrate the actions and emotions of the characters. As I frequently said to my students: "The audience cannot read your mind. You have to find ways to let them know what you are thinking and feeling. It is not enough to know and understand your character, you must let the audience see, hear, and feel it. Even a character that is hiding his/her feelings must let the audience know somehow."

Step Six: Character (See Appendix 3)

A director must be familiar enough with the characters to communicate impressions to the actors. The natural progression of rehearsals should move the actors a step or two beyond the director in terms of character development. In order to come to an understanding of the characters, the director must do a form of character analysis for *each* of the characters in the play, even the minor ones. Below is a technique for analyzing the character of the play. For minor characters, especially in a play with a great many characters, it may be sufficient to simply prepare the "Summary adjectives" (see list below) for each character. Remember that each actor will be looking to you for help. If you ignore anyone, the play will suffer. There is an old maxim for the theatre that says that a production is only as good as its weakest part. In addition, I am including a form of character analysis to be given to the actors so that they can do some homework for themselves.

Textual evidence. Skim the play for each character making three lists of quotations:

1. What the character says about her/himself.
2. What the other characters say about her/him.
3. What the playwright says about her/him.

Again, when you have completed this, look at your lists of quotations and *draw conclusions*:

- *Desires.* What does the character most want? (Super objective). Characters may appear to want material things, but this is superficial; what they really want are usually intangibles such as power, love, self-respect, security, etc.
- *Will.* Will is a character's relative inner strength or weakness. Is the character strong-willed, or weak-willed, or some gradation in-between? Describe.

- *Values.* A character's moral stance. How honest is he with himself? With others? What sense of moral responsibility does he have toward others? What is the moral code that governs his behavior? What is his sense of integrity? How far will he go to get what he wants?
- *Obstacles.* Who or what stands in the character's way, preventing him from attaining his goals? What must he do to overcome these obstacles? Does he succeed?
- *Decorum.* The character's physical appearance. What he looks like, his manners, and his poise. How does the character see himself? (Self-image). Your impressions of the character's decorum should be an extension of your understanding of his inner nature. How does the outer reflect the inner character?
- *Summary adjectives.* Make a list of at least twenty-five adjectives describing the character. This can be fairly easily accomplished by going back over your notes for this section and pulling out adjectives you have already used. Look at your list and *draw conclusions*.

A Character Biography (A Worksheet to Be Given to Actors)

The question most frequently asked by actors is: "once I am cast in a role, how do I begin preparing for it?" The most obvious answer is by developing a detailed study of the script and the character. I call this process: "Getting into the head of the character." This mental work is as much a vital part of the actor's homework as learning lines and blocking. The most important thing that an actor can do is to learn to *think* like the character. This is Stanislavski's "magic If" – "*If* I were this character, what would I do?" and "*If* this character were me, what would I do?" To do this you must come to an understanding of the psychology of the character and the factors that have gone into creating his/her personality. *Then* an actor must translate these psychological roots into the goals and actions, intentions, and motivations that he/she can use in playing the part. This is simply using "cause and effect" to help one inform the creative, intuitive, imaginative self. In other words, one must use one's left brain to stimulate and inform one's right brain. The most important question that Stanislavski asked himself all his life was: "where does inspiration come from?" His entire search for acting methods focused on finding techniques to help the actor create an atmosphere in which creativity and inspiration could happen.

This analysis is broken into an organized set of fundamental questions intended simply as a guide for the thought process in building the life of the character in the imagination. Do not think of it as merely an assignment. That would be counterproductive because it would not be motivated by one's desire to understand and play one's character – it would be motivated solely by a desire to get it done by a deadline. This would completely negate the creative process. Try to think of this project as an actor's *tool* to assist them in preparing for a role.

Always answer each question as thoroughly and thoughtfully as possible. Short answers often inhibit depth of thought and so inhibit depth of character. Be more interested in quality than quantity. There is no set length for this project. When people ask me how long it should be I invariably answer "as long as it takes". Do not accept "does not apply" as an answer unless you can explain *why* you think the question is not applicable.

Who Am I? A Character Biography

Character Biography

Answer the questions given on this outline. Do not use a "Question/Answer" or "List" format. This should be written in a "Narrative Prose" format. (*Note: Quick, short answers usually betray superficial thinking concerning character.*) You are trying to build the life and soul of a person completely different from you. Take some time and answer the questions in detail, giving lots of examples along the way. You may find answers to these questions directly in the play. At other times you will need to speculate using your knowledge of the circumstances of the play to create the word of the character.

Note: The biography should be from the point of view of a character in the middle of the play, *while* the action is taking place but *before* it has concluded.

1. When and where was your character born? Is anything in your character's behavior significantly influenced by this?
2. Where did your character grow up?
3. What do you consider to be your character's "home"?
4. Who are your character's parents? Where are they from? What are they like?
5. How does your character feel about his parents?
6. What was your character's happiest childhood experience? Details!
7. What was your character's unhappiest childhood experience? Details!
8. Does your character have any brothers or sisters? What are they like?
9. Which family member is/was your character closest to? Why?
10. Who were your character's close friends as a child? Why?
11. What were your character's favorite toys, activities, hobbies? Why? Details!
12. What was school like for your character? Did he like it? What were your character's best/worst subjects? Why?
13. Is your character intelligent? Does this have anything to do with his schooling? Why? Why not?

14. Who has been the biggest influence on your character's life outside of his family?
15. Is your character a friendly person (outgoing and gregarious)? Is he a shy person (timid and withdrawn)? Why?
16. What is your character's ethnic origin? Is this a factor in their life? Why/Why not?
17. What was/is your character's worst nightmare? Best dream?
18. What was the best present your character ever received? Why?
19. What was the nicest thing your character ever did for someone?
20. What was the nicest thing someone ever did for your character?
21. Is your character mentally and emotionally stable? Why? Why not?
22. What brought you to the place you are now? (Physically, mentally, emotionally)
23. What have you been doing for the last week, month, year?
24. What would you like to be doing in the next week, month, year?
25. Does your character show his feelings or hide them? Give examples.
26. What has been the high point in your character's life so far?
27. What has been the low point in your character's life so far?
28. Does your character have any enemies? Who and why?
29. Has your character ever been in love? Explain.
30. What are your character's major strengths and weaknesses?
31. What kind of people does your character like to be with? Why?
32. What kind of people does your character avoid? Why?
33. Is your character a consistent person? Does he always say what he means and do what he says? Why? Why not? Give examples.
34. How honest is your character with himself and others?
35. What are your character's immediate goals? (This can be translated in scenework as "what does your character hope to achieve in the scene you are doing.)
36. What are your character's long-range goals? (This can be translated in scenework as "what does your character hope to achieve by the end of the play?")
37. What stands in your character's way?
38. How will your character overcome his obstacles?
39. Does your character have any secrets? Give examples. (Unacceptable answer: "If I told you, it wouldn't be a secret.")
40. Is your character a product of his upbringing? Why or why not?
41. If your character could change one thing about himself, what would it be?
42. What are your character's eccentricities? (e.g.: talking with hands, shuffling feet, biting fingernails, avoiding eye contact, etc.)
43. Who would your character be if he could be someone else?
44. What is your character's attitude toward life in general?

45. What would your character be if he/she were:
    - An animal. Why?
    - A color. Why?
    - An element. Why?
    - A machine? Why?
    - A sound? Why?
    - A taste? Why?
    - Which of these best sums him up? Why?
46. Do you have any distinguishing speech habits?
47. What kind of clothes do you wear? How do you feel about the way you dress?
48. How do you feel about your personal appearance?
49. How do you feel about your circle of friends and your place in the circle?
50. How do you feel about your husband/wife/lover?
51. What is your occupation (if any) and how do you feel about that?
52. What sort of people do you work with and how do you feel about them?
53. Do you make a comfortable living (or perhaps just the opposite)? How does that make you feel?
54. How is your health? How do you feel about that?
55. How old are you? How do you feel about that?
56. What is your favorite color? Why?
57. What is your favorite food? Why?
58. What is your favorite time of day? Why?
59. What is your favorite gesture? Why?
60. What turns you off? Why?
61. What turns you on? Why?
62. What is your favorite curse word? Why?
63. What is your least favorite word? Why?
64. Under what circumstances do people see you at your best?
65. Under what circumstances do people see you at your worst?
66. At what tempo do you live life? Explain.
67. What is your favorite place to be?
68. What are your hobbies?
69. How would you describe your posture?
70. Is your eye contact with others usually direct? Why or why not?
71. How do you feel about physical contact with others?
72. How does your body language tell others who you are?
73. Prepare a list of at *least* 25 adjectives that best describe your character. The simplest way to do this is to re-read what you have already written and simply pull adjectives from what you have already said about yourself.
74. Look at your list of 25 adjectives and write a paragraph on conclusions that you can draw about the character from the list of words you have chosen.

Personal Connection

Consider carefully your feelings about the character you are playing. What do you have in common with the character? What are the differences between you and the character? Since you are the one who will have to play the character onstage using your voice and your body and your life experiences, it is important to consider how much you and the character are alike. An actor needs to develop empathy for his/her character. Remember that characters are representations of human beings and all human beings have some common ground. Find and list the connections which will help you to portray the character. Sometimes this is very easy, sometimes you will have to dig deep to find life experiences that compare with those of the character.

Synthesis

Now that you have spent a lot of time and mental energy in examining your character in ways designed to give you a new depth of perspective, go back and read over what you have written with the purpose of answering this final question: What, specifically, have you discovered through this analysis that will help you in playing him/her? Recognize also that there is no right or wrong answer to this question. Different actors will find different things useful. You, personally, may find something particularly helpful this time, and yet find that something else is more helpful next time. There may be sections that are not as helpful as others. The important thing is that you have considered many new ways of looking at your character and are now better able to flesh it out.

Step Seven: Idea (See Appendix 2)

Now that you have gotten deeply into the emotional guts of the play, step back and try to see the objective or intellectual side. What does the play mean? *What is the playwright trying to say to his audience?* What are the themes of the play?

- *Meaning of the title*. Many writers try to express the idea or theme of the play with a metaphorical title. What does the title tell you about the meaning of the play? *Who's Afraid of Virginia Woolf?* for example; or *Private Lives, The Lion in Winter, Hayfever, West Side Story,* or *True West*.
- *Philosophical quotations*. Skim the play yet again and make a list of the quotations that seem to express the author's philosophy. Is there a character that seems to best embody the theme? Is there a single line that embodies it?
- *Conclusions*. What is the play about? What is the theme? Is there a clearly defined intent? Why did the playwright write the play? What was he trying to say? Is it a simple message or a complex one? Does the play have

universality? Is its message relevant to a modern audience and will it continue to be relevant to audiences in the future? Is there something about this play that you feel needs to be brought to a modern audience? Is there something that speaks to you?

- *Concept.* Anything that you do to any play in terms of conceptualizing needs to serve the essence of the play. When you understand the action and theme of a play, you can do to it what you will as long as you are faithful to those principles. (And as long as you don't violate the copyright laws.) If, for example, you decide that *Romeo and Juliet* is about breaking down the barriers of forbidden love, it might actually work to have a black Romeo and a white Juliet. The concept serves the theme and action of the play. Too often, concepts are layered onto plays without a full understanding of the play. These productions soon run into trouble. I love a good, bold concept that takes chances and shows guts, but only if it helps to illuminate the play that was already there to begin with. One of the most obvious examples of this in recent years is the Baz Luhrmann, Leonardo DiCaprio, Clare Danes version of *Romeo and Juliet*. When I first saw this movie in a theatre it was very soon after its release. The row in front of me was loaded with teenaged girls who had obviously come to see their main heart throb, Leonardo DiCaprio. By the time the movie was over, almost every one of those young girls was openly in tears! I thought to myself, "Say what you will about Shakespeare, but when was the last time you saw one of his plays cause open weeping among teenage girls?" The movie had been drastically modernized and conceptualized with guns and gangs and cars and love scenes in swimming pools. But the language had not been changed at all. It had something to say to that audience and it still does.

I have learned that it's hard to kill Shakespeare. As long as the language is understood and even halfway competently delivered, it almost doesn't matter what you do to it. It's hard to kill. I was in a production of *The Comedy of Errors* where the director had decided to place it in post-civil-war America and one of the twin brothers had been brought up in the South and one had been brought up in the North (Syracuse, NY). Of course, the mistaken identity was blown from the moment you heard the southern accent of the Southern Antipholus. *But for some reason, it didn't matter to the audience.* I was also in another production of that same play that was designed to be performed on a game board and with costumes in the Italian style of Fellini's film *8½*. It made absolutely no sense and those design elements were never referred to in the play. *But for some reason, it didn't matter to the audience.* I could go on, particularly about a post-apocalypse *Macbeth* concept, which had the characters dressed in remnants of a formerly technological society, most of which didn't read past the first row. But, as I say, it's hard to kill Shakespeare!

Step 8: Synthesis

Each creative person finds those things that work best for them. The things that work for you may not work for someone else. Conversely, the things that work for someone else will not work for you. A synthesis is a drawing together and a summation. Which parts of this analysis worked best for you? Why? Which parts were not as effective? Why? The main reason for creating a synthesis such as this is to help you the next time you do a preparation for a show you are directing. You can refer to this and see which of the analysis areas were most useful to you.

Final note: By the time you have finished this preparation, you will be an expert on the play. You will know it backward and forward. There are, of course, a great many things still to be discovered through rehearsals, but you will now have a solid starting point for communication with actors and designers.

Remember that *this analysis is not designed to stifle your creativity – it is designed to stimulate it*. Your actors may seem to you agonizingly slow at catching up to your knowledge of the play at first, and this is how it should be. They will be starting from nothing and building a life for their characters. Be patient. The most important quality for a director to develop is patience. Lead and guide and never forget that you don't have all the answers. There are ideas that haven't come to you yet. There are creative inspirations that you and your actors will discover throughout the process of rehearsing. Don't try to do everything at once. The production must evolve slowly, with the addition of each artist giving it another creative kick, until all of the elements mesh into a single whole. You must learn to respect the creative abilities of those who are working with you, when to assert yourself and when not to, when to speak and when to remain silent. If you come across to your actors as dictatorial or tyrannical, you will lose their respect. If you come across as uncertain and tentative, you will lose their respect. You must earn the respect of those with whom you work, or the production will suffer. A director must have control, but must also maintain unity and harmony.

Note: this chapter contains material from: *Play Directing: Analysis, Communication, and Style*, 7th edition by Francis Hodge and Michael McLain; Routledge, 2009. Reproduced by permission of Taylor & Francis Group.

Bibliography

Clurman, Harold. *On Directing*. New York: Macmillan, 1972.
Cole, Toby, and Helen Krich Chinoy, eds. *Directors on Directing*, 2nd rev. ed. Indianapolis, IN: Bobbs-Merrill, 1963.
Cole, Toby, and Helen Krich Chinoy. *Directing the Play*. Indianapolis, IN: Bobbs-Merrill, 1953.
Dean, Alexander, and Lawrence Carra. *Fundamentals of Play Directing*, 5th ed. Long Grove, IL: Waveland Press, 2009.

Dietrich, John E., *Play Direction*, 2nd ed. Englewood Cliffs, NJ: Prentice-Hall, 1983.
Hodge, Francis, and Michael McLain. *Play Directing: Analysis, Communication, and Style*, 7th ed. New York: Routledge, 2009.
Miller, Arthur. *After the Fall.* New York: Viking Press, Revised Final Stage Version, Reset edition, January 1, 1964.
Seivers, W. David, Harry E. Stiver, Jr., and Stanley Kahan. *Directing for the Theatre.* Dubuque, IO: Wm C. Brown, 1974.
Vardac, A. Nicholas. *Stage to Screen: Theatrical Method from Garrick to Griffith.* Cambridge, MA: Harvard University Press, 1949.

7 Production Organization

Auditions

Audition Scenes

Before holding auditions the director needs to decide what materials will be needed. Do you want the actors to bring their own material? Do you want them to have pieces prepared in advance (meaning memorized)? Do you want them to read in pairs? If so, you should provide copies of some scenes for them to read. When doing this, it is wise to consider scenes involving multiple genders. I like to have scenes for two women, two men, and for 1 man and 1 woman. Sometimes I have scenes copied with multiple characters in case I get odd numbers. I also have monologues copied for either men or women. I don't like to have actors just reading monologues, because I like to see how they will work with another person, but sometimes you just don't have enough actors or enough material and you want to give everyone a fair chance. It doesn't mean that women can't read men's monologues or vice versa, it just means you are prepared for any eventuality. I am also not tied to gender identity either. If a male wants to read female or vice versa, then fine by me. Sometimes that kind of casting can really work. I also like to have enough copies of these scenes and monologues that I can hand scripts to two actors and tell them to go somewhere and read it over and then come back. If I only have one set of copies, then I will be waiting for them to come back before I can get another pair working. I also try to have at least one or two group pieces ready if possible. These, ideally are from the play you are casting but could also be from another work entirely. In fairness, it's probably a good idea to either use pieces from the object play, or to use pieces from other sources, but not both. The actors with the other sources will feel that the actors with the object play have an unfair advantage. It is also a very good idea for either you or your stage manager to write the name of each actor who is auditioning in the order that they show up. As they are given something to read, circle their name so that you are always aware of who is on deck with a script and who is currently reading for you. A simple check

DOI: 10.4324/9781003360216-7

mark will indicate who has read and who has not. If you have written the names in order of their arrival, you will easily be able to see who has been waiting the longest. If you have the luxury of time, you might be able to ask specific actors to read more than once in which case you give them another script with a new partner, and make another mark by their name to indicate how many times they have read. A good stage manager can help you enormously with this organization but you must have time to go over the procedure with them ahead of time. If you are not blessed with a stage manager, you will have to do this for yourself. One can keep all these balls in the air if one is organized but it also tends to take your attention away from the actual purpose for which you are there: namely to cast the play. You don't want to get so bogged down in the technical details that you aren't paying attention to the people who are reading at the time. That is yet another reason why it is always best to have a good stage manager to help with all of the details (see Chapter 15).

Time, Places, Schedule

Obviously, you will want to publicize the auditions well in advance. Clearly indicate the day, date, time, and location, as well as any special instructions such as parking directions, entrance doors, etc. Don't assume that anyone knows anything about the place you are working in. State whether the actors should have a one-minute monologue prepared or be cold-reading from the play. Enterprising actors like to find the play in advance (if it is available) and give it a read. Find a space that has heat (or AC) and at least one working bathroom. Ideally, you will also want an audition venue that affords several "break-out" spaces for actors to go and prepare. These should have at least a modicum of sound-proofing so that you aren't assaulted with the sounds of people in another room screaming at each other. It's also a good idea to make sure that there are no other people in the building for these reasons or at least that they are warned. Actors will want to know what the rehearsal time commitment will be. Try to set at least a tentative rehearsal schedule. People have many other life commitments that may make it hard for them to commit. A little diplomacy here will help. Let them know that you are flexible and that rehearsals will be custom tailored around the needs of your group. Do let them know when the technical and dress rehearsals are, because it is an unwritten rule in every theatre group in the world that those dates and times are sacrosanct and *everyone* is committed to them.

Actor Audition Notes

Take good notes so you can easily remember each actor. I usually note the physical attributes of each person such as height, weight, hair color, hair style, distinguishing characteristics. I also try to note any scheduling conflicts – "Gone to sister's wedding on the 8th". Some organizations take a photo of each auditioner. This isn't always possible and can be cumbersome unless well organized. I usually try to make notes that will jog my memory ("Tall, half head shaved, pierced nose and lip"). I also make qualifying notes on each actor about their apparent good and bad qualities: "Reads well", "Difficulty reading", "Pronounced lisp", "Cherubic quality", "Youngish for the role", "Good energy", "Nice feel for _____".

I also try to see each actor as a character in the play and will make a note. In other words, I try to cast everyone in what I think are the roles they fit best. I know it sounds harsh but I usually rate each actor with A, B, or C. A is "in", B is "maybe", and C is "out". I usually try to give five or six lines on my note page to each actor, but I allow enough space on my note sheet if I go over.

Audition Forms

Some theatres will have a standard audition form; however, I try to use my own if they will let me. Audition forms have a pretty standard format. A couple of examples are given in Appendix 8. They should include name, date, address, phone, email, height, weight, hair color, etc. It is important to have a way to contact an auditioner so that information is important. Ask about special skills: Do you juggle, play an instrument, sing, do gymnastics, etc.? Many theatres want to know if an auditioner is willing to work backstage if not cast. You might list the options: lights, sound, set-building, house, box-office, etc. Ask auditioners to list any conflicting dates between the start of rehearsals and the opening of the show. I usually ask them to list what days and times of day are best for them to rehearse, including weekends. Do they have a work schedule that might be difficult to get around? Can they get off work during the last week before the show if they ask far enough in advance? It is common for someone to not be cast simply because their schedule is not compatible.

I also ask them to list relevant theatrical experience on the back of the sheet being selective as to "representative" roles. Of course, they may attach a résumé and headshot if they have one. If you know that there are going to be special skills needed in your show, indicate what they are: "Dance experience welcome", "jugglers needed", "guitar player needed". This information should also go in the publicity for the auditions. It is important to ask questions related to any show-specific needs, such as: "Are you willing to cut your hair?", "Are you willing to appear partly nude?" "Do you object to the use of strong language?", "Do you have any stage combat experience?", etc. Trigger warnings may be needed for certain sensitive situations in the play but audition forms can be customized to fit those circumstances. Intimacy is a very sensitive issue in this day and age and should be treated carefully, of course, but most definitely given a trigger warning at auditions.

Rehearsal Schedules

It is of paramount importance to set a definitive rehearsal schedule as early as possible. You might start with a tentative one until you can meet with everyone and get it approved. It is vitally important that everyone knows when rehearsals are and for which ones they will be called. Be as detailed and specific as possible. I frequently set a rehearsal schedule for the entire rehearsal period at once rather than scheduling a week at a time. Humans are creatures of habit and so try to set a *pattern* for rehearsals such as "All rehearsals begin at 7pm", Weekend rehearsals are at 2pm", "We will be rehearsing Monday, Wednesday and Friday and Sunday afternoons", etc. Establishing a pattern means that, even if I don't have my schedule with me, I know, if it's Wednesday, I have to be there at 7pm. If you break these patterns, do not be surprised if someone fails to show up because: "I thought we were always at 7pm on Wednesday!" A rehearsal schedule should include the following information:

1. Date
2. Day of the Week
3. Time
4. Place
5. Event ("Block Scene 1 & 2", "Run Act II", "Work Act I".
6. Call list with separate times if possible ("Puck and fairies at 7, Oberon at 8").

Note: "Blocking" has been discussed earlier. "Working" a scene or an act is when you work with something in detail, stopping and starting and going back to run something again. Note: It is always preferable to *run* something right after you have *worked* it, just to help cement the details in the actors' minds. "Running" an act or a scene is where you try to get through it without stopping. Other designations might include "stumble through" which is attempting to run something without stopping but knowing you may have to stop and start anyway. Technical rehearsals are usually numbered: 1st Tech, 2nd Tech, etc.). and may not have every actor called. Dress rehearsals are similarly numbered. Some directors schedule a "dress parade", which is not a rehearsal but a chance for designers to see the costumes on the actors in front of the set and in appropriate lighting conditions for the first time. Color in lighting can change the appearance of colors in pigment, so it is important to see the costumes and scenic pieces in correct lighting conditions. Some schedule a "crew view" in which the play is run in its entirety solely for the running crew, who almost never get to watch a rehearsal from the front.

Props

Props List: Hand Props

The actor's version of scripts from Dramatists Play Service and Samuel French includes a list of props in the back. These are the props used in the first production. This can be a good starting point. I always skim the play looking for props called for by the playwright. It is amazing how much smoking goes on, for instance, in Noel Coward scripts. It was such a cultural convention for Noel Coward's era, that it is hard to imagine doing one of his plays without it. It certainly poses a problem if you do want to eliminate smoking. Hand props are those used by the actors that are held in, or manipulated by hand. Put together a rough list of hand props early so that your technical people (or in fact, you yourself if you don't have a prop crew) can start looking for them. The best prop people are those who love to go to thrift stores and antique markets. My mother practically found a second career for herself as a prop hunter for a theatre group she worked with because she had a lot of contacts in the antique and secondhand goods market as well as several friends who ran pawn shops. She always amazed people with her ability to find some of the oddest things (a cross that shot fire out the top, for instance).

Props List: Set Props (See Appendix 9)

Set properties are those large pieces that form the basis for the obstacle course in the ground plan, usually but not always defined as furniture. Set props can also be things such as rocks, tree stumps, fences, garbage cans, juke boxes, pin-ball consoles, etc. I had a designer who never made a distinction between hand and set props. However, most of the real world divides them up that way. Many theatres have an inventory of furniture in storage. It is often possible to borrow set pieces from another theatre. It may also be possible to borrow items from thrift stores and other businesses, but some may have been burned by irresponsible theatre companies who either failed to return items or returned them damaged. I worked for a college theatre that had the same initials as a local summer theatre. When we went looking for furniture, they saw our initials and practically denied us entrance. A good director will insist the company act responsibly and return things in a timely manner, offer program mention, offer tickets, etc. It is always a good idea to try to foster good will with local businesses. Also, if you are planning to alter the item in any way, for instance painting or re-upholstering, something, *get permission first.*

I create these lists, at least in a preliminary way, at the same time I do my script prep. It gives me talking points at first design conferences. Since I also demand input into the groundplan, it also helps me to communicate my needs at those conferences. I used to drive one of my scene designers crazy because she kept telling me that I was designing the set for her which was her job and so I was stifling her creativity. After many years of working together, I finally made her understand that the relationship between the blocking plan and the groundplan were so organic that I needed the input there in order to make the other happen. In my opinion, it is impossible to block a production in advance on paper, without having an established groundplan.

Scenery

1. *Number and type of required locations.* If the scenic designer has not come prepared with this list, or if you do not have a scene designer, then you need to do it. Playwrights are often very good at providing this information, particularly as the acts and scenes change. When I directed *Harvey* by Mary Chase, the script indicated three acts and three changes of location. The first act was in the library of the Dowd family mansion, the second act was in the lobby of the sanitorium, and the third act was back at the library. This was seemingly simple, but required a massive scene change. The very elaborate Victorian library set had to completely go into hiding while the sterile and gleaming modern hospital took the stage, and then reappear when the action moved back to the library. *Noises Off* by Michael Frayn famously has three acts that change from the setting of the realistic interior of the house, complete with a second story and a staircase, to the *same set* as seen from behind in the second act, then back to the realistic interior in the third. It almost always requires some sort of turntable to rotate the set. This is why very few small theatre groups attempt this show. Shakespeare notoriously deals with many different locales, but moves between them with very few set pieces and often a place is described very quickly by the characters and then left to the audience's imagination. Many multiple settings require great ingenuity in scenery and moves at such a pace that often a complex groundplan for each location is not possible. I got around this when I directed *A Midsummer Night's Dream* by having many of the fairies costumed as things such as rocks and stumps and trees and fallen logs. I created a living groundplan which could easily move between each exterior scene and sometimes even within the scene (to great comedic effect, I blushingly add). The point is that a detailed analysis of entrances and exits and required locations is crucial to begin creating a groundplan and then blocking the show.
2. *List of required scenic pieces (doors, fireplaces, beds, etc.).* These are often dictated by the location. A bedroom probably needs a bed. A farce usually requires a fair number of doors. A Victorian mansion probably

requires a fireplace. Again, what you are looking for are those things mentioned in the script or required by the playwright. It is possible to change or consolidate locations, even though something else is called for by the playwright. When doing *Mrs. Warren's Profession* by George Bernard Shaw, we found that one scene that took place in the house according to the script could easily take place in the garden set from the previous scene. Walls are not always needed to indicate a realistic interior, but frequently work best. I have seen realistic interiors delineated by a skeletal outline of the house, behind which are seen scenic paintings of exteriors or even just a sky cyc. Usually there is some non-realistic and almost impressionistic reason for doing so, but it can also work to show the outline of the walls of a house by simply hanging window frames and pictures along what would be the path of the walls. I once saw a production of *The Rhinocerous* by Eugene Ionesco produced by a college theatre in which the set consisted of metal scaffolding that was covered with butcher's paper upon which had been painted a fanciful and cartoonish exterior of a Parisian street. As the play progressed and more and more people were transformed into Rhinoceri, they literally and gradually began to tear the paper from the scaffolding. By the end we were left looking at nothing but metal scaffolding which resembled nothing so much as cage bars. It was truly ingenious and awesome. It usually just takes some imagination to solve even the most difficult scenic problems.

Costume Notes

1. *Script requirements.* Once in a while, a playwright will delineate costume ideas. Most of the time, while I'm sure they have distinct ideas about what their characters look like, they don't give descriptions. Only George Bernard Shaw, who seemed to have an opinion about everything concerning his plays, seems to give any real detail concerning costumes.
2. *Director ideas.* The costume designer and director work together to establish the look of the characters. In theatres with no costume designer, actors often find their own costume. Sometimes there is an inventory of costume pieces from which to choose, although it can be difficult to find appropriate sizes. In these cases, the director can offer an opinion of the actor's choice: "I like those pants, but not that shirt." As an actor, I have gathered many costume pieces over the year from various eras that fit me. As a result, I have opera cloaks, frock coats, formal wear from several different periods, and rough western shirts that could easily be seen in an Elizabethan period. I have several of my own pairs of shoes in various styles and a pretty good assortment of hats. You cannot, however, expect all of your actors to have extensive personal collections. The best

you can do, at the early point of your preparation, is to jot down rough ideas concerning each character. As I am color blind, I usually confine my ideas to shapes and textures. I did take a costume course in college and have several fine textbooks with lovely examples of the look for different costume periods. An excellent resource is Lucy Barton's *Historic Costume for the Stage*. It contains hundreds of simple illustrations of historic periods – a good director should have some familiarity with historic costume.

Lighting

1. *Script requirements*. Many playwrights will give concrete ideas as to the time of day each scene takes place. Some will even go into detail such as: "four hours later", or "the next morning". There may be clues as to the use of candles and other practical methods of achieving lighting effects. Look through the script for anything in the text or stage directions that will indicate what the playwright thought about the lighting of a scene. In Arthur Kopit's *Indians*, for example, Buffalo Bill says, "Back again. Always knew this is where I belonged. The heat of that old spotlight on my face!" Well, there's a clue.
2. *Director ideas*. You will obviously have your own ideas about what lighting effects are needed for each scene. Your study of the play will have given you ideas for mood or other effects that lighting can supply. If you are color blind, like me, you will be dependent on others for a sensitivity to color. My sensitivity is mostly to light and dark. I am a fan of old movies and I always marvel at how they used lighting in those old movies to achieve effects. The backlight, in particular to highlight the silhouette of a head, a key light on the face of a romantic lead. The use of shadows and darkness to provide emphasis and mood. I think the old black and white movies, particularly, knew how to use light and dark to touch emotions and give emphasis. Watch for the darkness and shadows, in particular. It is almost a lost art. When color came to the movies, they needed a lot of light in order for the colors to register on the film. The amount of light washed out the darkness until visionary filmmakers such as Stanley Kubrick actually invented lenses, films, and cameras that could function in low light. See Kubrick's *Barry Lyndon* in particular.

Sound

1. *Script requirements*. Playwrights rarely specify music for their plays. Even Shaw seemed to shy away from this area. They do, however, pay attention to sound effects: a gunshot, a dog barking, someone knocking

on a door, a plane flying over, etc. These will be noted in the text of a play as well as the stage directions. List what will be needed. An important decision is whether the sound effects will be recorded, performed live, or be a combination. Recorded gunshots rarely sound authentic. Slapping two boards together can produce an adequate sound. Even an actual gun going off sometimes doesn't sound quite right to an audience, who have been brought up on the sound of gunshots from TV and film. There are many online resources for finding recorded sound effects.

2. *Director ideas.* Music is another story altogether. I am a big proponent of using music (themes and scene bridges, as well as pre-show, intermission, and finale music) to set a mood. I once directed a production made up of bits and pieces from e. e. cummings theatrical works entitled *Think Twice Before You Think*. I used the avant-garde music of Lori Anderson almost exclusively for themes and bridges. It was a magical marriage of surreal minds at work. To this day, it is one of my favorite stage efforts. I think both e. e. and Lori would have been happy with the blending. I did another show with very dark overtones by a well-known Canadian playwright named George F. Walker entitled *Better Living*. I used music by another Canadian, Leonard Cohen, for themes and bridges. There is a dark streak that sometimes runs through Mr. Cohen's works that seemed just particularly appropriate for the play. It captured the moods very well and got much attention – another of my very favorite marriages of play and music. Another show I did was set in Moscow about American students at the Moscow Art Theatre in the eighties entitled *Mockba*. I went in search of Russian rock music and found a real treasure trove, mostly by the Russian artist, Boris Grebenshikov who had been called "the Russian Bob Dylan". It was just absolutely the right touch of fairly modern sounding and yet foreign music and was a great complement to the show. We also found the Russian equivalent of "top forty radio" which we recorded and used in several backgrounds.

I've worked most of my career in a college setting and was covered by the educational exemption for copyright law. When selecting music for a show, be aware of copyright law. It is against the law to use musical pieces without paying a royalty fee or at least getting an artist's permission. Disney, in particular is very strict about anyone using music that they hold the rights to. It's well known in the theatre world to "beware of the Mouse". One way around this is to find a musician or two and get them to write something for you.

Make-up

1. *Script requirements.* Playwrights do not give many textual clues about make-up except when something is unusual. Even then there isn't a lot

of detail. In Ionesco's *Rhinocerous*, for example, the characters gradually transform into Rhinoceri. I have seen this done in many different ways from the literal addition of horns and gray skin, to simple masks and helmets. Since Ionesco was drawing a broad metaphorical parallel with the rise of the Nazis and fascism, the masks and helmets idea seemed to work the best, although it was not very subtle. I was involved with a production of Grimms' *Fairy Tales* which involved a lot of animal characters. The costumes and make-up for this show were amazing and incredible as we had a rabbit, a crow, a donkey, a turtle, and many other characters. I directed a production of *A Midsummer Night's Dream* in which we made some of the fairies up as inanimate things such as rocks, tree stumps, small trees, even mounds of earth. These characters literally became parts of the set which could move and change places. The effect was frequently startling for the human characters and often hilarious.
2. *Director ideas*. As indicated above, you can certainly see how the director's vision plays into the creation of the world of these plays. The responsibility for make-up often falls to costume crew. In some theatres, character make-up is left to the actors. This can be good and it can be bad. Sometimes actors think they know more than they do and you end up with a garish mess. Other times actors know virtually nothing at all and so you get virtually nothing at all. I think I would rather have virtually nothing at all than the garish mess. Once in a while you get someone who knows what they are doing and then that person becomes most helpful to everyone else. That is a very nice place to be. But if you are going to do a play where you know that there will be extreme make-up demands, try to find a specialist to come in and help out. A *Christmas Carol* springs to mind.

Publicity

There is a terrific book called *Subscribe Now* by Danny Newman about the necessity for selling the show. He postulates "Would you rather have a beautiful production, or a full house?" He also postulates that you should plan to spend some money on publicity if you really want to sell your show. Most TV and radio stations will be happy to sell you ad time but are much more reticent to just give it away. The same applies to print media as well. Posters are somewhat effective, but an ad in a newspaper (yes, they still exist) or on the internet (Facebook, Instagram, etc.) are much more effective. So, first you have to ask yourself, "Who's going to do it?" If the answer is you, you are probably already biting off more than you can chew. Ideally you should have someone in your organization (Hah, you say. Organization?) who is responsible for helping out with publicity. Writing the copy, getting the photos taken, scheduling the actors and the photographer as well as the costumer, having the poster developed. In this age of internet access, it is much easier to access graphic material. But again, be careful of violating copyrights! Call the TV stations to see about news reports, possible ad time, etc. Same with radio. Find all of the print sources that carry public calendars for the arts and get yourself hooked up with them. Write letters to organizations and offer discounts for groups. This can work for schools, senior living establishments, etc. As you can readily see, managing publicity could easily be a full-time job and most professional theatres have people hired to do just that. Community theatres have to depend on volunteers, unless you can free up some money to pay a little bit to someone for this job. One way to raise money might also be selling ads in programs: another thankless job that requires vast expenditures of time. On the other hand, establishing relationships with local businesses can pay dividends in many other ways. Don't be afraid to remind them that buying an ad in a program can be used as a tax deduction. If you can get a large business to sponsor an evening of programming, they might be willing to send their employees and families to the show on those evenings. A subscription series in which people can buy tickets at a discount if they do packages of multiple shows or even an entire season is always a good way to help pack a house.

As with just about everything else involved in running a theatre, there are so many considerations for publicity that it can make your head spin. However, I have seen some small groups that began to get a reputation for quality entertainment in their area, and thus they developed a repeat audience. It is an amazing thing to see when people have so many reasons not to leave home and so many other ways to spend their entertainment money, that they will spend money on a night out at the theatre. A large part of that is giving them a good show. I don't mean always doing crowd pleasers. We've all seen that and there is nothing wrong with including one or two of those in a season, but you can give quality with lesser-known material and convince your audience to trust you to give them an evening of entertainment. I once asked my dad what he thought entertainment meant and he answered, "I like to laugh". Well, who doesn't? I see my dad as an almost typical audience member but you must also remember that sometimes people like to cry as well. If not, why are there such disciples for the soaps. My great aunt used to call them "the agonies". Why do people like to cry? There's great catharsis in a good cry. Never sell your audience short.

This can be more task oriented. List the things that need to be done and who you think can and will do them.

Programs

In addition to listing the cast and crew, programs should include information necessary for the audience to understand what they are about to see: a list of characters, the time frame (period, day, time, elapsed time, etc.), and warnings about the use of special effects: strobe lights, smoking, gun shots, etc. It's considerate to include the running time, length of intermission(s), and where the restrooms are located.

A character/cast list is required, as well as a list of every crew member and position. Be sure the names are accurate (how does the actor/crew member want to be listed?), spelled correctly, and using the correct pronouns. Directors should also provide a list of individuals or groups that require special thanks. These are usually businesses or persons who have loaned items, people who have worked outside of the normal expectations, people who have provided services or time, etc. Programs may also need special notes for certain odd show requirements such as "gunshots will be used in this production" or "Smoking will be simulated in this production", whatever special requirements you feel you need to warn your audience about. Finally, a director's note is often included though that is not a necessity. It can provide additional contextual or historical information, insight into the director's vision, or simply set a mood. A favorite director's note I wrote for a particularly crazy comedy consisted of the word "blah" repeated over and over again, occasionally interrupted by some cliché phrase like "wonderful crew" or "long-suffering wife", etc. I like to read director's notes although many don't. It's best to avoid such clichés as "It has been a long, hard road" and "We hope you enjoy". Of course, you hope they will enjoy it. Do you really need to say that?

Bibliography

Barton, Lucy. *Historic Costume for the Stage*. Boston, MA: Walter H. Baker, 1969.
Brockett, Oscar G., Robert J. Ball, and Andrew Carlson. *The Essential Theatre*, 11th ed. Boston, MA: Cengage Learning, 2016.
Brockett, Oscar Gross. *The Theatre: An Introduction*, 4th ed. New York: Holt, Rinehart & Winston, 1979.
Carter, Conrad, A. J. Bradbury, and W. R. B. Howard. *The Production and Staging of Plays*. New York: Arc Books, 1963.
Cole, Toby, and Helen Krich Chinoy, eds. *Directors on Directing*, 2nd rev. ed., Indianapolis, IN: Bobbs-Merrill, 1963.
Cole, Toby, and Helen Krich Chinoy. *Directing the Play*. Indianapolis, IN: Bobbs-Merrill, 1953.
Dean, Alexander, and Lawrence Carra. *Fundamentals of Play Directing*, 5th ed. Long Grove, IL: Waveland Press, 2009.
Dietrich, John E. *Play Direction*, 2nd ed. Englewood Cliffs: Prentice-Hall, 1983.
Dolman, John Jr., and Richard K. Knaub. *The Art of Play Production*. New York: Harper & Rowe, 1973.
Downs, William Missouri. *The Art of Theatre: Then and Now*, 4th ed. Boston, MA: Cengage Learning, 2017.
Hagen, Uta, and Frankel Haskel. *Respect For Acting*. New York: Macmillan, 1973.

Hodge, Francis, and Michael McLain. *Play Directing: Analysis, Communication, and Style*, 7th ed. Nrw York: Routledge, 2009.

Seivers, W. David, Harry E. Stiver, Jr., and Stanley Kahan. *Directing for the Theatre*. Dubuque, IA: Wm C. Brown, 1974.

Vardac, A Nicholas. *Stage to Screen: Theatrical Method from Garrick to Griffith*. Cambridge, MA: Harvard University Press, 1949.

Whiting, Frank M. *An Introduction to the Theatre*. New York: Harper & Brothers, 1961.

8 Directors and Design

The Goals of Design

Designers turn the words and thoughts of the play into pictures and sounds. Theatre communicates both visually and aurally (heard language), and the designers' creations can greatly enhance our experience.

The four goals of theatrical design are to provide information (where, when, what, how), underscore the emotional life of the play, help to tell the story, and reveal the world of the play (the total environment in which the characters live).

By "providing information" the designer answers four fundamental questions:

1. *Where are we?* The place in which the play is set can be real or fictional. Whether real or imagined, our "suspension of disbelief" makes us want to believe that the place could exist. Design must support that illusion. Design tells us if we are indoors or out, in public or in private, in a rich or a poor environment, etc.
2. *When are we?* Without words, design can tell us the era in which the play takes place, sometimes the exact year, season, and time of day. Architecture and furniture can be clues to a historic period or era. Season can be indicated by such things as Christmas decorations, autumn leaves, etc. Many designs show us the time of day by representing the light of the sun or moon through the use of colored light. Sometimes, even a clock on the set can tell us exactly what time it is. A famous example is *Night Mother* by Marsha Norman in which the main character tells her mother she is going to commit suicide at midnight and there is a clock on the wall steadily counting down to that hour in real time. Other indications can be the type of clothing the characters are wearing. If, for instance, all of the characters have to take off their heavy coats, scarves, and gloves as they enter, we can assume that it's cold outside. I was once in a show called *When Ya Comin' Back Red Ryder* by Mark Medoff which is supposed to take place at the edge of the desert in New

Mexico in the summer. We were all dressed in hot weather clothing such as shorts, T-shirts, tank-tops, etc. Unfortunately, we were doing this play in an outdoor venue in Colorado in September and one weekend was particularly cold, rainy, and blustery. We had to pretend it was burning hot and we were dying of the heat. It was a real test of our acting skills and we were silently cursing the audience which dutifully showed up in coats and scarves huddled together for warmth. The show must go on! Another unfortunate decision I was involved in was a production of *The Lion in Winter* by James Goldman, which is supposed to take place at the Christmas Court of Henry II. We were all dressed in furs and boots in July! The show must go on!

3. *What is going on?* The design can tell us what is happening in the development of the story as the locations change and we see time passing. I saw a set design which featured a broken child's high chair in a corner of a realistic living room. As the play progressed, we learned the couple living there had lost a child to cancer. We recognized that by simply seeing it.
4. *How is this being presented?* Design also tells us how reality will be interpreted. The style tells us if the play is going to be realistic, romantic, surreal, or very theatrical.

In addition to answering the basic questions, the design can also:

- *Underscore emotion.* The design influences our mood psychologically by using the elements of design: color, line, mass, and texture. Bright, cheery colors, for instance, let us know that there is a lightness and frivolity to follow.
- *Tell the story.* Stories develop from scene to scene. The design helps us follow the journey by revealing the progression of locations. The world of the play involves, of course, the specific information discussed above, but also involves the *values* of the society or world in which the characters live. We imagine not only the world that we see on the stage, but the world as it exists *off* the stage. Where do the characters go when they exit? Where are they coming from? A good design implies the life of the *whole* world of the play through the use of all the communicative elements, and speaks to us both consciously and subconsciously. Often, the religious, political, and social environments of a play are reflected in its design.

The Elements and Principles of Design

I believe that every good director should have a fundamental knowledge of design and be capable of speaking the language of design with designers. For that reason, I will attempt to provide some basics of design. In many cases, amateur directors will also be dealing with amateur designers and may have to help them to understand the sort of thing that they are looking for.

The four fundamental elements of design are: color, line, mass, and texture. We respond to color both psychologically and physiologically. We have come to associate certain colors with certain moods and responses since childhood. Conditioned responses to color: "Red Hot Mama", "I'm a bit blue today", "purple-faced with anger", "green with envy", "heart of gold", "gray day", "a black mood", etc. We often refer to colors as being either "warm" or "cool". Reds, oranges, and yellows are often seen as warm while greens, blues, and violets are often seen as cool. There are three basic colors that cannot be created by mixing other colors together. We call these the "primary" colors. They are red, yellow, and blue. Black is the presence of all the colors, white is the absence of all color. The color spectrum is generally thought to be red, orange, yellow, green, blue, indigo, and violet. Above the range of human ability to see is ultra-violet and below that range is infra-red. Both are invisible to the eye. Color has three basic properties: hue, intensity, and value. Hue is the name of the color itself. For instance, Red by itself and not mixed with anything else is a pure hue. When we mix equal amounts of two primary colors, we create a new hue. Red and blue mix to create violet, for instance. Yellow and red create orange. Blue and yellow create green. The intensity of a color is its relative brightness or dullness. The value of a color is described by how much white or black is added to it. Its value is raised when white is added and lowered when black is added. We call these variations "tints" or "shades".

A line is the connecting mark between two points. Line is considered to have six basic properties. These are: path, width, continuity, sharpness, length, and direction. Each of these properties of line work on us psychologically, the same way color does. Path describes the way a line moves from one point to the other. There are straight lines, curved lines, zig-zagged lines, etc. Width describes the thickness of a line. A thick line feels heavier than a thin one. The continuity of a line is the consistency of a line's movement on its way from one point to another. Lines can be continuous or they can be broken. Broken lines make us feel jumpy and tense, while continuous lines have a certain security in relation. A line's sharpness is its distinctness. Distinct lines are different from fuzzy ones. Sharp lines feel hard and precise, while fuzzy lines feel soft. A line's length implies its duration. Long lines have a feeling of grace and stability, while short ones often feel jumpy and unfinished. The direction of a line describes where a line is headed in relation to where it starts. Lines can move in one of three directions: vertically, horizontally, and diagonally. Vertical lines are associated with strength because we often see them in the structural members that hold things up, such as columns. Horizontal lines are associated with evenness, balance, and serenity. Diagonal lines are often associated with instability and unpredictability.

This is often because we imply gravity at work and a diagonal line looks like it is about to fall over.

Mass describes the apparent weight of an object. We describe the mass of an object by its volume and its shape. The volume of something is the amount of three-dimensional space it takes up. The shape of something describes its form (circles, squares, cubes, irregular shapes like trees, etc.). We often see shapes as distinct from their surroundings because they appear to have edges. We call this the outline of an object. The area surrounding the object is the "background". In art we hear the terms "figure" and "ground", meaning the object in focus and the world surrounding it. Texture describes what we think something would feel like if we were to touch it. Texture can be rough or smooth, hard or soft, etc.

The five principles of design are those properties that are used to organize the elements into a composition. They are: focus, balance, proportion, rhythm, and unity. Focus describes how the design elements are used to guide our eyes to look where the designer wants us to look. Oddly enough, line is the easiest element of design to use to manipulate where we look. Balance describes how designers arrange the masses of the scenery into a composition that plays with our sense of symmetry.

Balance is the equal distribution of apparent weight on either side of a center. Symmetrical balance would have each side exactly mirroring the other. Asymmetrical balance is achieved when the apparent weight on the two sides of the center feels equal, although the masses are not identical. Imbalance is frequently used to make us feel uneasy. When things don't balance, we sense that something is wrong and our psychological inner tension is increased. Oddly enough, symmetrical balance works very well for comedy, while asymmetrical balance works for serious plays and imbalance works for tragedy. No one really knows why this is so. My theory is that we automatically see the world in balance and when it is not, we feel uneasy.

Proportion is the relative quantities of color, line, mass, and texture in relation to the whole composition. Proportions change when things are either larger or smaller than we think they should be. A clown's large shoes are "out of proportion" to the rest of his body. We often view things in relation to our own size. Things that are much larger than us can be intimidating or overwhelming, often frightening. Things that are smaller than us are no threat to us and we feel in control of them, even fond of them.

Rhythm is the repetition of the perceived elements in a design. When something repeats frequently, we say it has a rhythm. This can be perceived visually as well as aurally. We hear our heartbeat and recognize a rhythm. We also recognize a rhythm in the visually repeated pattern of a picket fence, for example.

Unity describes the way in which all of the elements are organized to form a coherent and aesthetically pleasing whole. We can't always tell when something is truly harmonious because we are used to that. But we can easily tell when something is out of place.

A metaphor that might help is that design is using the elements of design to make building blocks while the principles of design help you to arrange the blocks into a recognizable structure. In design, as in every art, there is a lot of room for differing interpretations of the proper visual way to present the work.

The Designer's Process (See Appendix 18)

Analyze the script focusing on several key concepts: physical needs (entrances, fire-escapes, etc.); locations (the library, the parlor, the bedroom, a park, etc.); how many and what specifics are mentioned in the script. Specifics can be changed by mutual consent. Multiple set plays are often consolidated in one setting – create a character/scene plot showing which characters appear in which scenes. This is particularly important for costume designers. Dialogue can give character visual clues ("I'm so sloppy today"). Understand the action: who wants what and what do they do in order to achieve it? Setting reflects, enhances, and supports the action. What is the time element: year, season, time of day (climate)? What sound effects are called for? What are the moods of the play?

Research the world of the play such as the history of art, architecture, interior decoration, furniture, clothing, differing forms of illumination (candles, gas lanterns, oil lanterns, torches, etc.). Go to the library and look for books with photographs or use Google to find illustrative images – sometimes just for metaphor, mood, color, tone; other times for specific locations, props, molding, wall treatments, etc.

Design Conferences

Design conferences involve the whole production design team.

1. *Preliminary concept*, usually described by the director with ideas thrown about by designers.
2. *Initial sketches, doodles.* Sketches are generally quick impressions designed to communicate ideas and concepts. One of my favorite examples of sketches gone awry is in the movie *Spinal Tap* where one of the characters sketches a set for their onstage rock concert by drawing what he sees as "Stonehenge" and then writes "22" next to it. Of course, when the set is built and they see it for the first time at the opening of a concert, the "Stonehenge" set is only 22 inches high.
3. *Solidifying the production design concept.* First drafts and white models, renderings and color swatches – color coordination is important. The designs are approved and all go back to the drawing board.

4. *Finalizing the designs.* Technical drawings, plots, charts, renderings, perspective drawings, full color models (ground plan, front elevation, cross section, working drawings, costume plot, light plot, instrument schedule, cue sheets, sound plots, etc.).

Going to Work on the Show

Once designs have been agreed upon, it is time to begin the work of making them into reality. This can now involve a myriad of technicians and artists such as: a technical director who oversees the building of the show, carpenters, scene painters, costumers, master electricians, control board operators, electrics crews who hang, circuit, focus, and color the lights, costume crews, properties crews, sound crews, load-in crews, running crews, stage managers, dressers who help the actors into their costumes, and so on. The actual building and running of a show can involve scores of people. Community theatres often do not have the luxury of being able to field all of these workers and so are dependent on volunteers to help make the production happen. Many jobs are doubled and sometimes trebled. Usually, the people who fill all of these jobs are the true backbone of a theatre and what they accomplish is nothing short of miraculous.

Choice of Theatre Space

If there is a choice, the kind of theatre space envisioned for the show needs to be addressed as well. There isn't always the luxury of a choice, but the five basic kinds of theatre spaces are:

1. The proscenium arch theatre
2. The arena theatre (theatre-in-the-round)
3. The thrust theatre
4. The black box theatre
5. The open space theatre.

The proscenium arch theatre has the audience facing the stage, with a framed opening through which the stage is viewed. Years ago, this frame was thought of as a picture frame which meant that the audience was literally watching a "moving picture". The word "proscenium" comes from the Greek "pro skene", meaning "in front of the scenery". The Greek "skene" was a building behind the playing space from which the performers entered. At some point, someone got the idea to paint the likeness of a background on the face of this building and "scenery" was invented. The proscenium stage is generally raised up a few feet and the audience area is raked up toward the back of the auditorium to facilitate sight lines. In the early days of the proscenium, the stage itself was often raked up as it went away from the audience. Hence, actors moved literally "upstage" and "downstage". Representational theatre is based on the convention that what you see on stage "represents" real life. This led to the idea of the "fourth wall", a concept that assumes the audience is looking into the acting space through an invisible fourth wall. It is sometimes easier to believe what we are seeing if we feel that we are literally peeping into the world of the characters. Presentational theatre is where the separation between the audience and the stage is deliberately broken and characters frequently talk directly to the audience. When the illusion of "reality" is broken like this it has been thought that it destroys the audience's "suspension of disbelief". What often happens, though, is that the audience is made to feel like "insiders" with the action.

Arena theatre refers to theatre where the audience completely surrounds the playing space. This places the audience closer to the action and fosters a more intimate and less formal relationship between the audience and the actors by removing the four walls and allowing the audience to observe from any angle. A drawback is that one can see the audience on the opposite side of the space which can sometimes hurt the illusion of reality for an audience. This configuration involves minimal scenery and scenic pieces that are very low and can be seen over. It is customary for the audience seating area to be in tiers to afford better sightlines. The performers must enter through the audience. Aesthetic distance describes the condition in which the audience is close enough to the stage to be emotionally involved, yet far enough away to remain physically apart. We all feel uncomfortable when someone comes too close. There is an appropriate distance at which we do not feel our space is being "invaded". Arena theatre often comes dangerously close to breaking this comfort zone.

Thrust theatre is where the audience sits on three sides of the performing space. Many classical theatres are thrusts: The Greek stage, the Elizabethan stage, the court theatres of France, etc. Usually, a back wall is used for scenery and for entrances and exits. The performers can also enter through the audience, as in the arena.

Black box theatre is literally a large, empty room painted black, in which almost any audience/stage relationship may be set up using moveable risers. It is an extremely flexible space, usually equipped with all the technology of a standard theatre (lights, sound, traps, flies, etc.). This flexible space was created as a rebellion against the proscenium that had dominated for centuries. It grew out of a desire to experiment with the audience relationship. One of these experiments was "environmental theatre", which often had the audience move their seats as the performance took place all around them. I saw a production of *The Hobbit* at the University of Texas where the audience sat in rotating seats in the center area while the action progressed as a "journey" around the outside of the space.

Open space theatre is literally theatre performed in spaces not originally designed to be performing spaces, such as warehouses, factories, gymnasiums, cafeterias, street corners, etc. The idea here is to take the performance to the audience rather than vice versa. This concept grew out of the political theatre of the 1960s, which was often performed in the streets to make anti-war statements.

Choices in Scenic Design

There are five standard kinds of scenic design:

1. Box set (realistic interior)
2. Realistic exterior
3. Two-dimensional painted scenery ("wing-and-drop")
4. Unit set
5. Projected.

Box sets or realistic interiors are a representational "slice of life", literally looking into a room with the wall facing the audience removed. "Drawing room plays" is a term often used for plays set in the "living" room of a family house.

A realistic exterior is a realistic representation of an outdoor setting, such as a park, street, country road, mountainside, etc.

Two-dimensional painted scenery is painted on flat surfaces. These surfaces can be fabric stretched on frames called "flats" or large expanses of cloth hanging from a pipe, which are called "drops". "Wing and drop" scenery combines the two styles. Flats, called wings because they are in the wings, are placed on the sides to represent buildings, trees, etc. Drops at the rear can be raised and lowered in front of each other to change the vista. Frequently, new wings are slid onstage to cover the previous ones. This change of view can be done in seconds and can be quite magical to watch.

A unit set is a permanent structure composed of many levels and areas that do not represent a literal place but on which many different places can be suggested.

Projected scenery is used in much modern scenery where it is projected onto surfaces with video and slide projectors. The development of powerful LED projectors, coupled with computers, allows for much more design freedom. Projectors are still quite expensive and require some expertise to use, but the possibilities are limited only by one's imagination. Much texture can also be added by the use of "gobos" fitted into lighting instruments. These range from simple images cut out of steel, such as leaves or windows, to revolving color images printed on glass. Moving images can simulate snow falling or clouds moving. Lights with LED sources have revolutionized the use of color in lights as colors and patterns can be changed instantly.

Sound Design

The Three Types of Theatre Sound

1. Sound reinforcement
2. Emotional reinforcement
3. Sound effects.

Sound reinforcement refers to the use of microphones to amplify actors' voices or musical instruments. The development of very small and accurate microphones has led to extensive use of reinforcement in modern theatre, not always to the benefit of a production. While improvements are being made all the time, a good system can be quite expensive. A more important consideration is whether a skilled engineer is available to operate the system. No reinforcement is preferable to bad reinforcement.

Sound can be used for *emotional reinforcement* in several ways:

Themes. A show may have one predominant theme to set an overall tone or different themes for each act that reflect the tone of the act. Music before an act often sets the tone for what is to come, while music concluding the act often makes a statement about what just happened. Themes should be dynamic but short. A main theme is generally established and then repeated at the breaks to provide mood. One of my tricks is to use music by the same composer throughout a show to help provide a thematic unity. I once directed a play about a group of exchange students studying theatre at the Moscow Art Theatre. I wanted to give a sense of what young people in Russia might be listening to in the modern era. I found some very vibrant underground rock music by Russian musicians which helped provide the atmosphere.

Bridges. These are longer pieces of music, often intended to sustain the audience's mood through breaks in the action from one segment to another. Keep in mind that a theme, repeated too often, loses its effectiveness as a statement.

Underscoring. Common in movies and television, but rarely used in theatre, underscoring is music which plays during or "under" a scene. If used, it is important to set volumes low enough so the music does not cover or distract from the actors' voices and play on the audience's sub-conscious.

Pre-show music. This is music that plays when the audience enters the theatre and is designed to transition them from their lives outside the theatre into the world of the play they are about to experience. Pre-show music generally fades out about 3–4 minutes before the show starts in order to set it apart from "theme" music. Audiences have indicated to me that they truly appreciate this attempt to bring them into the world of the play from the moment they enter the theatre. I highly recommend the use of pre-show music to help set the mood. When I directed the comedy *Light Up the Sky* by Moss Hart, a satire of the theatre and theatre people, I used a lot of the music from *Forbidden Broadway*, which is broadly satirical of Broadway musicals. It helped to set the tone. We had the audience laughing before the play started.

Sound effects can also be used to help tell the story. Recorded sound effects involve pre-recording all the effects and playing them back during performance. Computers have made this much easier than when magnetic tape was spliced together to form more complicated strings of sound. Many sound effects libraries may be found online. Computers now allow much more complicated recording, splicing, and mixing to be done without all of the manual work of literally cutting tape and gluing it together. One of my jobs in college was creating show tapes using the splice and tape method. One of the hardest sounds I had to create was from a George Bernard Shaw play entitled *Heartbreak House*. The script called for the sound of a Zeppelin flying overhead. I recorded an aquarium motor at a much faster speed and then played it back at a slower speed which slowed the sound down and deepened the tone. It was perfect for the ominous quality of a German war machine flying overhead.

When pre-recording is not possible or effect does not sound authentic, it is necessary to produce those sounds live. Many sounds do not reproduce well in recordings such as gunshots. It is quite preferable to use a blank gun offstage. One show I did called for the sound of a bicycle offstage. We found that the sound of an old mechanical hand egg beater made quite a decent substitute. This is quite an art form for movies in the occupation of a "Foley artist" – a person who produces sounds by various means that are then recorded. The light saber sound for *Star Wars* is an example (which was recorded by hitting the support cables of a tall antenna with a wrench) as well as the "voice" of Chewbacca, the Wookie. In the famous *War of the Worlds* radio broadcast by Orson Welles and the Mercury Theatre, they wanted an ominous sound of the spacecraft opening. They got a large mayonnaise jar and placed it in the bottom of a toilet with a microphone and slowly unscrewed the lid. For an excellent illustration of the process, there is a movie that was made for TV in the 1960s entitled *The Night That Panicked America*. While the plot is a bit cheesy, the faithful reproduction of the radio studio in the broadcast of the play is nothing short of brilliant. It is one of the most accurate depictions of the way radio broadcasts used to work that I have ever seen. The gentleman who played Orson Welles as well as all those who portrayed all of the other Mercury Theatre actors are nothing less than brilliant.

The Sound Plot

A sound plot is a list of cues and their location in the script. If a director has a clear idea of where and when he/she wants a sound cue to happen, it is a good idea to create a sound plot indicating those moments (see Appendix 12).

Cues can be divided into two lists: music and effects. Obviously, these sounds are brought into design production meetings and played for all to hear. Directors may have strong opinions about sound and lead the way in their selection, or they may just want to have the designer choose things and approve or disapprove them.

Costume Design

Good costume design tells us:

1. *where* the action is set. Is the action indoors or out? What is the climate? Is the action public or private? Are the characters rich or impoverished? Costumes can even tell us if the action is in a particular country or city. For instance, Texans might wear boots, workmen might wear hard hats, a rich man might wear a well-cut suit. Those living in colder climates tend to wear heavier fabrics and more layers; warmer climates allow for lighter fabrics and fewer clothes.
2. *when* the events take place. Costumes can tell us the era or even the decade, the season of the year, and the time of day. Many periods of history are defined by their silhouette (the bold outline of the costume). There are many costume books for the stage that contain illustrations of the various eras of history.
3. *who* the characters are. Costumes can give us a lot of information about the characters, such as personality, ethnicity, nationality, vocation, social and marital status, religious affiliation, psychological profile, and state of mind. These things generally fall into several categories:
   - *Gender*. In most eras there is a bold distinction between what men and women wear. Our modern world doesn't often make such distinctions.
   - *Age*. This can often be determined by a quick look at a person's attire. Young people are more concerned with how they look and fitting in. Older people may try to look younger through the use of make-up or the style of clothing.
   - *Economic status*. This can be revealed by what a character wears. For instance, it is easy to see the difference between an expensive men's suit and one purchased off the racks at Walmart or a thrift store.
   - *Relationships to other characters*. This can also be communicated through costume choices. Family ties, military allegiances, social affiliations, etc. can be indicated. Frequently designers use color to link together groups of characters. In the old movies, the good guy always wore a white hat. Scottish clans have unique patterns of plaid that are practically the equivalent of wearing a name tag.
   - *Telling the story*. Costume changes, even minor adjustments to costume, can help to indicate the changing circumstances of the

character. A quick example is *Waiting For Godot* and the degeneration of the clothing that mirrors their continuing fall from grace.
- *How the action is (or is not) like apparent reality*. Costumes are primary indicators of the style of a production. One quick glance can tell us if the story is realistic or not.
- *Underscoring the emotions of the play*. Like the set designer, the costume designer can manipulate the design elements to influence our emotional response to the characters in the same way that they influence us psychologically (our associations with the color red, for example as being fiery and bloody; yellow as being bright and cheery, blue as being melancholy, green as being envious, etc.).

Lighting Design

When plays were performed outside in the sunlight, the impression of the changes of light in the story was created by the playwright's words: "Light thickens, and the crow makes wing to the rooky wood" (Macbeth); "What light through yonder window breaks ..." (*Romeo and Juliet*); "O now be gone, more light and light it grows" (*Romeo and Juliet*). The audience knew if it was supposed to be night or day by the words and behavior of the actors. In 1879 Thomas Edison developed the incandescent light bulb, and only 11 years later, in 1890, the Savoy Theatre in London introduced electric lighting on the stage.

Any creative art involves both artistry and craft. The artistry is the designer's vision of the final product as seen by the audience. The craft is in the use of the tools of the trade. The tools of the lighting designer have become increasingly technologically complex. The lighting instruments, the color media, the instrument accessories, the control equipment (which has now become computerized), form a field of study in theatre that can take a lifetime to master. The development of low voltage, low wattage LED light sources has created a revolution in the way lights are made and used for the stage.

The controllable qualities of light are: distribution, intensity, movement, and color. *Distribution* refers to several elements: the direction from which the light is projected, the quality of the light (sharp or diffuse), the character of the light (texture: smooth, even, patterned, hard, soft, etc.), and the area that the light has to cover. When we focus lights, we determine their quality and character by changing the focal length of the instrument and adding patterns or diffusion media. *Intensity* is the actual amount, or level of brightness, of the light that strikes the stage. This is controlled by the use of dimmers. *Movement* of lights involves the timed duration of a light cue: the movement of onstage practicals such as lanterns or flashlights; the actual movement of a lighting instrument (varilights, follow spots, etc.).

Color is perhaps the most powerful of the qualities in its mood-enhancing power. Color media allow the designer to literally "paint" with light. The old color media were called "gels" because they were literally once made of a gelatin-like substance that could dissolve in water. Though they are not made of gelatin anymore, we still use the term. The newer method of changing color in lights media is created by the use of many multiple LED sources of varying colors and the ability to create differing hues and tints by the mixing of them.

The basic functions of stage lighting are visibility, selective focus, modeling, and mood. *Visibility* is the most basic, and simply means that the audience must be able to see the actors. However, visibility is selective, and it takes light to do that in an enclosed space such as a theatre. We can literally make audiences look where we want them to by lighting some areas and not others. This is called *selective focus*. One famous designer said that he pays as much attention to where the light *isn't* as to where it *is*. The intensity, direction, and color of a light can highlight one part of the stage while suppressing another, or make an actor emerge as a focal point onstage while everyone else is in shadow. In musicals, focus is often accomplished by the use of follow-spots, bright lights mounted on pivots to literally follow an actor as he moves around the stage. *Modeling* describes how we see in three dimensions because of our ability to see the subtle shadings of light and shadow and color that surround an object. Lighting designers can deepen the shadows and accentuate the highlights to sculpt our perception of objects on the stage (try putting a flashlight under your chin to see the effect of changing the direction of shadows). The use of sidelight and backlight can sculpt bodies by enhancing edges and is used a lot in dance. *Mood* means that the designer must work closely with the director and other designers to establish the moods of the play. Intensity, direction, movement, and color can all be manipulated to create subtle psychological effects on the audience.

Note: The information in this chapter is drawn from my experience teaching a course entitled "Introduction to Theatre" and was compiled from a variety of sources, including*: The Art of Theatre: Then and Now* by William Missouri Downs, *Another Opening, Another Show* by Tom Markus and Linda Sarver, *An Introduction to the Theatre* by Frank M. Whiting, *Theatrical Design and Production* by J. Michael Gillette, *History of the Theatre* by Oscar G. Brockett, and *The Theatre: An Introduction* by Oscar G. Brockett.

Bibliography

Barton, Lucy. *Historic Costume for the Stage*. Boston, MA: Walter H. Baker, 1969.
Brockett, Oscar G., *History of the Theatre*, 10th ed. Boston, MA: Pearson, 2007.
Brockett, Oscar Gross. *The Theatre: An Introduction*, 4th ed. New York: Holt, Rinehart & Winston, 1979.

Brockett, Oscar G., Robert J. Ball, and Andrew Carlson. *The Essential Theatre*, 11th ed. Boston, MA: Cengage Learning, 2016.

Carter, Conrad, A. J. Bradbury, and W. R. B. Howard. *The Production and Staging of Plays*. New York: Arc Books, 1963.

Clurman, Harold. *On Directing*. New York. Macmillan, 1972.

Cole, Toby, and Helen Krich Chinoy, eds. *Directors on Directing*, 2nd rev. ed. Indianapolis, IN: Bobbs-Merrill, 1963.

Cole, Toby, and Helen Krich Chinoy. *Directing the Play*. Indianapolis, IN: Bobbs-Merrill, 1953.

Dean, Alexander, and Lawrence Carra. *Fundamentals of Play Directing*, 5th ed. Long Grove, IL: Waveland Press, 2009.

Dietrich, John E., *Play Direction*, 2nd ed. Englewood Cliffs, NJ: Prentice-Hall, 1983.

Dolman, John Jr., and Richard K. Knaub. *The Art of Play Production*. New York: Harper & Rowe, 1973.

Downs, William Missouri. *The Art of Theatre: Then and Now*, 4th ed. Boston, MA: Cengage Learning, 2017.

Gillette, Arnold S. *Stage Scenery: Its Construction and Rigging*. New York: Harper & Brothers, 1959.

Gillette, J. Michael. *Theatrical Design and Production: An Introduction to Scene Design and Construction, Lighting, Sound, Costume, and Makeup*, 7th ed. New York: McGraw Hill, 2012.

Hodge, Francis, and Michael McLain. *Play Directing: Analysis, Communication, and Style*, 7th ed. New York: Routledge, 2009.

Parker, W. Oren, and Harvey K. Smith. *Scene Design and Stage Lighting*. New York: Holt, Rinehart & Winston, 1968.

Seivers, W. David, Harry E. Stiver, Jr., and Stanley Kahan. *Directing for the Theatre*. Dubuque, IA: Wm C. Brown, 1974.

Vardac, A. Nicholas. *Stage to Screen: Theatrical Method from Garrick to Griffith*. Cambridge, MA: Harvard University Press, 1949.

Whiting, Frank M. *An Introduction to the Theatre*. New York: Harper & Brothers, 1961.

9 The Visual Tools

Much of the information in this chapter comes from Dr. Francis Hodge's book *Play Directing: Analysis, Communication, and Style*. These ideas and concepts had an immense impact on me as a beginning director and helped me see the thousands of variables that exist when illustrating the action and story of a play for an audience as well as actors. As I learned visual methods of sending messages to an audience, I realized how an actor must use the subtleties of communication in a kinesthetic way. Every movement on the stage should be telling the story, illustrating the intentions and actions of the characters, and symbolically leading the audience in their understanding of the ideas and emotions of the play. There should be no throw-away movements. Everything counts, everything has a purpose, and anything that doesn't is simply distraction. I believe that I learned more about acting from these concepts as I ever did from any acting class I took. The concepts in the visual tools, I believe, come closer to illustrating what Stanislavski meant by the "Method of Physical Action" than any of the systems that purport to teach it.

I have found that, due to a need to work quickly, it is helpful to begin rehearsals (after obvious first table reads just to make sense of the script), by blocking the show completely. Some directors prefer to block in an improvisational way, which means making things up as you go. This method can work out quite well but my experience is that, since it involves so much trial and error, it takes far too much time. If one has the luxury of time, this technique can prove to be much more organic. I, however, have never had that luxury. I block the entire show in advance, on paper, and spend early rehearsals giving this blocking to the actors, with the understanding that things may very well change as new ideas occur. This pre-blocking helps one to imagine what the production will look and sound like on the stage. This has often been called "seeing the show with your mind's eye". As a practical matter, you must first get a handle on the groundplan: the arrangement of the objects on the stage. The director must have input and decision-making power when it comes to the groundplan. The blocking is the organic physicalization of the action within the environment of the play. Action is the forces in conflict with the characters. Telling the story to the audience must involve the visual clues that are being sent as well as the auditory clues. Shakespeare's audience may have said that they were going to "hear" a play. Modern audiences say that they are going to "see" a play. Our modern world is so visually oriented that we are often confronted with images everywhere we go. I would never begin rehearsals until the designs for the sets are well under way. I want my actors to imagine letting their characters live in those imaginary environments.

The visual tools for illustration of the action are groundplan, composition, gesture, properties and their use, picturization, and movement.

Groundplan (See Appendix 17)

The groundplan is primarily a device for communicating ideas and symbols to the audience. It is also a useful device for helping the actors to discover ways to illustrate the action. Some primary rules for creating a groundplan are:

1. Break up the space by creating an "obstacle course" through which the actors must move to help illustrate the action. A bare stage gives an actor nowhere to go to get away from the other characters in a scene of great conflict. Placing obstacles on the stage allows a character to put something tangible between themselves and another character. A bare stage doesn't lend itself to illustrating the symbolic separation of the characters, while an obstacle course does.
2. An obstacle course must consist of at least five acting areas defined by two sit-down positions at least six feet or more apart. This sit-down rule applies best with realistic interiors but the same concept can be applied to other forms of drama. I have found that the rule actually works in realistic exteriors and non-realistic forms of theatre as well but needs to be applied with imagination. In the case of non-realistic or exterior scenes, the areas don't necessarily need to be defined as sit-down positions, as long as they can be used to physically (and psychologically) separate the characters. A long, unbroken path across the stage is not possible in an obstacle course because the movement would be broken up with many side-jogs. This helps to illustrate the tensions and conflicts within the scene. The six-foot rule is, quite simply, determined as the distance that the audience psychologically sees two characters as being *apart* (two arm spans equals roughly six feet). The reason for the five acting areas is not as clear except that it is not an even number and so throws off our sense of symmetry. Obviously, one can have too many obstacles when all movement is inhibited, and too few where there is virtually nothing for the characters to hide behind. The sit-down positions idea obviously springs from the realistic tradition of the "drawing room" as the main area for character interaction. As mentioned earlier, it is my experience that, with a little imagination, the obstacle course can consist of things other than sit-down positions.

3. The main function of the obstacle course concept is to create a symbolic tension on the stage. Tension is created in the mind's eye by breaking up the stage picture in non-symmetrical ways. Using diagonals helps to indicate tension. If a kitchen table is placed dead center onstage and parallel to the proscenium, not much tension will be generated and blocking potential will be extremely limited. The movement pattern in such a case will almost necessarily be circular around the table. But if you turn that same table on a diagonal, move it off center to one side, and counter it with another object on the other side of the stage, then you have broken up the natural path of vision and created tension. The eye (from the audience's perspective) tends to read things from left to right. It's just the way we are programmed. Use the diagonal principle whenever possible. A good groundplan will encourage this. The same principle can also be used in the line of the set to provide subliminal tension by breaking up long, uninterrupted expanses with architectural jogs.
4. The objects on the stage should be placed free from the walls. If, as is common, all the furniture is placed against the walls, the compositions created will force actors to face the walls, not having a path behind the furniture and with no obstacles in the center to break up the movement patterns. It may not be logical in the sense of how rooms are normally arranged, but it will help create striking and different movement patterns to illustrate the tensions of the characters and the story. The goal of stage composition is to create tension arrangements, which open space doesn't do. A good question to ask is, "Can the characters physically move completely around an object?" Many fresh compositions can be obtained by allowing characters to separate each other on opposite sides of something. One thing I have noticed in my television-watching life is that most if not all sit-coms follow this rule. Watch *Friends*, or *Frazier*, or *The Big Bang Theory* among many, many others and you will find the concept of the obstacle course in use constantly.
5. Don't put everything in one horizontal plane of the stage. By using several planes (commonly defined as foreground, midground, and background) and placing objects in these areas, you will be encouraging a greater use of the depth of the stage. The same applies to the vertical planes to utilize the width of the stage (defined by left, center, right). Utilizing the entire stage as you place objects encourages more complex and illustrative blocking, as well as eliminating repetition.
6. Pin down the corners. Place something in each of the downstage corners. This encourages the use of the corners. We were taught that these are sit-down positions, which are good to have, but I have found that it doesn't need to always be so. It can be any object as long as it encourages the use of those areas of the stage. I have even placed a window or an entrance in a downstage corner. The important thing is that they are areas for the actors to use.

These rules can be used for exterior scenes and even non-realistic plays, although it requires some imagination to find objects that would realistically exist in an exterior (rocks, tree stumps, fallen trees, railings, trash cans, fireplugs, etc.). Very rarely have I found a play that resists use of these concepts. Plays with many multiple scenes can present challenges because, if quick changes are needed, it can be difficult to move a lot of things on and off the stage. But, multiple-scene plays tend to automatically avoid the stagnation that can come from being locked into the patterns of movement forced by a boring groundplan.

Composition

Composition is generally defined as the physical arrangement of neutral bodies in space for the purpose of symbolically illustrating the action of the play and the relationships between the characters. A director wants to control the visual pictures the audience will see. It is so easy on film to zoom in on something to make the audience look at it. But we can't do that onstage. For that reason, we try to create pictures on the stage that will transmit messages to the audience. I found that, as an actor, once I learned the concept of "focus", I became a much better actor. I learned when my character should have focus and when I should be assisting other characters by "giving" focus in various ways. A stupid or selfish actor tries to "steal" focus by always demanding that the audience be looking at him/her. While I do think it is true that characters continue to listen and react physically to everything going on, there are variations of extremes that can ruin the progress of the story by diverting the focus from where it should be. The actor's general rule of thumb should be that, if an audience member should happen to look in their direction, they will see a character actively engaged in the story, but they shouldn't be made to look that way unless it's appropriate. In this way, actors learn to find ways to express themselves in small as well as large ways. Actors also, quite often, discover the power of "stillness". We are programmed to listen better when the speaker is not moving. For that reason, it is best for actors to avoid too much movement while speaking. These are "held compositions". This is not always true, but it is common for other actors to remain still while one is speaking.

Body Positions

Body positions convey different meanings. We are accustomed to speaking to each other face-to-face. In fact, that is so ingrained in us that we actually think we hear better when someone is facing us. It is harder to hear someone if they are facing away from us or speaking at a distance. We are programmed to perceive communication happening between two people when they are directly facing each other. Of course, it is not true that communication cannot go on when we are not facing each other. In reality it happens all the time. We are also programmed to see a person turned away from another as deliberately not wanting to hear them. "I am shutting you out" by turning away from you. This is, of course, accentuated by walking away. Two people turned away from each other send the message that neither one wants to speak to the other. All characters in a play are together, apart, or some gradation in between. Composition, then, is the manipulation of these three basics in order to illustrate the action (the conflict between characters. Body positions are often literally defined in relation to the audience which is traditionally on one side of the performing space in the proscenium theatre. How much of the actor is seen by the audience depends on how he or she is standing on the stage. We speak of "full face": straight out to the audience, "¼ right": right profile, "¾ right", and "back": turned completely away from the audience. This also applies to "¼ left", "left profile", and "¾ left". We (the audience) attribute many meanings from characters turned in these directions from us as well as from the other characters. The symbology usually relates to our perception of how completely a character is wanting to communicate with us.

Levels

The use of levels pertains to the actual head level of the character relative to the other characters. He/she is at the highest when standing (unless standing on something) and any variation that takes the head closer to the floor is a change in level. Most of the time we (the audience) perceive the highest head level as the one that takes focus. Of course, this is simplistic because there are lots of other variables.

Planes

There are many planes of the stage going upstage from downstage just as there are going from stage left to stage right. In a proscenium theatre, a person will appear to get smaller in relation to everything else as they move upstage. This is why downstage is often seen as the strongest position. Although, again, this depends on other variables.

Types of Focus

The actor must become aware that there are two main ways of giving focus. One is eye focus with one character looking directly at another. If several characters are all looking at one other, then the audience will tend to look that way as well. The second focus is line focus in which one character gives focus by pointing or even leaning in the direction of another. This is often emphasized with objects in the hand.

Diagonals

If two characters share the same plane on the stage with the same positions and levels, they will be seen to "share" focus. If one is upstage of the other then a diagonal is created. If the downstage character is looking at the upstage character and turned in their direction, the upstage actor will have focus. And vice versa. Notice how the tension is enhanced by the use of diagonals. Diagonals almost always help to enhance and illustrate tensions.

Triangles

Putting three bodies in a space automatically creates a triangle. Different compositions can be created by shortening or lengthening the legs of the triangles, changing the total area of the triangle, rotating the triangle out of symmetry, or breaking up the legs of the triangle with another character. Experimenting with those variables will suggest many different compositional meanings.

Space and Mass

Compositional meanings can be created by grouping multiple characters to one side of the stage in opposition to a single on the other. This would seem to suggest a sense of many against one. This is using space (the distance between them) and mass (the cluster of many forms together). Many differing meanings can be created by the manipulation of this ingredient.

Repetition or Support

When a group of characters appear to be behind another character in one area of the stage, they appear to be "supporting" the principle. A cluster of characters all in one area of the stage are "repeating" each other, as can a line of characters across the stage.

Note: I can't tell you the number of times I have seen a group of characters in a line across the stage in which I literally could not tell who was speaking. Now this is an extreme, but it is a clear example of not knowing how to create focus. This was exacerbated in one production I saw where the actors were all miked up and the sound came from the speakers behind us. When one spoke in the chorus line, you really couldn't tell which one it was. I originally thought this was done intentionally, but could never understand what purpose it would have had. I saw another production in my capacity as an adjudicator for the American College Theatre Festival in which the director had staged the show so that every scene was played down center. When one group of people were through talking, the next group would be brought down center. When more than two characters were speaking, they would all be brought down center into a line across the stage. It was extremely repetitive and very dull. I could not believe that someone with any training and experience would do that, unless some "historical" points were being made. I never discovered what that point was. It was simply dreadful and not very imaginative.

Climactic Composition

This is one of the most important concepts to understand, and one of the most abused. When two characters are less than six feet apart on the stage or even closer, they are in a climactic composition. This is so called because these are compositions that should be saved only for moments of climactic import. They should only be used in moments of either extreme love (an embrace), or extreme hate (a fight), or some small variation in between. These moments seem mostly to come at climactic moments within the play. The temptation to get two lovers very close together very early should be resisted because it will diffuse the dramatic tension. *If you overuse climactic composition, it loses its significance for an audience.* Trust me on this one, it works. But it is extremely difficult to resist and also difficult to keep actors from committing. I would only let Romeo and Juliet kiss maybe two or three times in the play; once at the party (and possibly not even there), once in the garden when it will be difficult to reach each other, and once in the bedroom scene after they are wed. At the end, neither is aware of the other until it is too late. The kiss then is not a mutual one. The audience should see them wanting to kiss, but not being able to until the moment is absolutely right.

Stage Areas

Obviously larger and smaller compositions can be made by limiting the amount of space used. The stage can roughly be separated in halves or quadrants. Limiting blocking to one quadrant will have an entirely different feel from blocking using the entire stage. Large stages accommodate these divisions easily. Smaller stages will present more difficulty and so one finds oneself using smaller divisions.

Use of Furniture

Furniture or other kinds of objects on the stage can be incorporated into compositions. Allow objects to become part of the composition instead of thinking of it as merely scenery to be performed in front of. Obviously, the objects interrupt the space, making the movement patterns adjust accordingly. In addition, an actor's apparent mass can be increased by having them find ways to tie into objects such as chairs.

Gesture

Up until now we have looked at composition with neutral bodies in space. Gesture adds animation. Gesture is the animation of the of the moveable parts of the body. Gesture usually takes place withing the sphere of the body, or the farthest extent to which the arms and legs can reach. The six-foot apart rule established earlier is basically the closest two things can be together before they are perceived as being "apart". If one extends one's arms out as far as they will go in either direction and the person standing next to you does the same, only allowing the tips of your fingers to touch, you will find, almost every time, that the distance is roughly equal to six feet. Words are one kind of symbolic expression, and gesture is another. Gestures are very important to an actor and help to convey the character's internal states and feelings; however, indiscriminate use of gesture will convey very little meaning. Therefore, the actor must be very selective to create meanings in the audience's mind.

Decorum is the outward appearance of a character. A character is defined by their decorum, how they hold themselves and move. A king moves and holds himself in a very erect and proper way because he has been brought up believing he is a symbol of power and strength. A ditchdigger moves like a man accustomed to using his body continuously in physical labor. Decorum is simple symbology. Of course, these are frequently based on clichés, but audiences understand them. Good actors are always looking for the physical keys for their characters: finding the appropriate decorum. When I played Richard Lionheart in *The Lion in Winter* by James Goldman, I had to overcome my own naturally bad posture and find a way to become a proper British soldier – *the* proper British soldier, in fact. I employed an ace bandage around my shoulders in such a way that pulled them back. It was a constant reminder to me to keep ramrod straight and helped me to assume that attitude as well. When I played a one-armed man ... well that one is fairly obvious. But the director decided that the character had lost his right arm. As I am right-handed, it meant that I had to learn to do everything left-handed. It was a reminder of just how much the character had lost. A very good friend who was an excellent actor said he never felt quite right about a character until he found the physical "key". Of course, one hopes that the audience can also see and feel the subtle meanings these things impart, but it's more important for the actor to find and feel them. An actor I worked with who was playing Richard frequently greeted other characters with one hand on their back, the other on their chest. He told me it was Richard's "kiss of death". I don't know if the audience perceived that, but it gave him a little sinister secret that helped him to internalize the character. I thought it was very cool.

Properties

While gesture helps to animate the neutral composition, hand properties help to enhance and expand the gestures. Properties can extend the length of the arm, make the hands and fingers active, produce sounds, and show states of nervousness. Everything an actor touches can be used to help express the decorum of the character. A cigar becomes not just a smoke, but a kingpin's scepter. A book can express a character's emotional state by the violence with which he closes it or slams it down on a table. A cane becomes a pointer. A coin becomes a finger fidget. Young actors, who frequently don't know what to do with their hands, can frequently be helped by giving them such an organic prop. Properties possess the inherent capability to help reveal inner psychological states.

Picturization

When you consider what the audience is seeing, what messages are being sent and received, it is often useful to think of the stage picture as a series of still pictures. Take a mental snapshot of any given moment on the stage and visualize, through the composition, what is going on between the characters, at least in a broad way. Try this for yourself involving something that you watch on TV. If you have the capability, pause the picture every once in a while, and examine the compositions you see. Are you able to see the relationships? Good visual storytelling will allow you to follow the story this way. Another trick is to watch something with the sound turned all the way down. Can you understand the story through the compositions, body language, and gestures? If not, the visuals are not contributing to the telling of the story. This is the basic concept of picturization. Even something as simple as the relative positions of the people on the stage should help illustrate the action.

By now you may be thinking you had no idea there were so many variables involved in creating a meaningful picture on the stage. You are right, my friend. It can be daunting, but sending visual clues is part of the job of a director who is actively involved in telling the story of the play. Consider all the variables! I have found that actors who are aware of the principles of composition very often become extremely helpful in finding the details that help tell the story. That is often why I say that I learned more about acting in my directing classes than I did in my acting classes. Audiences may not be able to tell exactly what it is that engages their imaginations when watching a play, but they will quickly become bored with stasis and repetition.

Movement

Movement is the transit of a character from one point on the stage to another. My rule of thumb is that characters (and actors) should not move unless they feel compelled to do so. There must be a reason, a purpose, an intent, behind every movement on the stage. Rarely, actors must be moved for technical reasons ("The fairies are dancing through here in a moment and so you need to be out of the way"). Movement takes place between compositions. A note about the artificial reality of the stage: people often do talk while they are moving. On the stage this can dilute the essence of the moment. It is distracting and takes attention away from the lines themselves. One thing you will find is that it is almost always more effective to have characters halt their movements to speak. Another rule of thumb is that a motion before a line calls attention to the line, while a motion after the line calls attention to the motion. This applies to gesture as well. If I slam a book down on a table and then say, "No!", the line is the highlight. If I say, "No!" and then slam the book down, the emphasis is on the gesture. If I say, "No!" *while* I am slamming the book down, it will probably obscure the line. You see how that works? Is it the way people behave in real life? No! But it should be the way they behave on the stage.

Movement must spring from the dramatic action. There are lots of variables involving movement on the stage. These are three basic types of movement as motivated by the actions of a character:

1. Movement *toward* another character. This can be but does not necessarily have to be seen as "aggressive" motion.
2. Movement *away* from another character can be seen as a "retreating" motion.
3. Stasis, no motion or simply standing one's ground.

All three types of movement can be activated by body position and gesture. In fact, motion can be reduced to its smallest component which is simply turning the head either forward or away, for example.

When I have time to play with a scene, I will do an exercise called "Cat and Mouse". I tell one actor to move toward the other one with every one of his lines. The actor is then to use a forward arrow to mark in the script which of those "felt" like an appropriate movement. If the movement did not feel right, no mark is to be made. The actor can only move while speaking and must stop at the end of each line. Next, I tell the other actor to move away from the other on each of his lines and make appropriate marks in the script. Then, we reverse the exercise, having the actors do the opposite forward/backward motion and make appropriate marks. It is important for the actor moving away to understand that they do not need to back-up, simply to move away. Again, when no motion "feels" right, they make no marks. At this point, their script has four different notations: forward marks, away marks, no marks, and instances with both marks on the same line, indicating that both directions felt right. They then repeat the scene a third time just following their marks. When they reach a line with both marks, they are required to choose one option. When one actor reaches the other and has no more room to move forward, it becomes a circular motion around the other actor. *Most of the time, the actors are simply amazed that the scene has essentially blocked itself.* This exercise takes a fair amount of time to work. One should do it when one has allowed enough rehearsal time to play.

A technique for blocking is to *diagram the movement* of a scene on the blank opposing page of the script by drawing (or xeroxing) a copy of the groundplan and then showing the movement by indicating with a character's initials, where they started and using lines with arrows, showing where they moved and stopped. Then one marks the points in the script where those moves happen. When I'm blocking a play, I don't do it exactly that way, but do use a master groundplan with coins for each character (some people use plastic figures). I make blocking notations in the script in the usual way – "A x's L to behind center of couch". The notations I have made in the script are good enough to let me know what I've done, and I don't really need the groundplan with the blocking lines and arrows to remind me. One of the advantages of the page-by-page illustration with the lines and arrows was that, when finished, you could actually overlap each page of the groundplans and see what was called the "master movement plan" which seemed to be a spaghetti jumble of lines on the groundplan. It very quickly revealed which areas of the stage you were not using very much or where you were over-using areas (see Appendix 14, 15, and 16).

Playwright's Movement

Sometimes a playwright will indicate a movement in the script which seemed important to them. Again, always make a distinction between those actually written by the playwright and those written by the Stage Manager of the first production. You can usually tell because a playwright will give qualifying words such as "Charges angrily toward" while a Stage Manager would notate that as "S. x's to Z." When an "X" is used in blocking notation it means "crosses" meaning "crosses the stage". Character names are indicated by initials with periods after them while upstage and downstage will be "U" and "D" and left and right by "L" and "R". Shakespeare gave very few stage directions with major duels fought with the description "They fight", while

George Bernard Shaw could go one for paragraphs describing bits of business. What you use depends on what you want. You want to be faithful to the playwright, when possible, but your groundplan may be quite different from the one they were working with.

Variables of Movement

1. *Speed* of a movement is often an expression of a character's inner state or intention. Inexperienced actors are frequently not aware of the expressive possibilities of the speed of a movement, and so tend to do all moves at the same rate of speed.
2. *Movements in series.* A character's moves in succession can, ultimately, lead to a build in intensity. There are many other meanings that can be derived from movements in a series. A character may be trying to sneak up on another character, or even just sneak away. A character may be trying to "trap" another character by denying them an obvious escape path. A character may be uncertain of intention and so the movements will be wandering and random.
3. *Movement related to dialogue.* As mentioned earlier, a move before a line accentuates the line. A movement after a line accentuates the movement. This is often called "pointing" as a device for establishing emphasis. Volume may be related to movement as well. A slow, deliberate movement may be accentuated by an appropriate tempo in speech. And vice versa. It is almost impossible to move slowly when delivering an angry line. Many times, I have said to actors that their bodies are lying. This is usually when there is no character intensity in a movement to match the intensity of a speech.
4. *Quantity of movement.* Movement on every line can often kill it as a tool for expression and illustration. The decision when to move and how much movement to use is a delicate one and requires a sensitivity to the intentions of the characters and their internal states. There are exceptions to this: when blocking for the arena or thrust stages, it is nearly impossible to keep an actor "open" to the audience since almost everywhere they turn, their backs will be to someone. In those instances, I have often found it very useful to use more movement. This, in turn, keeps opening them up to different sides of the stage composition as they move. Another oddity of arena theatre is that characters often find themselves facing the audience. Ingenuity in creating the groundplan will give them logical opportunities to do so. In this instance, it is not a negative thing to place some objects "against the walls". Again, pay attention to the idea that a movement *on* a line is often distracting and can actually make it hard to understand the lines. (Most of the time when an audience member says he could not "hear" an actor what he

really means is that he could not "understand" the actor. This can be because of poor diction, or it may also be that lines are distracted by movements.) This means that the actor needs to feel when it is important to move and when to hold still. But I have found a general rule of thumb to be that *the lines will lead the blocking*. If you know what a character's intentions are, then it will be logical how to illustrate them in movement. Young actors are often afraid to trust their instincts, which can lead to a lot of under-illustration or erroneous illustration. They will need guidance. On the other hand, experienced actors will need no prompting once they realize that you trust them to use their instincts. I once directed a short scene between two women and so thoroughly trusted the actors to play with their instincts that I gave them a starting point on the stage and an ending point and told them to do anything they wanted to do as long as they ended up where I designated. They had a lot of fun over successive rehearsals and gradually began to arrive at a pattern of movement that worked for them and felt just right and so they often repeated it. I gave them a rehearsal where I told them that they couldn't do anything exactly the same way they had done it the night before. At first, they were very uncomfortable, but eventually they complied. At the end they discovered one or two new things, but basically indicated to me that they had arrived at something that felt "right" to them and wanted to go back to using it. Of course, I agreed. But we did have some fun while they were exploring the possibilities. Many times, one can very clearly see what *doesn't* work more easily than what *does*.

The Promptbook

Your promptbook is a binder with your script which contains your blocking notation and notes as well as your notes and diagrams of the groundplan as well as notes on props, lighting, sound, etc. I have found it extremely useful to copy my script and reduce it a little, giving me ample margin space in which to write. I also use one page per sheet instead of duplexing my script. This gives me a blank facing page for notes. I also make absolutely certain that my page numbers correspond to those given the actors. Sometimes this means that I have to indicate for myself where their pages start and end by drawing a line across the page at those intervals. There is nothing worse than saying: "Everyone go to page 12" when everyone has a different page 12. Shakespearean scripts avoid this because every line is numbered and the act and scene divisions are very obvious. If you retype the script for yourself (strongly recommended), you will need to find a way to justify your page numbers with everyone else. If you have a stage manager (very highly recommended) make sure that they understand that they need to keep a similar promptbook. It is the stage manager's job to record the blocking as rehearsals progress, including any day-to-day changes. At any moment you should be able to turn to the stage manager and say, "What was that movement we did there yesterday?". The stage manager is also responsible for script management and needs to make sure that everyone is aware of script cuts and changes. I had a community director who kept saying, "I hope someone is writing this down because I'm not". If you are not going to write things down then you damned well better be sure your stage manager knows that he or she is the one you are depending on to do so. If you are unlucky enough to not have a stage manager, then it is the director's responsibility to keep up with these things. If not, there will be chaos and a lot of time and effort will be wasted. If you have an inexperienced stage manager, you will find that it would be very beneficial to spend a few days with them prior to rehearsals explaining what you expect from them.

Blocking for Thrust and Arena

The basic rules of blocking for the proscenium stage include the idea of never turning your back to the audience and keeping your face visible to the audience at all times. While I do not necessarily subscribe to this rule, it is a generally accepted one. However, when you put the actor into the audience, as is the case in both thrust and arena theatres, you quickly notice that it is impossible to keep an actor from turning their back to the audience since the audience is on all sides. The solution is quite simple: don't hold a composition for long lengths of time! In other words, keep your actors moving. Also be aware that vocal projection falls off when the back is to the audience, so vocal projection and articulation of words becomes even more necessary in cases where you must have actors turned away. I probably don't need to point out the other obvious thing about this kind of theatre: it is even more important for the actor receiving the action, to help the audience understand the impact of what is being done. The reaction to a line becomes almost as important as the line itself when the audience cannot see the person speaking the line. Since the audience will always be looking at someone who doesn't necessarily have compositional focus, it also becomes very important that the reactions be tempered to account for that fact. I once had a director whose theatre was permanently arranged in a form of shallow thrust. He never understood the need for breaking the "back to the audience" rule and so basically staged most of his shows with actors pushed to the back of the stage in a very forced kind of "proscenium" staging. One really needs to understand that the proscenium rules don't work in thrust and arena theatres and that it's OK for actors to have their backs to the audience. In fact, watching a show in this kind of theatre becomes a different experience on each side and so the director needs to move around while directing in order to see each of those different perspectives. The ultimate effect of these types of staging helps the audience to feel much more involved in the action and so can be very exciting forms of theatre.

Some Thoughts on Blocking

Blocking needs to be carefully thought out. It is not just random or haphazard. Leaving it totally up to the actors is very risky unless you are blessed with very experienced actors. Even then, they may not be able to place their focus on the big picture. The forces of conflict and the interplay of tensions between the characters must be physically illustrated using the visual tools. The strongest of these is blocking. Blocking is *your vision* of the action of the play and the illustration of the story and sub-text. The main difference between your focus as a director and the focus of an actor, is that you are focusing on *all* the characters, while an actor is mostly focused on his or her own. This is why the study of directing is a good one for actors, because it begins to make you aware of the interplay of actions between all the characters. You suddenly begin to think about how you want the other actors to react to what you are doing instead of just concentrating on what you are doing. This is called "finding the other". Many people say there is a contradiction here. If an actor is thinking about the other characters, then how can they be "in the moment" or "in character"? I disagree because I think characters are *always* considering what the others are doing from their own perspective, the same as real people are. Either way, it doesn't hurt an actor to consider the other characters and it is essential for the director to consider them.

This chapter contains material from: *Play Directing: Analysis, Communication, and Style*, 7th edition, by Francis Hodge and Michael McLain (Routledge, 2009). Used by permission of the Taylor & Francis Group.

Bibliography

Carter, Conrad, A. J. Bradbury, and W. R. B. Howard. *The Production and Staging of Plays*. New York: Arc Books, 1963.
Clurman, Harold. *On Directing*. New York: Macmillan, 1972.
Cole, Toby, and Helen Krich Chinoy, eds. *Directors on Directing*, 2nd rev. ed., Indianapolis, IN: Bobbs-Merrill, 1963.
Cole, Toby, and Helen Krich Chinoy *Directing the Play*, Indianapolis, IN: Bobbs-Merrill, 1953.
Dean, Alexander, and Lawrence Carra, *Fundamentals of Play Directing*, 5th ed. Long Grove, IL: Waveland Press, 2009.
Dietrich, John E., *Play Direction*, 2nd ed. Englewood Cliffs, NJ: Prentice-Hall, 1983.
Dolman, John Jr., and Richard K. Knaub. *The Art of Play Production*. New York: Harper & Rowe, 1973.

Hodge, Francis, and Michael McLain. *Play Directing: Analysis, Communication, and Style*, 7th ed. New York: Routledge, 2009.

Seivers, W. David, Harry E. Stiver, Jr., and Stanley Kahan. *Directing for the Theatre*. Dubuque, IA: Wm C. Brown, 1974.

Vardac, A. Nicholas. *Stage to Screen: Theatrical Method from Garrick to Griffith*. Cambridge, MA: Harvard University Press, 1949.

10 Acting Exercises

I had a professor who said the use of words involves the sense of taste. Until an actor becomes attuned to the use of language and words as something to be tasted and savored, the language is sterile and unexpressive. "Taste the words", he would say.

Another professor likened the use of spoken words to music. "Find the music", she said, meaning find the ups and downs of tone, volume, register, etc. "Use all of your voice". Listening to some of the past greats such as John Gielgud, Ralph Richardson, or Laurence Olivier will quickly help one to discover the incredible variety of expression in the human voice.

Most playwrights know this. A good playwright hears the words as well as writes them and gives us little clues as to how they are to be said. This is also the reason plays are meant to be spoken and heard rather than just read.

Acting Exercises

The following are wonderful "out of the box" exercises that can help actors discover nuances of character and action. Give them a try if your schedule allows time for experimentation. It almost requires scheduling special rehearsals just for experimentation, which few organizations have the time for. They are very creative and fun to do and help to move rehearsals beyond the ordinary.

Always run the scene normally once before every exercise for familiarity and once after. It is vitally important for the actors to discover how to use their new-found knowledge or instincts and put them into action. Do not skip the final step of running the scene normally at the end.

DOI: 10.4324/9781003360216-10

Voice Overs

This exercise helps actors to discover the physicality of a character without using one's own voice and memory to deliver lines.

1. Run through the scene for familiarity with characters A and B.
2. Assign two different actors to read the lines while characters A and B physically perform the scene. Perform the scene physically acting with the external voices.
3. Run the scene again normally.
4. Have you discovered anything new?

Voice Overs (Alternate)

1. Same thing with actors using their own *recorded* voices.

Silent Running

1. Run through script for familiarity.
2. Begin working through the scene with the actors communicating the intent, emotions, and nuances trying to communicate everything from emotions to line nuances totally without speaking. This will take some time and will not be easy. Don't give up. Go all the way through the scene.
3. Run the scene normally.

Repeat

Repeat until you feel a motivation (dramatic action/intention focus).

1. Run through script for familiarity.
2. Each line of the scene is charged with an intention. The person receiving the action may not continue the scene by speaking his or her line, until they feel that the action directed toward them by the previous line has compelled them to react/respond/reply. If the partner does not respond or react, then the initiator of the action will have to try again until the impetus to respond is felt. When the scene continues, the roles are reversed. This will, again, be very time consuming and difficult to work through but, if played honestly, the forces at work will become palpable. (*Note*: It may be necessary to change tactics with each repeat.)
3. Run the scene normally.

Throw or Pass (Instinctive Physicality Kinetic Action Focus)

1. Run through script for familiarity.
2. Using a soft ball, bean bag, or even a small pillow, actor A must pass the object to actor B with each line *in the manner of the line*.
3. The obvious variant to this is to do the same thing, only instead of passing the object, it is now thrown.
4. Run the scene normally.

Hands On

This is a tension and "feel" game. Actors seldom actually put their hands on each other and so cannot feel the physical tensions that exist between them. This exercise gives them an opportunity to tangibly feel the tensions. Note: Some people are sensitive about touching other people or being touched, so it is a good idea to let them know ahead of time what is required here:

1. Run through script for familiarity.
2. Actor A sits facing actor B with the palms of their hands together. This is often best done as a "lines off" exercise, with eyes closed, which means it is used later in the progression of rehearsals.

The actors are to feel the tension of each line as they push against each other. This may be repeated several times playing with the pushing dynamic each time until the actors begin to feel a "pattern" emerging in the tension they feel between them.

3. A variant to this exercise is to have the actors grasp hands, changing the tension game into a "pulling" dynamic.
4. A second variant has the actors place the palms of one hand together and grasp hands with the other. This now becomes a fairly complicated game of "Push" and "Pull". Do not graduate to this exercise before completing at least one of the other variants to establish the "feel" of the game.
5. Run the scene normally.

Balance–Wrestling

This is a "tension" variant with a "win/lose" overtone.

1. Run through script for familiarity.
2. Each actor stands facing the other with their opposite foot forward. The outside edge of the feet should be touching. This puts one leg forward and the other back. They also grasp opposite arms in a

handshake with wrists and forearms clasped. This is a classic wrestling stance and the object is usually to see who can force the other one to lose their balance. Obviously, the objective here is to feel the "tensions" of the scene and discover who "wins" and who "loses" or when a "draw" is reached.
3. Run the scene normally.

Singing the Lines

1. Run through script for familiarity.
2. Run the scene with each actor singing the lines instead of speaking them. Encourage the actors to take this seriously and match the quality of the singing with the quality of the line and the moment in the scene. It doesn't take a brilliant singer to do this. What is important is experimentation with the "tone" of each line.
3. Run the scene normally.

Note: I have had success with opera and musical singers by doing just the opposite of this. Have them speak the lines of the song rather than sing the lines. They begin to discover the meaning behind the words.

Melodrama

1. Run through script for familiarity.
2. In this exercise, each actor must approach the scene and the situations within the scene as if each line were the most important line of the play. In this way, every line is milked for its superficial emotional evocation. Actors begin to discover that (a) not every line is so important, and (b) some lines are much more important than they originally thought. I used to call this the "soap opera" exercise, but now very few people know what I mean.
3. Run the scene normally.

Opposites

1. Run through script for familiarity.
2. Ask each actor to decide on the overriding emotion for his or her character in the scene. Run the scene with each actor playing the exact opposite of the chosen emotion. When this exercise is done seriously, the actors will discover there are many other emotions that can work for a character in any given circumstance, sometimes even the opposite.
3. Run the scene normally.

Make 'Em Laugh

This one is usually just for fun and is used to shake up the "standard" way of playing something when it is beginning to get stale.

1. Run through script for familiarity.
2. The objective for each actor is to make the others laugh. It is a strong, clear objective and usually has nothing to do with the scene, but gives the actors the freedom to just have some fun. Many times, actors discover they have been taking the situation in the scene far too seriously and that there is room for humor.
3. Run the scene normally.

Extremes

1. Run through script for familiarity.
2. This is similar to the melodrama exercise. Everything must be played four times as large as usual. Sometimes you can pick out a specific element to push. For instance, you might say that you want the entire scene played as angrily possible, or with the crying or laughing all the time, etc. Many nuances can be discovered by pushing the envelope. It will also become very clear when a scene cannot be played in this manner or when focus on one emotion or attitude is too much.
3. Run the scene normally.

Switching Roles

1. Run through script for familiarity.
2. Quite simply each actor takes the opposite character. In this exercise, actors switch characters for a run-through of the scene. One of the surprising things they discover is that they haven't really been listening to what the other has been saying. By speaking another's lines, themselves, they hear more intimately what the other person is saying
3. In a variant of this exercise, actors switch roles but play the other character in the manner they want them played. This is a very direct means of communicating what you feel has been missing from the dynamic of the scene in the forces that you feel should be coming at you.
4. Run the scene normally.

Speaking the Subtext

1. Run through script for familiarity.
2. This is a very difficult exercise with several variations. The actors must decide their character's scene objective and, as they work through the

scene, articulate that objective before each line. "I want to make her love me", for instance, is spoken before every line. As actors begin to get comfortable with the idea, they can vary the phrase: "I want to make you love me, but you are so pigheaded!", etc.
3. An even more difficult variant of this is for actors to speak the subtext of each line after they speak the line. "I hate you" "(I don't really but I'm mad and I want you to see it")".
4. Run the scene normally.

Cat and Mouse: Attack/Retreat

When I have time to play with a scene, I will do an exercise called "Cat and Mouse". I tell one actor to move toward the other one with every one of his lines. The actor is then to use a forward arrow to mark in the script which of those "felt" like an appropriate movement. If the movement did not feel right, no mark is to be made. The actor can only move while speaking and must stop at the end of each line. Next, I tell the other actor to move away from the other on each of his lines and make appropriate marks in the script. Then, we reverse the exercise, having the actors do the opposite forward/backward motion and make appropriate marks. It is important for the actor moving away to understand that they do not need to back-up, simply to move away. Again, when no motion "feels" right, they make no marks. At this point, their script has four different notations: forward marks, away marks, no marks, and instances with both marks on the same line, indicating that both directions felt right. They then repeat the scene a third time just following their marks. When they reach a line with both marks, they are required to choose one option. When one actor reaches the other and has no more room to move forward, it becomes a circular motion around the other actor. *Most of the time, the actors are simply amazed that the scene has essentially blocked itself.*

Bibliography

Barton, Robert. *Acting Onstage and Off*, 6th ed. Belmont, CA: Wadsworth Publishing, 2011.
Benedetti, Richard. *The Actor at Work*. Englewood Cliffs, NJ: Prentice-Hall, 1981.
Brook, Peter. *The Empty Space*. New York: Atheneum Publishers, 1968.
Guskin, Harold, and Kevin Kline. *How to Stop Acting*, 1st ed. New York: Farrar, Straus & Giroux, 2003.
Hagen, Uta, and Frankel Haskel. *Respect For Acting*. New York: Macmillan, 1973.
Lessac, Arthur. *The Use and Training of the Human Body*. Pondicherry, India: Lessac Research, 1978.
McGaw, Charles. *Acting Is Believing*. New York: Holt, Rinehart, & Winston, 1980.

11 Playwrighting

I wrote this in the proposal for an honors playwriting class:

> It would seem fairly obvious that, in attempting to create a dramatic work in a course such as Playwriting, students are asked to understand the elements of the dramatic form and to exercise their imaginations in the use of them. One could argue that the playscript is the first true step in the process of creation in the dramatic arts. All other skills and imaginative constructs within our discipline originate with the work of the playwright. Without the Play, there is no Theatre. There is something elemental in the human psyche that demands an outlet for creative expression. One could argue that it is one of the basic human needs. In attempting to create something out of a blank page that will then become a completely illustrated, fully realized public moment of passion and emotion, one is reaching deep within one's fundamental make-up to attempt to understand the nature of creation.

To me the first and most important rule to follow in any endeavor in the theatre is this: In any form of published matter pertaining to your production, it is legally, ethically, and morally essential to include the name of the playwright! Far too often I see posters, advertisements, etc., with the name of the play and the name of the director and often the names of the main actors, *but not the name of the playwright*. You owe it to them to include their name on everything! *Where would you be without them?* In film, it is common practice for a production company to buy the rights to a fictional work outright. This gives them the right to do anything they want to with the material. In this case, the playwright loses all control of the work. But in the theatre, the playwright retains the rights to the work and *any* kind of change must be approved by them.

In this section, we will attempt to give a bit of a primer on the structure of a play as well as the writing process.

The correct name for someone who writes plays is *"playwright"*. The thing that a playwright does is called "playwriting". The term "playwrite" does not exist. This is a throwback to a medieval tradition of identifying a person as a "craftsperson" who has a well-practiced and highly successful skill as a "wright".

Aristotle, in his *Poetics*, written more than two thousand years ago, called a play an "imitation of an action". "Action" in this sense has come to be interpreted as "the significant events of life". In this sense, Aristotle was saying that plays are imitations of life; but not the everyday, mundane events of life – rather, the significant, dynamic, dramatic events of life. One could take two hours out of your day and script it and put it on the stage. But how interesting would that be? How much more dynamic to take those few moments that were the most important of your life and put those onstage?

In modern theatre, the word "action" is used to describe the things that one "does". Indeed, the dictionary definition of "to act" is "to do". Therefore, actions are the things that we do to, for, and with one another in the pursuit of our goals. Remember always that characters are goal-oriented. Action then, is what they *do* to get what they want.

In another definition of a play that I have read, the author says that the *essentials* for a dramatic work are: *conflict, emotion, empathy,* and *catharsis*.

Conflict. All plays must have conflict or they are not dramatically interesting or dynamic. It is the root and the essential ingredient of drama. People are put into conflict with one another in the pursuit of their goals. The fact is that, when all is said and done, a play lacking this element is weaker than one with it.

Emotion. Obviously, characters pursue their goals out of deep-seated needs and desires about which they feel passionately. If we as the audience come to understand and identify with them, then we can begin to feel some of the emotion that they must feel as they win or lose, succeed or fail, or all of the variations in between of those quests. Plays that lack the element of emotion (some often call it "passion"), seem also doomed to failure.

Empathy. The more an audience comes to feel for a character the more they may come close to feeling along with the character. When we can lose ourselves in another person's story to the extent that it makes us laugh and cry along with the character as he or she takes us on their journey (story), then the drama has truly succeeded. Plays tend to be more about emotion first, and intellect second. It isn't until after the events have transpired that we begin to think about them. In the same way, a character often doesn't have time to think, but must react and adapt quickly to the changing circumstances surrounding him or her, and then only has time to think after the "action" has transpired.

Catharsis. Somehow, some way, we feel better for having taken the journey along with the character. Sometimes we learn something, sometimes we just feel our emotions purged, sometimes we are just grateful that our lives aren't that bad. Whatever we feel, it should make us feel somehow more aware about ourselves and our world than when we first started. Some plays are intended to make us feel angry and to spur us to action. Brecht certainly thought so.

The story that is being told is often referred to as "the plot". The plot, of course, is the sequence of events that make up the telling of a story.

The Playwright's Tools: Dialogue, Stage Directions, Characters, and Actions

Dialogue. Plays, more than any other form of writing, are stories told almost completely through dialogue. Dialogue is, of course, the things that people say to each other. Therefore, it defines the medium as a *spoken* medium. Plays are not written to be read; they are written to be spoken. Dialogue is highly compressed and selected language. With only a few hours in which to tell an entire story, a playwright must find just the right words and sequences of words in which to express many things. Dialogue may seem casual and off-hand, but that is usually the work of hours of painstaking second-guessing to make the words resound with meaning, but sound like everyday speech. By the time we get a published script, it may have been rewritten scores of times. Each time a script is produced with the playwright in attendance, the script will undergo even more changes as the thoughts are refined and condensed even more. Tennessee Williams did not stop rewriting his plays until he died. Editions of his plays that have been published years apart show differences that indicate that he was always refining the dialogue.

Stage directions. Many of a character's actions are implicit in the dialogue. Shakespeare supposedly only wrote one stage direction "Exit, pursued by Bear", but in our modern world, we are much more visually oriented and many things can be done and expressed without actually speaking. Modern playwrights have become more attuned to this and often use stage directions (*written in parentheses and often italicized within the dialogue*) to give us clues to the physical illustration of actions. Often, stage directions also give us hints as to the intangible states of emotion of a character as the playwright felt them. These are exemplified by such stage directions as: (*crying*),(*laughing*),(*disgusted*),(*painfully*) etc. Stage directions can also give us major clues as to the pacing of a sequence of lines. Playwrights may implant such directions as (*pause*) or (*long pause*) or (*quickly*) or (*silence*) to indicate when to speed up or slow down, or how much time to take between things. I also have a theory that, since playwrights hear their dialogue as they write, the time that it takes one to read a stage direction is often also just the right amount of time to hold a pause.

Characters. Obviously, the characters are the fictional beings that represent the people of the story. They are the agents of the action for the story. Characters can be totally fictional or can be based on real people, but they are representations of real life with all of life's complexity. The more realistic and unique a character can be crafted by a playwright, the more it will have resonance for an audience. A good test of a character in a play is: if you can give one's lines to another without losing any sense of the meaning, then they are probably not very complex characters and only serve as mouthpieces for the playwright's opinions. A good slogan for the theatre might be "Characters are people too". This is obviously not true of comedy and farce. Often, the characters in a broad comedy are simplified into cartoon-like attributes. Although I have found that, if you try to describe the plot of a comedy such as, say, Neil Simon's *Barefoot in the Park* to someone, it begins to sound like a very serious play indeed: "A young married couple begin to discover how much they are incompatible and how different they are from each other which leads to their contemplation of divorce."

Actions. Characters have wants, needs, and desires and these are simply translated into goals. A major character is a character around which the action revolves. The character instigates the actions of the play by attempting to pursue a goal. Usually, the character encounters something standing in the way of achieving this goal and conflict is created. The character must then strive through a series of varying tactics to circumvent the obstacles to those goals. The outcomes are many but basically conform to the following:

- The character fails to achieve his goal. This is usually sad to us, because we have come to want to see them succeed.
- The character achieves the goal. We are usually happy about this, as is the character.
- The character changes the goal. A more complex answer and not always one that satisfies us but may, in fact, make the character happier.
- The character neither succeeds nor fails but is left completely unsatisfied. Contemporary plays exist where this is the solution (which is actually no solution) and the excuse is that it is more like real life, where there are no simple answers. This is well and fine, but we are often left feeling very disquieted and restless at such endings. If that is the desired effect, then it is usually a disturbing one.
- Postponement. The goal is not achieved, but the character vows to continue the quest. Sound like sequel fodder? It usually is. Although much comic effect can come from such an ending, in which we are usually left to ask ourselves how important the goal is to the character after all.

How do playwrights work? Usually very much alone. They tend to work in their heads, in their dramatic imaginations. Many times, a play can gestate inside of one's head for years before demanding to be put on paper. Where do playwrights work? On paper, on a typewriter, at a computer screen, in a lot of small notebooks, in a small room, in public. There are many ways to work. I know one who can't write anywhere but in his attic. Another I know has to write in the morning at his kitchen table. Many writers need to write every day. But there are those who do it in bursts as well. One playwright I know can't write until he has a deadline hanging over him. I often advise young playwrights to just sit down and write from beginning to end. Often, the act of stopping to work on pieces stalls the process and one can get mired down in the details without ever getting to the end. But I do know of some writers who start with an ending and then write all of the events that led up to it. I also know of some who use elaborately constructed outlines (called "scenarios"). Although some of those also say that they follow the scenario until things begin to change. Many playwrights admit that the real writing is in the rewriting. Once they get something down (a complete story arc), then they proceed to rewrite many times. After this, they usually try to get the play on a stage where they can see and hear it. Many playwrights have told me that the thing that sounds so good on the page will just fall completely flat on the stage. No one can really predict this.

Structure can be linear, where the arrangement of the events of the plot are arranged in a sequential line, usually chronological. This is probably the most familiar structure. There are variations. Structure can be continuous. where the chronological line is unbroken and the events unfold straight through from start to finish with no gaps in the timeline. Structure can be episodic, where the chronological line is unbroken, but here may be significant gaps in the timeline as the play jumps from hour to hour, day to day, week to week, year to year, excluding the relatively unimportant events that happen in between.

Plots can be simple or complex. There are many differences about the definition of these, but the main one seems to be that a complex plot has many story lines involving different characters interweaving throughout the story. A simple plot will tend to follow only one main character from the beginning of the story to the end.

Cinematic style refers to the idea that stories can be told out of sequence. This can be in the form of flashbacks, or can involve whole inversions (stories which start at the end and work back to the beginning). The scenes can be actual happenings, or totally imagined events in a character's warped sense of reality. Another definition of the cinematic style is a tendency to use a great many fairly short scenes. Of course, since Shakespeare also did this, it is hard to see it as exclusively "cinematic".

A contextual structure is rather rare. It is basically embodied by the idea of a number of different short stories being told apparently independent of each other, each one involving its own story line and sets of characters. Each one can stand alone and no cause and effect seem to logically lead from one scene to another. The only thing that ties all of the stories together is its subject matter. In this sense they are "contextually" bound together. One very modern example of this was seen recently in the movie *Love Actually*, which began life when its writer saw a number of people greeting each other at an airport and decided that a statement about the nature of love could be made involving a number of stories built around that premise.

Thematic plays tend to be organized in order to communicate a central idea. This is the playwright's point of view and has often been referred to as the play's "message". Writers often write out of a need to express themselves about deeply felt ideas and issues. Plays that seem to come from a merely "clever idea" may seem clever to us, but will inevitably make us wonder why we have spent our money and time on something that has no meaning for us. We audience members demand very little, but we do demand that, if we take the journey, there be some reward.

Note: The information in this chapter is drawn from my experience teaching a course entitled "Introduction to Theatre" and was compiled from a variety of sources, including: *The Art of Theatre: Then and Now* by William Missouri Downs, *Another Opening, Another Show* by Tom Markus and Linda Sarver, *An Introduction to the Theatre* by Frank M. Whiting, *Theatrical Design and Production* by J. Michael Gillette, *History of the Theatre* by Oscar G. Brockett, and *The Theatre: An Introduction* by Oscar G. Brockett.

Bibliography

Brockett, Oscar G., Robert J. Ball, and Andrew Carlson. *The Essential Theatre*,11th ed. Boston, MA: Cengage Learning,2016.

Brockett, Oscar Gross. *The Theatre: An Introduction*,4th ed. New York: Holt, Rinehart & Winston,1979.

Brook, Peter. *The Empty Space*. New York. New York: Atheneum Publishers,1968.

Downs, William Missouri. *Playwriting from Formula to Form*. Orlando, FL: Harcourt Brace,1998. (*A lovely explanation of play structure and formula. One of the best.*)

Downs, William Missouri, and Robin U. Russin. *Naked Playwriting*. West Hollywood, CA: Sillman-James Press,2004. (*The second edition of this book and not as clear as the first one in my opinion.*)

Downs, William Missouri. *The Art of Theatre: Then and Now*,4th ed. Boston, MA: Cengage Learning,2017.

Whiting, Frank M. *An Introduction to the Theatre*. New York: Harper & Brothers,1961.

12 Memorization

Memorizing lines has to be the most boring and tedious task facing an actor. It requires concentration. I find that I cannot concentrate with a lot of other sounds or visual stimuli. I need a place where I can be alone in absolute silence in order to devote my true concentration to the task. But it is also the most important technical task the actor can develop. For it is a truism that one cannot think or behave in character when all one can think about is remembering the next line. It isn't until this stage is passed and the lines become truly second nature that one can begin the process of trying to vicariously live the life of the character.

A student once said to me: "Why do you harp so much on learning lines? Memorizing isn't acting." I agree. But I firmly maintain that acting cannot really begin until the lines are 100% learned.

You cannot know the freedom of acting until the words are second nature to you; until you do not have to actively think about them; until you can be confident that the words will come out of your mouth when you open it without much conscious thought on your part; until that time, you can never truly know the freedom of creativity in acting. It is only after you have reached this stage that you can enter into your character, think those thoughts, feel those feelings, and move those moves. Your words come out naturally because they have become the most natural thing in the world. You don't need to think about them.

I often play a game with myself. I reach a stage where I stop bringing my script to rehearsal. I know actors who sit in the greenroom each night pouring over their lines until just before curtain. This is simple insecurity. You must trust yourself and put aside the fear of failure. If you can put all of that aside, try not to think about the lines and hit the stage confident that they will be there when you want them, then you have jumped to another level of consciousness in acting.

There is no hard and fast rule of memorization. In fact, to the best of my knowledge, there are no hard and fast rules anywhere in acting. It seems to be a truism that for every rule, there is an exception. Perhaps that is the nature of such an intuitive art form. However, there are a few techniques

DOI: 10.4324/9781003360216-12

for memorization that seem to work for many people. The first of these is *repetition*. The best way to memorize is by rote repetition. It should be done in a structured way, but there is no better way to memorize than by simply going over the material again and again until it has been planted in one's brain. The structure that I find most successful is to learn one line and then go to the next. Then I do the first two lines together and go to the third. Then do the first three and go to the fourth. Build the memory up in stages this way until a short section is memorized, then repeat this structure for the next group of lines. Then try to do a page at a time, repeating the pattern for each page. When you have memorized one page, start over at the top of the second page. Then repeat the first two pages and go to the next, etc.

The next concept is page visualization. This will not work for everyone, but most people try to "see" each page in their mind's eye, which gives them a visual reference for memorization. In this way, I often find I can pinpoint the placement of the line, even if I don't know it, on the page and scene.

The most productive of all the techniques is running lines. This can be done in a couple of ways. The first is with a partner. The best way to run lines is always with a partner. It is one of the most thankless and boring of jobs, so it can be hard to find a partner with the patience and giving nature necessary to spend hours going over lines. My wife helps me occasionally which I think is a testament to her generous nature. I hate running lines with others, but I know how. It is the human touch that is important here. A person can stop you and correct you, or give clues or mnemonic references to help you remember. They can also provide the opposite character's lines in a much more appropriate tone for the flow of the scene. The next wrinkle for running lines is to do it with a recorder. Much less preferable to running lines with a person, it is possible to use a small digital recorder to run lines. The key is recording all of the other characters' lines, either leaving a gap for your own lines or using the pause button liberally in playback. This can be a very effective way to run lines with yourself and can be done anywhere you can take your playback device. I plug my device into my car stereo and run lines with myself on my way to rehearsal or while running around town. It is difficult to operate the pause button in the car, and so I would discourage that. Better to record both your lines and the other characters lines and then just let it run on playback. Even this kind of repetition is extremely useful.

A word about phobias. For many people, learning lines can be the most terrifying part of acting. (There is even a hilarious and terrifying play, *The Actor's Nightmare*, written by Christopher Durang, that treats this subject in excruciating detail.) "How do you learn all those lines?" is a common comment in the dressing room after a show. Many people are convinced that they could not possibly do it. That suggestion in one's mind can become a block. Most of the time, the key to learning lines quickly and efficiently is simply overcoming that block. Anyone can learn lines. The human mind is an amazing organism. People have, under hypnosis, remembered the most amazing minute details of their early lives even down to things that they have read years ago. The mind is capable of a lot more than we ask of it. One can learn lines – we just have to unlock our mind. Develop a positive attitude and convince yourself that you can do it. Once you've done it several times, you will quickly begin to see how easy it is. Memorization is a skill that improves with practice. The more you do it, the better you get. Will you make a lot of mistakes in rehearsal while trying to learn lines? Of course! It's natural. All of the other actors are in the same boat. The trick to the mindset is just this: you will make mistakes and everyone expects it so it is no big deal. It has absolutely no relationship to your worth as a human being so you should not give it such importance in your mind. You screwed up a line in rehearsal? So what? You'll get it next time. It is also perfectly acceptable to ask the director if you can do something again. I know very few directors who will refuse such a request. I also try to play little mind games with myself. I will plant in my subconscious the notion that, if I screw up a line one night, I will never make that mistake again. That way, by making my mind focus subconsciously on the line that gave me problems, it automatically reminds me the next night. I seldom make the same mistake twice. However, there are times when a line or group of lines does seem to be a sticking point or a hang-up for you. The problem is usually one of interpretation. You do not have a fundamental understanding of what your character is saying and what motivates it within the circumstances of the play. Once the fundamental understanding is found, the line will be found. I'm not saying that this is always the case, but most of the time there is a reason that I am making the same mistake over and over again, and I try to find the underlying cause.

Another very unusual phenomenon for me is that I have often been able to learn lines in my sleep. By studying and concentrating hard for an hour before I go to bed, I find that my mind continues to work while I am asleep. It is a very strange feeling to go to sleep feeling shaky on a piece, and then wake up absolutely knowing it. It has happened to me on numerous occasions. All I can say is that, again, the mind is an amazing thing.

I have actually gone absolutely blank onstage only a few times in my years of acting. It is the most terrible feeling in the world. In such times, one relies on one's colleagues to help put one back on course. A professor of mine told me: "When you blank, don't try to ad-lib your way out of it, that usually makes things worse because it gets you farther off track. And besides, your lines will never be as good as the playwright's. The best thing that you can do is to jump to the next thing that you know, even if it means skipping some text." Most of the time, the audience really never knows when such moments are occurring and they go by so fast that no one will even notice. Many times, if you can't get back on track yourself, your scene partners will be able to jump a line or two and get you back on track. I have been a witness to a line screw-up bringing a play to a grinding halt only twice in my life. Most of the time, there is something that someone can do to keep the play going.

While on this subject, it should also be said that one should absolutely never let a mistake get you down. By dwelling on a mistake, you destroy your concentration and the rest of your performance will suffer. Put it out of your head and go on. We tend to build up our mistakes in our minds so that they are far worse to us than they really deserve to be. You cannot let a small flub destroy your confidence. Most of the time it is probably only worth a good laugh in the greenroom afterward.

13 Ethics and Behavior

One thing that seems never to be taught in any theatre course is attitude and etiquette. When one takes a role in a play, one enters into an unspoken agreement with a theatre company to fulfill certain responsibilities and obligations. Since these rules are seldom written out formally, it would behoove one to seek out senior members of a company and ask about rules of etiquette and behavior.

Of course, if one is not taught about ethics and behavior in the theatre, can one be faulted for not knowing any of these "unwritten rules"? For that reason, it would only seem appropriate for every theatre company to commit their ideas about proper rules of theatre behavior to paper. If these rules are then handed out to every participant, then an atmosphere of mutual respect for appropriate behavior can be fostered.

A question often asked is "what is a professional?" I have worked with some "professionals" who didn't seem to understand the idea of courteous behavior. Conversely, I have worked with a number of amateur theatre companies and actors who behaved in a thoroughly respectful manner. One could say, then, that professionalism is an *attitude*. It seems to me that all of these rules embody, in some sense, the concept of obligation and of responsibility.

Honor Your Responsibilities

If you agree to do something, then do it. Often you find that many people are depending on you. If you fail to meet your responsibilities and obligations, then you are letting down others, wasting time, and making the entire production suffer. Although it is not often voiced aloud, directors learn to identify those people that they know they can depend on from day to day and, consciously or not, these thoughts can enter into the decision-making process when casting or assembling a production team. I cannot say for certain, but I know that, in my course of instruction at the University of Texas, I was repeatedly cast through my years there by one particular director. I am fairly certain that at least part of the reason for that was because I got a

DOI: 10.4324/9781003360216-13

reputation for being "dependable". I never missed rehearsal, was always off book when asked, and always arrived early.

Here are examples of some of the responsibilities one is committed to when one becomes a member of any company:

Be punctual. Know when you are called to rehearse. In the theatre time is often money and if you are late then you are not just wasting time, you are wasting money. In the professional theatre, actors are often fined for lateness. A good rule of thumb is to arrive thirty minutes early to allow time for vocal, physical, and mental preparation and warm-up.

Never miss a cue. Whether it is an offstage line, or an actual entrance, you must pay attention backstage so that you are there when needed. Never keep people waiting on you.

Be quiet offstage. If you are making noise, it can adversely affect the concentration of others. Have respect for those who are onstage. The golden rule applies here: treat others the way you would like to be treated. It also helps your process and concentration to be watching the show and anticipating your entrance.

Never interrupt the director. If you are not working a scene with the director, and have ideas or questions they can often wait until a break or after the rehearsal. This does not apply, of course, while you are onstage working a scene.

Never walk in front of the director or other production personnel such as designers, stage managers, etc. It is distracting and rude. Always find a way to go behind people who are trying to concentrate on what is in front of them.

Be off book completely by the designated date. Nothing wastes more time in the theatre than actors who are not off book when they are supposed to be. Nothing (outside of being late or missing rehearsals) is ruder and more unprofessional. Most theatre companies will allow cuing well past the "off-book" deadline. "Off book" means that you do not need to carry your script. Obviously, the better "off" you are the better.

Obey all instructions from the director or stage manager. Never argue questions of authority in front of the company. Problems can be discussed at a later time. This is, again, a matter of according respect to those individuals who have the task of trying to keep all of the pieces together and make everybody happy while at the same time trying to produce a work of art. Someone has to have the final say and that someone is usually the director. Second to the director is the stage manager. During the run of a show, when the director is not backstage, the stage manager is the ultimate voice of authority. No one ever said that the theatre was a democracy.

Never leave a rehearsal without permission. A director may decide to go over a scene again and if you cannot be found, then you are wasting other people's time. If you need to go somewhere and know you have time to do so, always check with the stage manager before going. That way at least someone will know where you are.

Treat props and costumes with respect. Props should not be handled or moved except when needed. They should have a designated place to reside during rehearsals and performances and should be taken from and replaced in these places. If not, you may have to go onstage without a crucial prop. Costumes should always be treated with care; they are often delicate constructions and may rip or tear easily and be difficult to fix. Most theatre companies have rules prohibiting eating, drinking, and smoking while in costume. A good rule of thumb is to take a personal interest in the care of your own costume – that way it will be there and ready for you when you need it.

Treat technical crews with respect. Remember that you cannot do the show without them. Where would you be without lights? Where would you be without someone to fix or launder your costume? The technical people are as much a part of the show as the actor and they should be afforded equal respect.

Always be prepared. Bring those things to rehearsal with you that you will need (scripts, pencils, schedules, etc.) It is often not a bad idea to have a notebook in which you can put notes, schedules, handouts, etc.

Once you have agreed to something (schedules, hairstyles, etc) don't expect to be able to change it. It is often quite a logistical nightmare to put together a schedule encompassing all of the time constraints of thirty actors. When a final rehearsal schedule is achieved, any change you might want to make will most likely affect the entire cast. Of course, emergencies happen, but don't abuse the concept. When did you agree to the schedule? Generally, a director will have a first or second meeting at which he/she will present the final version of the rehearsal schedule. If you do not say anything at this point, then you have agreed to it. Why do I mention hairstyles here? I have actually had an actor refuse to cut their hair and one who suddenly showed up at rehearsal one night with their head shaved. This can be quite a cause for concern if the circumstances of the show call for long hair.

Professionalism is an attitude, a desire to work creatively and efficiently with a minimum of wasted effort in an atmosphere of mutual trust and respect. It is very much a self-discipline.

Leave your personal problems outside. The environment of the theatre involves building imaginary circumstances that mirror the life of the play. If you introduce your own life problems into this environment, it can only inhibit the work. Directors don't care how tired you are. If your character is supposed to have energy, they will expect to see energy.

Take notes when the director gives you notes. It shows the director that you care about what he has to say and are striving to accomplish what he is asking of you. It shows that you are listening and concerned. Don't rely on memory alone.

When rehearsal comes to a halt while something is being discussed or worked on, stay in your position and remain quiet. You don't need to freeze, but don't wander off and strike up a conversation with a friend. This will make it that much harder to pick up the thread of energy where it left off. Another useful rule of thumb to follow is to begin a scene several lines before the actual spot where it was halted. When a director works on a bit, he usually wants to see the bit performed when the rehearsal begins again.

Always do everything in your power to ensure the smooth running of the show. Remember the axiom: if you are not part of the solution, then you are probably part of the problem.

Suggestions from the Internet

I decided to try to find out what others have recommended as appropriate rules for the theatre. Fortunately, the internet connects people together in marvelous ways. And so, I asked the question on the "Theatre List" on the internet. Here are some of the responses. Note: each "voice" is set apart by quotation marks.

One contributor wrote:

"We do a contract something like this:

1. I will never miss a performance.
2. I shall play every performance to the best of my ability, regardless of how small my role or large my personal problems.
3. I will respect my audience regardless of size or station.
4. I shall never miss an entrance or cause a curtain to be late by my failure to be ready.
5. I shall forego all social activities which interfere with rehearsals and will always be on time.
6. I shall never leave the theatre building or stage area until I have completed my performance.
7. I shall remember that my aim is to create illusion, therefore, I will not destroy that illusion by appearing in costume and make-up off stage or outside the theatre.
8. I will not allow the comments of friends, relatives or critics to change any phase of my work without proper authorization.
9. I will not alter lines, business, lights, properties, settings, costumes, or any phase of the production without consultation with and permission from the director.

10. I shall accept the director's advice in the spirit in which it is given for he/she sees the production as a whole and my role as a portion thereof.
11. I shall look upon the production as a collective effort demanding my utmost cooperation, hence I will forego the gratification of my ego for the demands of the play.
12. I will be patient and avoid temperamental outbursts, for they create tension and serve no useful purpose.
13. I shall respect the play and the playwright, remembering that "a work of art is not a work of art until it is finished.
14. I shall never blame my co-workers for my own failure.
15. I will never engage in caustic criticism of another artist's work from jealousy or an urge to increase my own prestige.
16. I shall inspire the public to respect me and my craft through graciousness in accepting both praise and constructive criticism.
17. I will use stage properties and costumes with care, knowing they are tools of my craft and a vital part of the production.
18. I will observe backstage courtesy and shall comport myself in strict compliance with rules of the theatre in which I work.
19. I shall never lose my enthusiasm for the theatre because of disappointment or failure, for they are the lessons by which I learn.
20. I shall direct my efforts in such a manner that when I leave the theatre it will stand as a greater institution for my having labored there."

Another contribution was:

"These seem to me to all be very basic rules of rehearsal which everyone should know, but which I find myself repeating over & over when I work with adults, particularly. Not only does it bother me as the director, but the other actors who are prepared feel cheated by the fact that the other actor isn't prepared, as they suffer, too. Incidentally – when the adult in question doesn't get it through their head from me, the other actors are *very* effective in getting them to remember, whether through 'jokes' & gentle ribbing, or by well-timed friendly phone calls before rehearsals. Also – I heartily second the rule about letting the director direct!"

Yet another Internet response was:

"No matter what venue I work in, I always lay my unwritten ground rules out during auditions. Don't wait for the first rehearsal. Give everyone a knowledge of the kind of responsibility you expect from them with regards both to their own behavior as well as the cast's behavior in general. I find this solves lots of problems very quickly. You can even hand out on paper these 'unwritten' rules and policies so that they are no longer unwritten."

This respondent gave us another list:

> "Here's my list. Allowing the actor to focus on the performance is at the heart of these backstage rules of behavior:
>
> 1. In the dressing room, greenroom, or elsewhere: remember to keep the focus on the show itself.
> 2. No visitors, please. People not involved in the production must not be allowed backstage until after the performance. Concentration, writes Doug Moston in his book, *Coming to Terms with Acting* (Drama Books), is 'the ability or act of focusing all your attention or energy where you want or need it'. Thus, anything that interferes with actors' concentration can damage their performance and the show. Visitors, even well intentioned, are at best a needless distraction, and at worst a downright nuisance.
> 3. Children who are not part of the production do not belong in the greenroom or dressing room. They quickly grow bored, get underfoot, and in the way. They may pose a danger to themselves or others. And when their parent is onstage or helping with the set, they either go unsupervised or divert the energy of cast members. Forget the 'You won't even know they're here' ploy. You most assuredly will.
> 4. Keep it down. Einstein once said that energy can neither be created nor destroyed. That is not true backstage, however. Here energy is created – both the positive, focused kind that helps drive the performance, and the negative kind produced by such simple but often overlooked stressors as noise. Therefore, radios or stereos don't belong. Let's face it, it's almost impossible to find music that everybody likes, and so it's bound to bother someone. In addition, simple conversation has to compete with the sound level of actors speaking louder or straining to be heard. More important, ambient noise can obscure important communication such as the stage manager's warning of 'Places, please!' By the same token, it's wise to ask that actors keep their voices down and save their energy for the stage. Those who do vocal warm-ups should go into the restroom or outside. However, there is one important exception: if the cast does vocal warm-ups as a group, the focus on the performance is maintained and strengthened.
> 5. Stay focused. During the show, card games, cell phones and the like can help pass the time, but unless you're doing one of those big shows where the ensemble has twenty minutes or more between entrances, actors are usually better off conserving their energy and focusing on their next entrance. Card games also may lead to loud conversations that can fray the voice, and in some cases, can even be heard from the house (yes, I am speaking from experience, here).
> 6. Respect their space. It is, of course, simple courtesy not to shove others' clothes or personal items out of the way to make room for

your own. If there is a shortage of space, the stage manager should call everyone together to brainstorm a mutually acceptable solution. Respect others' mental space as well. For example, some actors prefer to be quiet before a performance. Be sensitive to this and don't try to strike up a conversation.

7. Actors need to clean up after themselves. Dealing with another person's mess is unnecessarily stress-inducing and can affect the quality of your performance and that can affect everyone in the show.
8. Keep your cool. An actress in heavy conversation in the dressing room did not hear her cue, and was seriously late for an entrance. By not paying attention she caused the show to stumble and created momentary panic among the other performers. That was problem enough, but the situation was compounded when she was bawled out as soon as she left the stage. Her subsequent performance was overheated and out of control as she worked off her anger. While it may seem logical to deal with bad behavior immediately, it's better for the show if you wait until after the final curtain. You'll be in control of your temper and will have had time to phrase your comments to best advantage. (In the case above, a chewing-out was probably unnecessary. The actress in question was well aware of her transgression and its effect on her fellow actors.)
9. Don't move it. A simple rule: don't move anything belonging to someone else without permission. 'I came backstage to make a quick change', recalls one actor, 'and my costume wasn't where I'd left it before the show started. I broke into a sweat, I panicked. I hunted for my costume for several minutes, and with my dresser's help finally found it on another rack where someone had moved it without telling me. I barely made my change in time, and when I walked out onto the stage, I was still jittery and well, I stunk.' Actors must be confident that when they look for a costume or reach for a prop, they have placed offstage, it will be there.
10. Button it up. 'Guess who's going to be in the house tonight?' an actor yelled as he came in the greenroom door. The celebrity was a well-known local director, and you can imagine how the news of his presence affected some of the performers. One forgot her lines; another actually padded his part. Ask the cast not to discuss who's in the audience, and certainly not to scan the audience for familiar faces to share with the others. The actor's focus should be on what's happening on stage, not out in the house. Backstage also is not a group therapy session. Actors need to remember their personal lives are just that personal. There are always exceptions, of course. Sometimes a traumatic event must be acknowledged. For the most part, however, it's best to leave one's troubles outside. Psychiatrists often encourage patients to become other-directed, to move beyond the preoccupation with self. How better to do that than in the ensemble environment of the theater?"

Here's yet another contribution from the Theatre List:

"The Golden Rule. Probably the best advice regarding backstage etiquette is simply to practice the Golden Rule: Treat others as you want to be treated and keep in mind why you're there."

Yet another contributor gave us this:
1. "Be aware that you may be asked to change your hair style and/or color if the part requires it.
2. Be aware that you may be asked to go on stage without your glasses (if you wear them) due to lighting problems.
3. You will be asked (at least in our community theater) to assist with the building, painting, or decoration of the set, as well as the strike of the previous show's set and your own set."

The following are further different contributions:

"Don't second guess the director and offer acting notes to your fellow cast members."

"Don't call the director after auditions and demand to know why YOU weren't cast."

"I have one – If you are a high-profile director/producer in a community theater environment refrain from speaking unkindly about other directors/producers openly. In other words, if you must gossip do so in the presence of close friends only and certainly not in front of your cast members or people who do not know you well. It is a very poor and unprofessional reflection on you and the theatre you represent."

"Oh, and another one for actors – leave the directing to the director. Do not attempt to direct your fellow cast members (it's just plain rude)."

"Maybe we should write these rules – maybe in really big letters in stone or bronze, to be posted in backstage areas everywhere. I suggest this because it seems to me that young performers are not learning (absorbing?) these rules any longer, a fact that makes theatre a lot less pleasant as it begins to resemble more and more our woeful disrespectful society."

"Whatever 'professional' and 'amateur' may mean, could we please stop using them qualitatively, implying that professional means all that is good, noble, and artistic, while amateur means all that is slipshod, piecemeal, and pedestrian?"

Bibliography

Moston, Doug. *Coming to Terms with Acting.* United Kingdom: Drama Publishers/Quite Specific Media (June 1, 1993).

14 Diversity

I am not an authority on equity, diversity, and inclusion (EDI) and if I were to try to pontificate about how to treat these things in the theatre, I would be sadly ignorant and come off as an idiot dinosaur from an earlier age. The best thing I can do is to point my readers in the direction of some wonderful resources.

The League of Resident Theatres provides one of the best and most inclusive resources I have found for exploring the issues of diversity and inclusion in the theatre. A wealth of information may be found here: https://lort.org/edi-resources.

There are now some very good reference books available about the concept of "intimacy coaching" for film and theatre that bring new awareness concerning what may and may not be done, and the idea of "permission". One listed in my bibliography is *Staging Sex: Best Practices, Tools, and Techniques for Theatrical Intimacy* by Chelsea Pace and Laura Rikard.

One of my favorite books about community theatre is Leah Hager Cohen's wonderful treatise entitled *The Stuff of Dreams*. In it she says:

> We were an unlikely family, those of us who came together and apart with each show, in ever-changing configurations. There were dancers and lawyers, professors and librarians, cooks and salespeople, doctors and carpenters, and mothers and fathers and grandparents. There were gay people and straight people, healthy people and damaged people, people you couldn't wait to be around and people who were plain scary … Community theatres tend to be sort of bastions for misfits, which isn't to say that they aren't also populated by the conventionally successful and adept, but that they are relatively welcoming and unexclusive places … Here are all these strangers coming together—for nothing profitable, nothing useful, nothing tangible or lasting, for nothing more than such stuff as dreams are made of—all because of some unnamable, unstanchable desire to imagine themselves into other people's stories and relate those stories to others.

I have been very lucky or perhaps I've led a somewhat sheltered life, but I have never been involved with a theatre company, whether educational, professional, or community-based, that seemed to care in the slightest what one's sexual orientation was, what the color of one's skin was, what ethnicity one belonged to, what social skills one had or lacked, what gender one identified as. It doesn't mean discrimination does not happen, but my feeling is that the artistic community involved in producing theatre is far less concerned with those issues than whether a person can find the light and remember the line.

I think theatre, by its very nature is an inclusive medium. The emotional vulnerability we are called upon to call up on a nightly basis creates more than usual bonds between people who are engaged in the activity of trying to elicit intense emotions in an audience.

For example, I just finished a run of Shakespeare's *A Midsummer Night's Dream* in which I played Peter Quince, the leader of the Rustics. In our cast, Oberon was played by a transgender woman who was simply outstanding in that role. Among the lovers, one was a transgender male, and another was a transgender woman. Everyone in the cast quickly lost track of who identified as what. When you remember that Shakespeare's actors were all males, some of whom were considered expert at playing women, and that the entire story centers on confusion of identities, it quickly ceases to matter. The story was about young love and lust and those were the qualities that emerged most prominently, as should be expected. The fairies were played mostly by children and no one in the entire company was stereotyped into any role on the basis of any kind of ethnicity. The truth was that no one cared. The only thing we cared about was capturing the magic that Shakespeare had created and telling the story to an audience. I feel that it was a very successful production.

When approaching the idea of diversity, one only needs to consider the best actor for that particular vision of the production. Maybe it would make an interesting statement to have a black Romeo and a white Juliet. Maybe it wouldn't matter a bit. But be aware that a choice such as that will be construed as fraught with meaning. I once considered doing a play by a Native American playwright but decided not to produce it because I felt it would be incorrect to cast a bunch of white teenagers as American Indians. I would never make such a decision without consulting the playwright, in any case. It was a wonderful script, but I knew I would be doing it a disservice because I couldn't cast it appropriately.

Sexual harassment is another important issue, and one to which little attention was paid in the past. The "Me Too" movement has made us all more aware of and sensitive to the roles of men and women in our society. In fact, now that we are taking the blinders off and seeing the incredible disservice that women have suffered at the hands of men in the entertainment business, it is simply appalling and one would be very remiss, indeed, not to pay attention to the requirements of plays that subject female characters to those indignities. Do we ignore those plays and simply not produce them? I think Tennessee William's *A Streetcar Named Desire* has something to tell us about the world in which those characters lived and is important for us in our understanding of the very nature of moral right and wrong in our collective past. I certainly wouldn't refuse to do that play because of its treatment of women. But I would make sure that all of the participants understood what they were getting into, and entered into the endeavor willingly and with consent. You would be sure to give the cast and audience context. Ibsen's *A Doll's House* is a depiction of a historical era in which women were treated very poorly but it is an accurate depiction of that time and is also a strident call for a change in the status quo. Ibsen was considered to be very progressive in that social milieu. In fact, there were purported to be riots in the streets concerning the issues of that play.

Bibliography

Cohen, Leah Hager. *The Stuff of Dreams: Behind the Scenes of an American Community Theatre*. New York: Penguin Putnam, 2001. (*One of the best overviews of community theatre history and philosophy that I have ever read.*)

Pace, Chelsea, and Laura Rikard. *Staging Sex: Best Practices, Tools, and Techniques for Theatrical Intimacy*, 1st ed. New York: Routledge, 2020.

15 The Stage Manager

The stage manager (SM) is very likely the most important single member of the company. The SM is charged with being the organizing force behind all aspects of setting up and running auditions, rehearsals, and performances. The SM speaks for the director when the director is not around and, as such, should be given due deference by every member of the company. Many times, stage managers are recruited for work on productions without adequate knowledge of the job. The director should be the one, in the community theatre setting, to train the SM and acquaint them with the expectations of the job. A good SM makes the production run smoothly and anticipates any and all situations that might arise. A poor SM will not ruin a show, but will drastically inhibit the smooth running of the production.

Everyone looks to the stage manager for answers: "What time is the call tomorrow?" "Am I called tomorrow?" "Did I move behind the couch on the line?" "Am I at Microphone number eight?" "Will there be water in the glasses?" An old joke about Stage Managers runs: "How many stage managers does it take to change a …. It's done!"

A stage manager coordinates and organizes all the different teams involved in the day-to-day running of a theatre production from rehearsals to performances and post-show. They liaise and communicate with the full company and organize each team to ensure the smooth running of a production. In consultation with the director, they create and set up rehearsal schedules and post actor calls. Needless to say, the SM is a virtually thankless job which is why they are due the most thanks.

In the professional world, it is not unusual to see stage managers moving into directing jobs, since they are the ones who manage the show after the director leaves. It is also a high "burn-out" job because the responsibilities and stresses are very high. In the professional world, the SM is also a member of the Actors' Equity Association, the professional actors' union. This is because they deal most closely with the actors including managing the actors time (which equates to pay) and levying fines for breaches of the rules such as lateness, missing costume fittings, etc. The degree to which this responsibility translates into a community theatre setting is variable,

DOI: 10.4324/9781003360216-15

to say the least, but the fact remains that a good SM is worth their weight in gold.

Duties of the Stage Manager

- Liaise with all departments and coordinate exchange of information.
- Create a prompt script compiled with notes on actors' cues and requirements for props, lighting, and sound.
- Manage the script changes and communicate these to actors and all other departments.
- Supervise alterations to the set and props between scene changes.
- Manage risk assessment to ensure the safety of the full company.
- Attend all rehearsals and performances.
- With the director, create a master calendar of rehearsals, target dates and deadlines, and performances.
- Conduct auditions with the director, including coordinating audition forms and information sheets.
- Handle script distribution and collection.
- Prepare cast and crew contact lists.
- Tape the floor for scenery locations in the theatre (for rehearsals) and spike the scenery onstage in the theatre (for performances). This requires the ability to read a scenic design ground plan.
- Open and prepare theatre or rehearsal space for all rehearsals (includes sweeping and mopping the stage, pre-setting furniture and props, etc.).
- Clean up after all rehearsals and performances spaces (includes returning props and furniture to storage as needed, backstage custodial duties, etc.). This can include cleaning up after actors, who should be directed to clean up after themselves. Anything they leave behind, stage managers must clean up, so police the space before actors leave and make sure they take their things with them.
- Close and lock the theatre or rehearsal space after all rehearsals and performances, including turning off all lights and closing and locking all doors.
- Record director's blocking in the production book and assist actors with blocking as needed.
- Take line notes when actors are off book and prompt actors as needed.
- Assist the properties team and coordinate rehearsal props and furniture as necessary. This also includes creating and maintaining a master props list.
- Develop preset lists and running order lists.
- Organize backstage storage areas for rehearsals and performances in co-operation with the technical director.
- Write and distribute daily rehearsal, production meeting, and performance reports in a timely fashion.

- Facilitate communication between production staff members as necessary for smooth production operations.
- Record all deck cues, lighting cues, sound cues, etc. and stand-bys in the production book in advance of the first technical rehearsal.
- Facilitate communication between production staff members and cast members as necessary, i.e., costume fittings, makeup orders, program proofing, etc.
- Manage the production callboard, including sign-in sheets, and announcements.
- Monitor actors' attendance and punctuality for all rehearsals and performances and deliver all pre-show time calls.
- Coordinate all scene shift rehearsals, technical, and dress rehearsals in cooperation with the director and other members of the production team.
- Supervise the work (as needed) of technicians, deck hands, and board operators.
- Organize and supervise special rehearsals for fight calls, dance calls, and special effects.
- Call all cues during the run of the show including light, sound, and deck cues.

Production Book Checklist (Not Necessarily in Order)

The production book is generally a loose-leaf binder that the stage manager keeps which forms the basis for all of the recorded production information that one might need to run a production from auditions through performances. The ideal should be that, if the SM were unavailable due to some extreme circumstance, one should be able to pick up the book and run the show. Of course, we all know that this is unrealistic, but it certainly would help for all of the available assistant stage managers to be familiar with the production book just in case.

- Rehearsal schedule
- Rehearal schedule changes (dated for synchronicity)
- Master production schedule (including all tech dept dates)
- Props lists
- Preset lists/charts (what goes where before the start of the show)
- Shift lists/charts (what gets moved where in the intervals)
- Contact sheets
- Cast list
- Crew list
- Lighting notes

- Lighting cue sheets (copies)
- Costume notes
- Sound notes
- Sound cue sheets (copies)
- Groundplans
- Audition sheets (copies)
- Bio sheets (frequently for programs, but also for publicity purposes)
- Check lists (pre show)
- Check lists (post show)
- Sign-in sheets
- Rehearsal reports
- Performance reports
- Duty rosters (who does what in the running of the show)
- Crew duty sheets (individual)
- Miscellaneous notes (make-up, special effects, etc.)
- Blocking script
- Cueing script
- Photo call list
- Rules and regulations (for the company)
- Theatre policies (for the specific theatre being worked in)
- Spare forms (see the forms book)
- Distribution list (who gets what on a regular basis)
- Category dividers
- Character/Scene chart (if necessary)
- Production meeting minutes
- Production meeting schedule
- Lock-up sheets (list of things that need locking up each night)
- Strike list (who does what at strike)
- To do lists
- Extinguisher/Alarm plans (where are they all located)
- SM kit inventory
- Clean script copy (in case copies are needed)
- Program
- Wrap-up comments.

Stage Manager's Rehearsal Kit Inventory

1. Bottle of pain killer
2. Box of assorted adhesive bandages
3. Package of poster putty
4. Two pencils
5. Pencil sharpener
6. Black magic marker

7. Packet of rubber bands
8. Container of paper clips, thumbtacks, bobby pins, safety pins, chalk
9. Sticky notes
10. Small pad of paper
11. Stapler and staples
12. Roll of adhesive tape
13. Roll of blue cloth spike tape
14. Package of assorted colored vinyl spike tape
15. Small package of tissues
16. Mat knife or package knife
17. Flashlight
18. Tape measure
19. Masking tape
20. Pair of scissors
21. Tweezers
22. 2 inch ace bandage
23. Package of 20 moist towelettes
24. One eraser
25. One highlighter pen
26. Instant cold packs

Bibliography

Dilker, Barbara. *Stage Management Forms and Formats*. Los Angeles, CA: Quite Specific Media Group, 1991.

Dolman, John Jr., and Richard K. Knaub. *The Art of Play Production*. New York: Harper & Rowe, 1973.

Downs, William Missouri. *The Art of Theatre: Then and Now*, 4th ed. Boston, MA: Cengage Learning, 2017.

Ionazzi, Daniel. *The Stage Management Handbook*, 1st ed. Canada: Betterway Books, first printing, 1992.

Kelly, Thomas A. *The Backstage Guide to Stage Management: Traditional and New Methods for Running a Show from First Rehearsal to Last Performance*. 3rd revised, expanded ed. New York: Back Stage Books, 2009.

Schneider, Doris. *The Art and Craft of Stage Management*. San Diego, CA: Harcourt & Brace, 1997. (*Possibly the most exhaustive record of blocking notation ever compiled anywhere. One might think too much, but lots to choose from.*)

Stern, Lawrence, and Jill Gold. *Stage Management*, 12th ed. New York: Routledge, 2021.

Appendix I
Sample of an Analysis of Given Circumstances
After the Fall by Arthur Miller

Environmental Facts

1. *Geographic location.* There is no one specific location for the play. It is set up to be seen in a flashback style in many different locations. The exact locations in which these flashbacks are set are not specified, only implied. Miller wants the freedom to be able to jump around in time and space from event to event in order to be able to create an emotional world in which Quentin ties events together in an impressionistic fashion. For this reason, he specifically states that the play is set "In the mind of Quentin". Specificity is not as important as the train of thought and emotion. The only things that are necessary to define place are symbolic pieces such as a bed, a wheelchair, a park bench, etc. Over all of these spaces we are to sporadically see the image of a concentration camp watchtower as if that single event is uppermost in Quentin's definition of his world.
2. *Date, year, season, time-of-day.* Again, specifics are avoided. The characters move in and out of the time sequences with complete selectivity, always determined by Quentin's stream of consciousness memory. Years can skip by in large units only to freeze on single minutes which repeat at seemingly random moments to highlight the juxtaposition of various memories and create commentary on them from Quentin's moral perspective. These occurrences are sewn together by Quentin's emotional needs at the moment. For instance, when he is castigating himself for his dying love for his first wife, he briefly recalls an instance where he felt he was lusting after a young woman who seemed to be idolizing him for something he said to her. It's his way of punishing himself. We must assume that we are in the realm of memory and that Quentin is not always in control of the sequence of events he remembers. This is the subconscious playing tricks on the conscious. An interesting device which is used only once is a brief "flash forward" at the end of Act 1. Quentin sees Maggie on the bed as she appears at the end of the play. We at once feel the sense of mystery about impending events and also

understand that all of the events Quentin is describing to us have already happened. We are left to wonder what constitutes the "present time" for Quentin, as everything that he describes has already occurred until we finally reach the end and realize that the "present" is just before he meets Holga at the airport for the final time. It is at that moment that we understand that the "problem" Quentin has told us he needs to solve is how he can possibly begin life anew with this woman. When he goes to meet her, he has made up his mind that the only thing he can do is to keep moving on, despite the weight of guilt he carries.

3. *Economic environment.* As in most of Miller's plays, we are dealing here with the middle-class American. Quentin is from a family which came to this country poor and worked its way up to middle-class comfort. Economic status seems not to bother Quentin. He is a fairly successful lawyer working for a large firm. He is faced with a moral dilemma when he is asked to defend some friends that have been branded "un-American" by the McCarthy hearings, even though they are not specifically described as such. When he takes the case, his firm asks him to leave them. This does not seem to affect his status economically as he eventually moves on to other cases, including handling the affairs of his second wife, Maggie (Marilyn Monroe). His concerns are more moral than economic.

4. *Political environment.* The formal political environment is dealt with here almost as a side issue. He is embroiled in the McCarthy hearings which places him in the vanguard of the political world of the mid-fifties and the House Un-American Activities Committee. But he seems almost untouched by it personally. It certainly does not spell doom for his career the way it has done for some of his friends. Miller is obviously touching on events that meant a great deal to him, but not wanting to dwell on them as he has larger issues to explore. He does not necessarily dwell on the flaws of the system, but on the flaws of the individuals who run them. He seems much more concerned with righting his own sense of morality than with righting the moral wrongs of the world. He sees the issue as one of personal responsibility. His larger question is always, "What are we to each other and what do we owe each other?" In this way he feels that he has always failed his fellow humans and isn't worthy of his life. He no longer sees himself as an earth mover. Instead of laying the blame for the wrongs of the world on others, he seems always to want to take the blame on himself. The larger implication in the play is that he is us, an everyman who has ruined everything he's touched and must come to terms with it if we ever hope to transcend. In a sense, this play was therapy for him, in which he tries to explain how he came to terms with his own evil side. He never actively preaches to us that we share his guilt and blame, but the parable is there. Instead, he seems

to take on all the blame himself. If people felt uncomfortable with this play, and in fact most all of his plays, it is because we do see ourselves in them. There are many times when his own personal experiences will not find common ground with the audience, but there are more of them than many of us would like to admit. This is not a political play. The implication is that we must all confront our own personal sense of responsibility to our fellow man, before the other things will fall into line.

5. *Social environment.* Quentin and Miller do not make a judgment on society as a whole in the same sense that they do not directly address the political environment. Miller obviously thinks that it would be too easy to make society a scapegoat for our own deeds and actions. Again, he sees the problems as dwelling deeply within ourselves; our humanity. He sees our only salvation as coming from within ourselves.

6. *Religious environment.* There is something very deeply religious in this play, in the spiritual sense. The crux of it lies in his speech about looking up for salvation and finding the bench empty. One can imply from this that Miller believes we will not find the answers to our problems by looking to God. This seems to have shaken his belief in the natural order of things. In a sense, what he is saying is that before we can look to God for salvation, we must find it within ourselves. He says that God's power is limitless love and that when we reach for that, we are only reaching for the power. The implication is that before we can reach for God, we must reach for the love. We must see our own imperfections and sins, and try to come to terms with them ourselves. *After the Fall* is about mankind's decision in the Garden of Eden to forsake God's protection, which at the same time means that he has assumed responsibility for himself. The play then becomes an earnest plea for us to look inside ourselves and see where our problems lie. He believes that we won't have to look very far if we are honest. He then points out that there are only two options after we have understood that we have an evil nature as well as a good one. One is to condemn ourselves; the other is to forgive and start over again trying to learn from our mistakes. Perhaps this is the true meaning of the concept of being "born again".

7. *A synthesis.* The major emphasis among all of the environmental facts would be the religious environment. Not the formal religious environment, but the informal one dealing with the morals of the main character, who we are meant to see as a kind of "Everyman", struggling with what a person owes to his fellow people. The moral dilemma is that we are all guilty of "sinning" and looking for our forgiveness and salvation from a higher sphere just isn't going to happen. We must face our sinful sides and find ways to forgive ourselves, or at least come to terms with our "fallen" state.

Previous Action

The play begins with Quentin talking to "the Listener". This is Miller's device to let Quentin talk directly to the audience. It is also evident that Quentin is talking to himself. Since the play is about Quentin facing up to and confronting himself, this is the most obvious conclusion. So, in a sense, the moments when Quentin is talking to the "Listener" are the moments of present action; they constitute the NOW of the play. In this sense, the play actually begins very near the end and everything that happens is memory being recalled by Quentin in order to illuminate the philosophical debate going on within his mind. All of these past moments lead us along the path of Quentin's evolution toward his ultimate decision about how he can go on with his life and go on with his new relationship with Holga. As the play culminates, Quentin comes back to the Listener and tries to draw his conclusions. It is at this point that he decides he will go on with his life and start over again, hoping he has learned from his past mistakes. In one sense he is caught in the middle of "To be" or "Not to be". In the end he decides to be.

Polar Attitudes

Quentin is obviously the major character. He is the one facing the dilemma that must be solved in order to go on living with some sort of spiritual peace. The entire play is his process of presenting all the evidence and acting as his own judge and jury. The environment is his own creation for it is the interior of his consciousness. His attitude at the beginning is one of unhappiness, confusion, even despair. He looks upon his life as being a total failure. He speaks at the beginning of the play about "having a bit of a decision to make". He says that he has hope although he doesn't understand where it comes from. He expresses his feelings about the hopelessness of things. He seems to be on the borderline between this hope and despair. The hope seems to involve his relationship with a new woman, Holga, in his life. His despair relates to his feeling that all of his past relationships have been failures and even, in some cases, leading to the ruin of others' lives. He proceeds to examine these relationships in great detail, sparing himself no pain. By the end of the play, we find that he has found that he is able to go on, to find new hope, to start over again. It seems to come from the strength he finds in Holga. He sees that she has been through some of the worst circumstances in human history (Germany in WWII) and managed to find a way to go on living and hoping. None of the other characters in the play can truly be seen as antagonists since Quentin makes it clear that he is own best antagonist.

Special World

Quentin's world is bleak and he does not see himself as being a human being worthy of the trust of other humans. It is my own personal thought that he is contemplating ending it all. In the end, he sees that we must all face our demons and put them behind us with the understanding that we must be better than we have been in our past and learn to forgive ourselves and try again. It is our own human spirit that can save us from ourselves.

Appendix 2

Sample of an Analysis of Idea

After the Fall by Arthur Miller

Quotations

These quotations were chosen by using a skim and scan reading of the play and allowing only the phrases that jumped off the page to be retained. It is a "stream-of-consciousness" technique.

1. A life, after all, is evidence (Quentin is a lawyer).
2. Despair can be a way of life; but you have to believe in it, pick it up, take it to heart, and move on again.
3. You never stop loving who you loved, why must you try?
4. No one has to be to blame.
5. A cemetery is like a field of mirrors in which people see themselves.
6. Maybe I don't believe that grief is grief unless it kills you.
7. Why feel guilty for telling the truth. Or is there something else behind it?
8. The trouble is ... telling the truth leaves you kind of ... cold.
9. Is that ever possible? To love and never lie?
10. I think we all understand it (Dachau), but we don't dare admit it. Or we would find it hard to go on living.
11. How can one ever be sure of one's good faith?
12. Survival can be hard to bear.
13. I no longer see some final saving grace! Some final hope is gone that always saved before the end.
14. No one they didn't kill can ever be innocent again.
15. It's a mistake to ever look for hope outside one's self.
16. I think one must finally take one's life in one's arms.
17. Remember ... when there were good people and bad people? And how easy it was to tell?
18. To admit what you see endangers principles.
19. If all of us are innocent, where does all this evil come from?
20. Or am I only calling evil what is only truth breaking out?
21. Is it altogether good to be innocent of what another does?
22. I don't know what we are to one another.

23. I think a man's got to take the rap for what he's done, for what he is.
24. If everyone broke faith, there would be no civilization.
25. When you've finally become a separate person, what the hell is there?
26. How few are the days that hold the mind in place.
27. You tend to make relatives out of people.
28. We are killing each other with abstractions.
29. What good is guilt if all it does is leave you pray to those who do not feel it?
30. I still can't believe all the hatred in this world.
31. The truth, after all, may only be murderous.
32. The evidence is bad for trust. And yet, how else do you touch the world?
33. (Morality is when) You tell the truth, even against yourself. You're not pretending to be … innocent!
34. There are no unimportant tears.
35. You oughtn't to have that power (the power to change people) unless you're full of love.
36. God, why is betrayal the only truth that sticks?
37. Decency is murderous! Speak truth not decency … I curse that whole administration of fake innocence! I declare it, I am not innocent! Nor good!
38. Isn't it necessary to say … to finally say … yes to something!
39. Can one ever remember love? It's like trying to summon up the smell of roses. You might see a rose, but never the perfume. And that's the truth of roses, isn't it? The perfume?
40. An event in itself is not important – it's what you took from it.
41. If there is love, it must be limitless; blind to insult; blind to the spear in the flesh. God! The same child's dream in both of us!
42. We are all separate people. I tried not to, but I see that now, honey, and I'm through pretending otherwise.
43. A suicide kills two people, Maggie, that's what it's for.
44. God's power is love without limit. But when a man dares reach for that … he is only reaching for the power.
45. We are very dangerous … people!
46. The wish to kill is never killed, but with some gift of courage one may look into its face when it appears, and with a stroke of love – as to an idiot child in the house – forgive it; again, and again … forever?
47. It does seem feasible … not to be afraid. Perhaps we could start from that.

Meaning of the Title

Miller is referring, here, to man's fall from grace in the Garden of Eden. Specifically, what comes after. Adam and Eve were corrupted by their acquisition of "Knowledge" (what the church wants us to see as "Sin") and forced to leave the presence of God. In this play, Miller is trying to come to terms with what he sees as his own "sins" (and mankind's). He comes to the realization that we all have evil within us and that "innocence" is something that we can never recapture. He feels that mankind is a brotherhood and that we should all be held responsible to each other. He then comes to the realization that one must start by admitting one's own sins and find a way to forgive oneself. He essentially discovers that, in contrast to the evil we all have, we must find the good as well. He sees that good side of humanity as the sense of brotherhood in which we are all in it together and we must help one another. He is saying that we should stop pretending "purity". One should not ignore one's sin but face it and move on from it, trying to learn from one's mistakes. But above all one must forgive oneself, find a way to learn to love and move on from there.

Philosophical Statements

The philosophical statements in the list above come mostly from the mouth of Quentin when he is talking to the Listener. Miller uses this device to draw moral conclusions about events that he feels were turning points in his life. This, of course, makes this a very autobiographical play. In a sense he is trying to illustrate the subjective emotions of the events and then to step outside of the sequential time frame and comment objectively on them and their meaning to him.

Quentin sees all of the good and noble things that he has come to honor become twisted and distorted into evil. He feels despair for humankind. The philosophical statements bear this out. They are full of references to good versus evil, truth versus dishonesty, innocence versus guilt. He begins to feel that the dividing lines between these things are growing less clear. Perhaps the two most important statements are: "Remember when there were good people and bad people and it was easy to tell the difference?", and "If all of us are innocent, where does all this evil come from?" We see Quentin's dilemma and we see his answer, an answer that he finds difficult to admit: that perhaps "good" is a rarer commodity than we admit and that what we take for good is often simply a disguise for evil and greed.

Perhaps the message of this play can be stated this way: we must all come to terms with the evil within us and hold ourselves responsible and accountable for our own actions (as well as inactions) and that only by doing this can we ever face the world without guilt. There is a lot of the "Jekyll and Hyde" concept in this message. Man is capable of both great good and great evil and it is within all of us and within all of us to control.

Miller's statement is obviously very personal, but the implication is that he sees both the dilemma and the solution as applying to everyone. The only way one can find self-respect is to acknowledge the dark side within us, striving to change it, and respecting the sanctity of the same struggle within everyone else. But it has to start within ourselves.

The interesting thing is that this seems to be a recurring theme with Miller. John Proctor, in *The Crucible*, is faced with standing up for what he believes in even if it means his own death. This is his statement of example for the others. Joe Keller in *All My Sons* faces up to his own sins and ends up sacrificing himself for them.

Miller was very obviously a man who was very concerned with the nature of right and wrong and with trying to help us to see our duty to ourselves and to the brotherhood of mankind.

Miller comes very close to preachiness with this play. It's original first draft was 1400 pages long and is a testament to the fact that he had a lot to say. It must have been a herculean task to whittle it down to the play we have today. The narrative device of speaking to the Listener can be dramatically ponderous unless the emotions beneath the ideas are intense. There must exist a sense of "do or die" in the struggle of Quentin to decide his own fate. It is not just a play about a man who wants to take a new wife, it is a play about a man who cannot see a way to live his life anymore. It is a struggle and must be seen as a struggle, an intense struggle. It has a very episodic structure, but the episodes are of sufficiently varying length, some short, some long, with no real rhythm established, that keeps it from feeling episodic. It is a deeply philosophical play that challenges us as we are made to feel the torment of the soul of Quentin.

Appendix 3

Sample of a Character Analysis

After the Fall by Arthur Miller

Note: I did one of these for each of the characters in the play but have only included one here: the character of Quentin. As there are a lot of minor characters, I decided to forgo the entire character analysis for each and only did the list of adjectives for them. I do believe that a director needs to be conversant with *every* character and actors should be encouraged to do the whole analysis for themselves.

Character: Quentin

Desires. Quentin's desires are very complex because they exist on both an intellectual and an emotional level. Intellectually, he wants to understand, in a very analytical way, his emotional confusion. He had deep feelings of guilt, failure, dishonesty, despair, and coldness. It is a moral dilemma in which he is trying to come to terms with the dark side of his nature; a side that he equates with the entire human race. At the beginning of the play, he says that he has met another woman but that he is afraid of beginning another relationship because all of his previous relationships have failed miserably. He has lost his ability to believe in "good". He has lost his ability to believe in himself and it is frightening him. Obviously, he would like to be able to go on living and find some happiness in living. That, I think is his main desire. He desires "Happiness". He feels that this is almost impossible because of his personal failings. He blames himself for everything. In fact, he even equates this with the concept of Jesus Christ accepting all of the sins of humanity. His mistake, here, is in taking all of the blame for everything. One might say he has a persecution complex, only the one doing the persecuting is himself. He says that he would like to be able to feel hope again, and then proceeds to illustrate, in event after event, why he feels that this is impossible. Finally, he comes to the realization that he must turn his back on his past mistakes (while never forgetting them) and try to go on. In other words, he discovers that he cannot look to others for forgiveness, he must find forgiveness within himself. This discovery helps him to find the strength to move on, especially given the example of his new love, who has experienced all of the tragedy of WWII and yet has found the strength and moral will to move on.

Will. Quentin is a bit self-indulgent in examining his "sins". He is very slow in discovering what Holga has already discovered. His self-doubt weakens his will to the point that the entire play is a long, involved struggle to finally find that he is, himself, ultimately responsible for his own forgiveness. In other words, he cries a lot over spilt milk. His guilty conscience gets in the way of everything he does in life and keeps him from seeing that no one can do it for him. He must find a way to move on with his life by himself. He equates this with an almost religious conviction that, like man after being ejected from the Garden of Eden, he is now on his own. This relates directly to the title of the play: *After the Fall.* Or after man's fall from grace, how did he find the strength and courage to move on? The fact that he does eventually decide to shoulder his own burden and begin again proves that his will is strong enough to overcome his paranoia. It takes him a long time to see it. This is not to say that this will all be obvious to the audience. They will undoubtedly have to go through the entire process of maturation with him. This, of course, is what Miller intends.

Values. Quentin's values are high. Perhaps too high for a human being. He sums it up when he says that "God's power is love without limit. But when a man dare reach for that, he is only reaching for the power." He feels that, like God, he should be capable of love without limit. *Maggie even accuses him of playing God*; after having said earlier that he was "godlike". The fact that Quentin wants so desperately to find his lost innocence proves that he is extremely naive concerning reality. The funny thing is that he is subconsciously aware of this. His sense of morality is high, but he feels himself too corrupted to be able to live up to his ideals.

Decorum. Miller tells us that Quentin is a man "in his forties". Other than that, we are left to fill in the blanks for ourselves. I think it would be a mistake to try to describe Quentin's look in terms of Miller's own physical appearance. We are to understand that this is not just Miller, but a modern everyman. Likewise, I feel that it would be a mistake to describe him as "handsome". His attractiveness to women is undeniable, but it is not his decorum, as much as it is his personality and his empathy that people feel. Above all, Quentin is a thinker. If any description of a person's outward appearance can hint at this, it would be acceptable and preferable, though it would be wise to avoid cliches. In some ways he is a pessimist and a cynic, yet this should not be a part of the physical appearance. There should be a capacity for scowling as well as beaming and there should definitely be worry lines. Quentin is definitely a worrier.

Character: Textual Evidence

The quotes here are arranged into two main categories: the things the character says about himself and the things that others say about him. There is an old adage in the theatre that a character is defined by what he says about himself, what others say about him, and what the playwright says about him. These quotes are derived through the process of skim and scan. This is an almost stream-of-consciousness skimming of the script, pausing only to underline those passages that fit the category. After the underlining (with pencil) is done, then the phrases are arranged into a list followed by a synthesis in which conclusions are drawn about the character.

What the Character Says about Himself

1. I felt I was merely in the service of my own success.
2. I do wonder sometimes if I am simply trying to destroy myself.
3. I have walked away from what passes for an important career.
4. It's outrageous to think of committing myself again.
5. A life, after all, is evidence, and I have two divorces in my safe-deposit box.
6. I'm a little afraid ... well, of who and what I'm bringing to her.
7. I think that my disaster really began when I looked up one day and the bench was empty.
8. A couple of weeks ago I suddenly became aware of a strange fact. With all this darkness, the truth is that every morning I wake up full of hope! With everything I know, I open my eyes, I'm a boy! For an instant there's some unformed promise in the air. I jump out of bed, I shave, I can't wait to finish breakfast – and then it seeps into me, my life and its pointlessness. And I thought – if I could corner that hope, find out what it really consists of and either kill it for a lie, or really make it mine ...
9. I don't know what to think of myself.
10. You never stop loving whoever you loved ... Why do I make such stupid statements! These goddamned women have injured me! Have I learned nothing!
11. I don't know how to blame with confidence, except myself.
12. I feel like a mirror in which she somehow saw herself as glorious [Felice].
13. Maybe I don't believe that grief is grief unless it kills you.
14. Is it simply that I am crueler than he? [His brother]
15. I don't know what the hell I'm driving at!
16. Why feel guilty for telling the truth! Or is there something else behind it.
17. The trouble is ... telling the truth leaves you ... kind of ... cold.
18. It's myself I don't believe in. I swear I don't know if I have lived in good faith ... And the doubt ties my tongue when I think of promising anything again.

19. Is that the fright? That I no longer see some final saving grace! Some final hope is gone that always saved before the end ...!
20. I feel ... unblessed.
21. I keep looking back to when there seemed to be some absolute; some duty in the sky ... and the world so wonderfully threatened by injustices I was born to correct! To believe! God, when I think of what I believed I want to hide! But I wasn't all that young!
22. To admit what you see endangers principle!
23. Why do I think of things falling apart?
24. I don't believe in blame, but if all of us are innocent, where does all this evil come from?
25. Or am I calling evil what is only truth, breaking out?
26. But I do pay attention. Just last night I read you my whole brief. [To Louise]
27. For instance, I walk through this slaughterhouse [Dachau] ... I don't feel quite innocent. Not quite guilty, either but ... How can I feel guilt for what I never did?
28. I don't want to know anymore! ... Yes! ... not to see! To be innocent.
29. I don't know what we are to one another.
30. I have lived through so much broken trust.
31. What am I looking for? Some simple-minded constancy that never is and never was?
32. I do resent being forever on trial. [To Louise]
33. I blame myself for everything. Isn't that obvious to you? [To Louise]
34. I am doing what you call an admirable thing because I can't bear to be a separate person. I think so. I really don't want to be known as a Red Lawyer; and I really don't want the newspapers to eat me alive ... I don't know how to say that my interests are no longer the same as his, and that if he doesn't change, I consign him to hell because we are separate persons!
35. I usually go right home. I've always gone right home. [To Maggie]
36. I don't sleep with other women, but I think I behave as though I do.
37. I'm defending Lou because I love him, yet the society transforms that love into a kind of treason, what they call an issue, and I end up being suspect and hated.
38. I would ask myself – maybe I'd even be brave enough to ask you – how I had failed. [To Louise]
39. ... or am I not guilty enough? Is that the horror now?
40. I'd have stuck it out to the end but I hated the danger to myself.
41. I still can't believe all the hatred in this world.
42. The evidence is bad for trust. But how else do you touch the world!
43. I am bewildered by the death of love. And my responsibility for it.
44. I feel I saw my truth – for one split second, with Maggie. I think a man stepped through this fog of praise and blame, all good and evil fell away,

and neither justified or damned I saw myself. I've lost my way back to that vision; it's as though I had armed myself against it. As though I cling to some power I fear to lose, and must, if I am ever to see that truth again.
45. ... there is a fraud involved; I have no power ...
46. It's that I can't find myself in this vanity anymore.
47. I hadn't had a woman's praise.
48. The first honor was that I hadn't tried to go to bed with her! She took it as a tribute to her "value" and I was only afraid! [About Maggie]
49. What the hell am I trying to do, love everybody?
50. I am afraid to mourn ...
51. If I could let in the memory of love – how it pressed me toward her like a wind in my back!
52. The future ... I've been carrying it around all my life, like a vase that must never be dropped.
53. I see the guilt, but where is Quentin?
54. She had the truth that day, I brought the lie – that she had to be "saved"! From what! Except my own contempt!
55. ... to live in good faith, if only with my guts! To ... yes! To be good no more! Disguised no more! Afraid no more to show what Quentin, Quentin ... IS!
56. I declare it! I am not innocent! Nor good!
57. I am not sure what we are upholding anymore – are we good by merely saying no to evil? Isn't it necessary ... to say ... to finally say yes ... to something?
58. My bitterness is making me a stranger to myself.
59. I saw clearly only when I saw with love.
60. Maggie, I keep a log. I know what I spend my time on.
61. I can't make a decision anymore without something sits up inside me and bursts out laughing.
62. We are all separate people. I tried not to be, but I see that now, Honey, and I'm through pretending otherwise.
63. We loved each other's innocence in order to love ourselves.
64. That I could have brought two women so different to the same accusation – it closed a circle for me. And I wanted to face the worst thing I could imagine – that I could not love.
65. I know how to kill – I know ... I know ...
66. But it does seem feasible ... not to be afraid. Perhaps we could start with that.

What Others Say about Quentin

1. You changed my life. [Felice]
2. But the way you talked to him; it made him act so dignified. [Felice]

Sample of a Character Analysis 141

3. I'll always bless you, always! [Felice]
4. Liar! Judge! [Maggie]
5. But I didn't mean to depress you so.
6. It's simply that, from the moment you spoke to me I felt somehow familiar, and it was never so before. [Holga]
7. You can't believe in anyone, can you? [Holga]
8. When you grow up, I hope you learn how to disappoint people, especially women. [Mother]
9. I almost feel honored to have known you. [Louise]
10. Lou's not like you, Quentin; you ... can function in the rough and tumble of private practice. [Elsie]
11. You don't pay any attention to me. [Louise]
12. You have no conception of what a woman is. [Louise]
13. You don't really see any woman. Except in some ways your mother. You do sense her feelings; you do know when she's unhappy or anxious, but not me. Or any other woman. [Louise]
14. She [Elsie] says you don't seem to notice when a woman is present.
15. What the hell are you so guilty about? [Mickey]
16. Every time I begin to assert myself it seems to threaten you. [Louise]
17. I'm beginning to think you don't want me to be happy. What do you want, revenge? [Louise]
18. You look like ... you could sit for hours under these trees ... thinking. [Maggie]
19. You were probably frightened. [Louise, *sarcastic*]
20. You have to decide how you feel about a certain human being, that's all. For once in your life. [Louise]
21. You are unbelievable! [Louise]
22. But – you are honest. [Louise]
23. I love the way you eat. You eat like a Pasha, a Grand Duke! [Holga]
24. I feel sometimes ... that I'm boring you. [Holga]
25. He wants a life! [Mother]
26. What are you, a stranger? Who are you? [Father]
27. ... the way you looked at me ... like ... out of yourself! [Maggie]
28. You wanted me to be ... proud of myself ... Didn't you? [Maggie]
29. I know who I am! I'm Quentin's friend! [Maggie]
30. You're like a God! [Maggie]
31. I bless you, Quentin! [Maggie]
32. That's you! To live the truth. [Maggie]
33. What you want! Always what you want! Chrissake, what are you! [Father]
34. You haven't even the decency to ... [Louise]
35. Why ... why are you do ... cold? [Maggie]
36. You should look at me ... like I *existed* or something. [Louise]
37. You're the first one that believed in me! [Maggie]

38. You're like a little boy. You don't see the knives people hide! [Maggie]
39. You don't want to *see* anything! [Maggie]
40. You lost patience with me. [Maggie]
41. You're still playing God! [Maggie]

Synthesis

One interesting thing that seems to surface after an examination of the list of quotes is the sense of things always taking place in the present. When Quentin speaks about himself, he often uses the "I" of the first person, but occasionally he addresses the universal with "You" although it's plain in these moments that he is still speaking about himself. This is, in a sense, his attempt to equate himself with the rest of humanity and vice versa. Perhaps he finds comfort in the fact that he is not so different from the rest of humanity. This is odd, because at times he seems to feel so distant from everyone else. It is all tied up in his concept of being a "separate" person. He starts off denying that people should be separate, feeling as he does that there should be a web of experience and emotion that ties us all together. Yet at the end of the play, he admits that he has become a separate person and that he is through pretending otherwise. I believe that he has come to the realization that he must find his peace with himself and that he should not look for it in any other entity. He calls it, "taking one's life in one's arms, like an idiot child". He has always looked for approval, judgment, admiration, criticism, etc., in others. Now he has come to the conclusion that he must find those things within himself before he can become a part of the greater whole. The cynical thing about the play is that Quentin says he no longer believes in "the greater whole". This is a very self-serving philosophy. The ironic thing about the play is that people really do identify with Quentin's dilemma. This must mean that, at some level, his moral confusion really is a human constant.

Summary List of Adjectives: Quentin

These have been arrived at by a skimming of the analysis section above and taking those words out which seem to describe the character the best. By the time one has done the analysis to this point, it should be pretty easy to come up with a list of adjectives.

- Self-indulgent
- Self-critical
- Confused
- Afraid
- Thinking

- Passionate
- Guilt complex
- Paranoid
- Naïve
- Cynical
- Corrupted
- Pessimistic
- Worrier
- Cold
- Cruel
- Responsible
- Practical
- Bitter
- Disappointed
- Disillusioned
- Conservative
- Emotional
- Objective
- Distant
- Moral
- Professional
- Honest
- Open
- Dependent
- Intelligent
- Insecure
- Neurotic.

Appendix 4

Sample of an Analysis of Dialogue

After the Fall by Arthur Miller

Word Choice

These words were chosen after a skim and scan of the script, using a pencil to underline those words which caught the attention and seemed unusual or characteristic of the play.

Decision	Crueler	Moron
Concentrate	Guilty	Idiot
Destroy	Goddamned	Divorce
Evidence	Hell	Innocent
Committing	Lie	Heaven
Presumption Justified	Truth	Unblessed
Condemned	Acceptable	Paradise
Verdict	Reassured	Married
Despair	Faith	Principles
Draining	Uncertainty	Subpoenaed
Darkness	Moral	Respect
Hope	Know	Testify
Pointlessness	Fright	Lies
Unnerves	Grace	Illusions
Blame	Murder	Evil
Grief	Beautiful	Ashamed
Monster	Mystery	Accomplice
Treacherous	Now	Laughable
Psychoanalysis	'cause	Fraud
Rib	Joke	Disguise
Deceiving	Beautiful	Betrayal
Trust	S'uze	Mourn
Automatic	Miracle	Future
Inhuman	Hysteria	Complicity
Dream	Abstract	Posture
Solidarity	Struggling	Contempt
Communists	Dying	Impersonating
Brotherhood	Aberration	Decency

Injustice	Burden	Bitterness
Conspiracy	Honest	Stranger
Swindled	Kill	Proud
Reactionaries	Accusation	Respectable
Civilization	Power	Meaningless
Integrity	Suffering	Cautious
Soul	Blind	Nervous
Conscience	Stranger	Ashamed
Constancy	Vanity	Cold
Threaten	Tart	Adore
Retaliation	Praise	Suspect
Separate	Helplessness	Dangerous
Bewilders	Hypocrisy	Vulgar
Decision	Complicated	Fag
Consequences	Murder	Survivor
Patience	Enemy	Failure
Pretending	Honor	Eden
Suicide	Destruction	Forgive
Lazarus	Knowledge	
	Alone	

Synthesis: Word choice

The words selected in this list definitely follow the ups and downs, the highs and lows of Quentin's emotions. They also seem to imply a very dark mood. Most of the words have negative connotations, from "destroy" to "failure". An examination of the list also turns up a lot of words that expose a sense of opposites: good vs evil, truth vs innocence, despair vs hope, pointlessness vs meaning, blame vs forgiveness, failure vs success, honor vs shame, paradise and Eden vs hell, married vs divorced, the past vs the present, blindness vs vision, civilization vs political morass, fear and ignorance vs knowledge, struggle vs decision. I think this paints an accurate picture of the state of Quentin's being. He is violently confused to the point of abject despair. He does not see any clear distinction any more between good and evil, right and wrong. It is not that he sees evil as being good, he actually sees it the other way around: evil is actually disguised as good. Right is simply a façade for wrong. Quentin is engaged in a struggle; a battle with himself to determine the truth of his existence. He is actually engaged in a quest for what he considers be his lost innocence. He equates his loss of innocence with the rest of mankind. At one point he talks about the indefinable web that bonds all of mankind, and he is confused because he believes he sees that web disintegrating. This quest for innocence is his way of looking for some relief for the terrible guilt complex that he has encased himself in. He blames himself for everything, even to the point of taking personal responsibility for the breakdown of his marriage to Louise, the death of his best friend, Lou, and the eventual suicide of Maggie.

The dialogue words also deal with intellectual and emotional abstracts philosophically such as conscience, truth, faith, decency, morality, principle, civilization, integrity, and so on. It is this search for universal truths that raises the play above the level of the simple story of a man who is in the throes of deep depression.

Several other distinguishing features develop upon examination of the list. The speech of the character of Maggie, for instance, is full of crudities and imperfections of speech, which are intended to show us her common, uneducated upbringing. The use of swear words such as goddamned, tart, hell, etc., play up the passion and struggle and frustrations of the characters. Quentin uses goddamned a lot. This is a subtle or not so subtle form of symbolism involving the religious overtones of the play. Quentin feels forsaken by God and his use of this common vulgarity points up his feelings of condemnation.

Phrase choices

Again, these have been selected by the skim and scan technique.

- Spur of the moment.
- Service of my own success.
- A life is, after all, evidence.
- Two divorces in my safe-deposit box.
- The bench was empty.
- Take it to heart.
- You never stop loving who you loved.
- Like a field of mirrors in which the living merely saw themselves.
- Like sawing off his arm.
- You owe one another a death.
- To love, and never lie?
- Like swallowing a lump of earth.
- I hear your wings opening, Quentin.
- Some final hope is gone that always saved before the end.
- Hang by my hair.
- Cuts the strings between my hands and heaven.
- Some duty in the sky.
- With her two bare faces hanging out.
- To admit what you see endangers principles.
- Drawing down the lightning.
- The day the world ended and nobody was innocent again.
- If all of us are innocent, where does all this evil come from?
- Truth breaking out.
- Bow its head like an accomplice.
- Why is the world so treacherous?

Sample of an Analysis of Dialogue

- She's not your rib.
- As soon as I said "I had been", stones.
- Everything is one thing.
- Wake up all the sleeping dogs again.
- Some brotherhood opposed to all the worlds injustices.
- She has taken your soul.
- You are a monster.
- Like an idiot child.
- I do resent being forever on trial.
- Stop this injured innocence.
- Don't want the newspapers to eat me alive.
- This is when I go blind.
- Light up the sky.
- How few are the days that hold the mind in place, like four or five hooks holding up a tapestry.
- Everything suddenly has consequences.
- How brave a homely woman has to be! How disciplined of her not to set fire to the museum of art.
- Now there's a truth; symmetrical, lovely skin, undeniable.
- What a miracle! A woman of my own!
- We were suddenly standing on two distant mountains.
- She was just there, like a tree or a cat.
- I thought of you …. Like a stranger I had never gotten to know – is it enough to prove a case, even win it – when we are dying?!
- He's a moral idiot!
- I am drowning, throw me a rope!
- Trying to keep the home fires burning.
- And in the morning a dagger in that dear little daughter's heart.
- Or is it simply that my heart still beats.
- I am bewildered by the death of love.
- A man stepped through that fog of praise and blame.
- You eat like a Pasha, a Grand Duke.
- There are no unimportant tears.
- And suddenly it fell, like some great man had died, and you were being pulled out of me to take his place, and be a light, a light in the world.
- Good men stay, although they die there.
- I can't find myself in this vanity anymore.
- I should have agreed she was a joke, a beautiful piece, trying to take herself seriously.
- Her helplessness tore my heart.
- Suddenly there was someone who … could not club you to death with their innocence.
- It isn't fraud, but some disguise.

- If I could let in the memory of love – how it pressed me toward her like a wind in my back!
- A future. And I've been carrying it around all my life, like a vase that must never be dropped.
- It's like they're eating you.
- You're not a piece of meat.
- To live in good faith if only with my guts.
- I curse the whole high administration of fake innocence.
- Are we good by merely saying no to evil?
- Sing inside me.
- Contemptible like all truth.
- Covered like truth with slime, blind, ignorant.
- The blood's fact, the world's blind gut ... yes!
- It's all true, but it isn't the truth.
- That's the truth of roses, isn't it? The perfume?
- That wishing girl, that victory in lace.
- That we conspired to violate the past, and the past is holy, and its horrors are holiest of all.
- You're like a flag to me.
- I'm a joke that brings in money.
- If there is love, it must be limitless; blind to insult, blind to the spear in the flesh.
- A suicide kills two people, Maggie.
- God's power is love without limit. But when a man dares reach for that ... he is only reaching for the power.
- It closed a circle for me.
- I wrote it down like a letter from hell.
- And her precious seconds squirming in my hands, alive as bugs.
- The footfalls of my coming peace.
- Always in your own blood-covered name you turn your back.
- Who can be innocent again on this mountain of skulls?
- Our hearts have cut these stones.
- Not in some garden of waxed fruit and painted trees, that lie of Eden, but after, after the fall ...
- The wish to kill is never killed.

Synthesis: Phrase Choice

An examination of the phrases in the play reveals a very heightened language, a poetic word-play that speaks volumes in its compactness. Miller has drawn pictures for us with words by using similes and metaphors couched in the apparent style of everyday speech. It is interesting to note that Quentin waxes most poetic when he is talking to the Listener, but it is by no means restricted to those moments. "With her two bare faces hanging out" is much more euphemistic than "I could see her breasts". It is also much more comic. This light touch is exactly what is needed at that point to keep the image from becoming overtly sexual. One interesting thing that occurs to me at this time is that the play opens and closes with the word "Hello". It is not at all unusual for things to begin with that word, but to have the play close with it, however, casts an entirely different light on the subject. With this one word, Miller is telling us that Quentin has decided to try to begin anew. Critics have been hard on Miller in this play for his weakness of structure. I do not think there can be any doubt, however, that he can still use language like a poet. To make us feel the realism of the characters and the situations while still getting away with lines such as, "How few are the days that hold the mind in place, like four or five hooks holding up a tapestry".

There is great imagery here, and Miller takes us into this mental space with ease and efficiency. The old cliché, "A picture is worth a thousand words", I believe is just as true for this play. The action is heightened by the use of metaphor and speaks directly to our hearts.

Dialect or Unusual Characteristics

Miller uses several devices to reflect the patterns and sounds of everyday speech. One of these devices is the use of common vulgarities. By having Quentin use curse words in moments of great passion, he seems to be simply a normal human being. This is augmented by the fact that Quentin is harder on himself than we would be. Miller also used the device of having Maggie use improper forms of grammar in her speech, and distorts words by the use of unusual contractions. This is an attempt to make us see that she is basically an uneducated person. The other unusual characteristic is the use of pauses. This is often indicated by Miller in the use of three dots (...) and by the use of dashes generally in the middle of sentences to indicate a pause in the thought process of the character.

The character either searches for the proper word, or simply pauses emphasize the next thought. Often, in Quentin's stream-of-consciousness these pauses are used to indicate a coming revelation or discovery. This is, of course, not an unusual characteristic of everyday speech, but it is an unusual device for a playwright. Miller uses it copiously to emulate real speech, and to hint at the ongoing confusion in Quentin's thought processes. Miller has, in this sense, given us real speaking dialogue.

Appendix 5

A Sample Dramatic Action Analysis

Scene Breakdown

Act II, Scene 1, *The Lion in Winter* by James Goldman
Unit 1: Alais and Eleanor
Alais singing to Eleanor: "Hold me close and never let me go."

Eleanor wants to gain Alais' sympathy by playing the beaten wife. Alais tries to needle Eleanor with her relative youth and favored status with Henry. Eleanor's pathetic ploy works and Alais is won over.

Unit 2: Henry, Alais, Eleanor
Henry: "They sky is pocked with stars …"
To
Eleanor: "I'm rather proud, I taught her all the rhetoric she knows."

Henry dismisses Alais while reminding her of her status as a non-entity. Alais belittles both of them for their manipulation of her.

Unit 3: Henry and Eleanor
Henry: "So you want me back."
To
(She reaches out, takes his hand and kisses it) Henry: "Don't do that."

Henry is lording his superior status as her jailer over her in a smug and pompous way. Eleanor is acting beaten down and pathetic to put him off his guard.

Unit 4: Henry and Eleanor
Eleanor: "Like any thinking person …"
To
Eleanor: "I'll stand by it, why?"

Henry goads Eleanor as he reveals his plan to get the Pope to annul her so that he can marry Alais. Eleanor plays dumb as to his motivation, trying to get him to reveal details of his plan.

Unit 5: Henry and Eleanor
Henry: "A new wife, wife, will bear me sons."
To
Eleanor: "I know; that's why I saved it up for now."

Henry reveals his plan to foster a new son to succeed to the throne. He is essentially discarding Eleanor's part in his life and his kingdom. Henry accuses Eleanor of using his sons against him. Eleanor belittles him for turning his back on her even though she loved him.

Unit 6: Henry and Eleanor
Eleanor: "Oh Henry, we have mangled everything we've touched."
To
Henry: "I loved you."

Eleanor seduces Henry into admitting that he loved and still loves her. Henry confesses his love for Eleanor.

Unit 7: Henry and Eleanor
Eleanor: "No annulment."
To
Eleanor: "Nothing I could do to you is too wanton; nothing is too much."

Eleanor berates Henry for his torturous treatment of her. She reveals the fault in his plan, that he doesn't have time to execute it before she and his sons will move against him to oppose it. She calls what she thinks is his bluff. She insists that he can't win.

Unit 8: Henry and Eleanor
Henry: "I will die sometime soon ..."
To
Henry: "She forbids it."

Henry confirms that he sees that Eleanor as well as his sons and the king of France will oppose his plan and then reveals the flaw in her plan. He can't afford to let them oppose him and so will jail all of them. Eleanor realizes that she has revealed too much and tries to shame Henry. He refutes her and belittles her little power play.

> **Unit 9: Henry and Eleanor**
> Eleanor: "Did your father sleep with me or didn't he?"
> To
> Eleanor: "We couldn't go back, could we Henry?"

Eleanor desperately tries to keep Henry from going ahead with his plan by begging and pleading with him and then attempting to humiliate and embarrass him by claiming that she slept with his father. She is trying to hurt him and it works but has the effect of driving him away. She loses the battle.

Summary of Scene

They want to feel each other out on the issue of succession. They also want to find out if there is any love left between them. Henry is fed up with his sons and has devised a plan to annul his marriage, marry Alais, and have another son. Eleanor thwarts this plan by making him see that he will have opposition from her as well as the sons and the king of France. Henry realizes that he will have to lock them all up if he wants to succeed. Eleanor realizes that she has said too much and has lost the battle.

Appendix 6
Sample of a Character–Scene Chart
After the Fall by Arthur Miller

Actor/Scene Chart

Page	Act I
6	Quentin monologue (entire ensemble in non-speaking tableau)
7–8	Quentin, Felice
8–10	Quentin, Dan, Ike (Felice, Maggie, one line each)
10–13	Quentin, Holga
13–17	Quentin, Mother, Ike (Dan non-speaking)
17–18	Quentin, Holga (finish of previous scene)
18–21	Quentin, Elsie, Lou (Mother, Father brief cameo)
21–23	Quentin, Louise (Father, Mother 3–4 lines)
24–28	Quentin, Mickey, Lou, Elsie (Louise a few lines)
28–30	Quentin, Louise (Holga, a cameo with one line)
30–36	Quentin, Maggie, crowd
36–42	Quentin, Louise (Mickey, Elsie, cameo with lines)
41	Quentin monologue
42–43	Quentin monologue (Holga cameo, Maggie one line)

Page	Act II
44–47	Quentin, Holga, Maggie, Carrie, Mother, Felice, Louise, Father, Dan
47–53	Quentin, Maggie (Mother and Dan one line cameo, Felice cameo)
53–59	Quentin, Maggie (crowd, Father, Dan, Mother one-line cameos, Louise, Chairman, Harley Barnes)
59–63	Quentin, Maggie (crowd, Elsie, Mother, Father, Dan, Clergyman)
63–70	Quentin, Maggie (groups of men, maid, secretary
70–71	Quentin, Maggie (crowd of men, Mickey, Lou, Felice, Father, Mother
78–79	Quentin, Maggie
	Quentin, Maggie, Holga, ensemble

Appendix 7

Samples of Rehearsal Schedules

Note: These examples do not start at the beginning of rehearsals, since these are revised versions after rehearsals had started. They are included here only as an example of the appearance of a schedule and the information contained.

Rehearsal Schedule for *Dracula* by Steven Dietz

(As of: September 8, 2012)

(*Always date things, that way if anything has to change, everyone will know which is the most recent schedule*)

(All rehearsals will begin at 7:30pm in the Main Theatre unless otherwise noted below. RH = Recital Hall)

Sept	11	Tues	Finish reading Act II
	12	Wed	7:30–8:30 Block pp 29–39, 8:30–10:30 Block pp 39–46
	13	Thurs	7:30–8:30 Block pp 3–18, 8:30–10:30 Block pp 18–29
	16	Sun	2pm, Run Act I
	18	Tues	7:30–8:30 Block pp 47–62, 8:30–10:30 Block pp 92–98
	19	Wed	7:30–8:30 Block, pp 62–66, 8:30–10:30 Block pp 65–74
	20	Thurs	7:30–10:00 Block pp 74–92
	23	Sun	2pm, Run Act II
	25	Tues	7:30–10:00 Work Act I, pp 29–46
	26	Wed	7:30–10:00 Work Act I, pp 3–18

	27	Thurs		7:30–10:00 Work Act I, pp 15–29
	30	Sun		2pm, Run Act I
Oct.	2	Tues		7:30–10:00 Work Act II pp 47–66
	3	Wed	RH	7:30–10:00 Work Act II pp 65–87
	4	Thurs	RH	7:30–10:00 Work Act II pp 87–98
	7	Sun		2pm, Run Act II
	11	Thurs	RH	7:30–10:00, Work problem scenes TBA
	14	Sun	RH	7:30–10:00, Work problem scenes TBA
	16	Tues	RH	7:30–10:00, Work problem scenes TBA
	17	Wed		7:30, Stumble-through Act I, LINES **COMPLETELY OFF**
	18	Thurs		7:30, Stumble-through Act II, LINES **COMPLETELY OFF**
	21	Sun		2pm, Stumble-through whole play, LINES **COMPLETELY OFF**
	23	Tues	RH	7:30, Work-through Act I
	24	Wed		7:30, Work-through Act II
	28	Sun		2pm, Run-through
	30	Tues	RH	7:30, Run-through
	31	Wed	RH	7:30, Run-through
Nov.	1	Thurs	RH	7:30, Run-through
	2	Fri		Set Load-in, no cast call
	3	Sat		Set Load-in, no cast call
	4	Sun		Set Load-in, no cast call
	5	Mon		7:30, Run-through
	6	Tues		7:30, Run-through
	7	Wed		7:30, Run-through
	8	Thurs		Tech: Call 6, go 7
	9	Fri		Tech: Call 6, go 7

10	Sat		Tech: Call noon, go 2pm
11	Sun		Dress: Call 6 go 7:30
12	Mon		Dress: Call 6 go 7:30
13	Tues		Dress: Call 6 go 7:30
14	Wed		Performance
15	Thurs		Performance
16	Fri		Performance
17	Sat		Performance

Rehearsal Schedule for *Mockba* by Ginger Lazarus

(As of September 5, 2003)

Note: All rehearsals will begin at 7pm unless otherwise noted.

Mockba Rehearsal Schedule

Date	Day	Place	Actor Calls
Sept. 16	Tues	Wright	7:00–8:30 **Block II14** All called except Laskin, 8:30–10 **Work monologues** Laskin, Lyubov, Jessica, Bogachov
17	Wed	Wright	**Work-through Act I and Run.** All Called
18	Thurs	Wright	**Work-through Act II and Run.** All Called except Tatiana
21	Sun	Wright	3 pm **Run-through Acts I and II.** All Called
23	Tues	Wright	**Work-through Act III and Run.** All Called
24	Wed	Wright	**Work-through Act IV and Run.** All Called except Tatiana
25	Thurs	Wright	**Run-through Acts III and IV.** All Called
28	Sun	Wright	3 pm **Run whole show, Lines OFF!** All Called
30	Tues	Wright	**Run whole show** All Called
Oct. 1	Wed	Wright	**Run whole show** All Called
2	Thurs	Wright	**Run whole show** All Called
*3	Fri	Wright	Possible additional Run-through

5	Sun	Wright	3 pm. **Run whole show** All Called
6	Mon	Wright	TBA – Work selected scenes
7	Tues	Wright	**Run whole show (Crew View)** All Called
8	Wed		**No Rehearsal**
9	Thurs	Wright	**First Tech Call: 6, Go: 7pm**
10	Fri	Wright	**Second Tech, Call: 6, Go: 7pm**
11	Sat	Wright	**Possible Third Tech, Call: 12pm, Go: 1pm**
12	Sun	Wright	**Second Dress, Call: 6, Go: 8pm**
13	Mon	Wright	**Final Dress, Call: 6pm, Go: 8pm**
14	Tues	Wright	**Opening Night: Actors Call: 6:30, Go: 8pm**
15	Wed	Wright	**Performance: Actors Call: 6:30, Go: 8pm**
16	Thurs	Wright	**Performance: Actors Call: 6:30, Go: 8pm**
17	Fri	Wright	**Performance: Actors Call: 6:30, Go: 8pm**
18	Sat	Wright	**Performance: Call: 12:30pm, Go: 2pm**
18	Sat	Wright	**Performance: Actors Call: 6:30, Go: 8pm**

Appendix 8

Sample Audition Forms

Note: Audition forms can be customized for the needs of each show. These are "generic" examples. Show-specific needs can be addressed in the forms, such as, "Are you willing to cut your hair?", or "Do you object to the use of strong language?", or "Do you have any stage combat experience?" or "Are you willing to appear partly nude?". Those are all situations that I have actually seen on audition forms. One gentleman found that the play in question contained a lot of instances of the Lord's name being taken in vain. He expressed that he could not do that on stage. I explained that I could not, in all conscience, rewrite the play for him and that it was my belief that the words would not be spoken by him, but by his character. After some thought, he surprised me by going ahead with the audition. I cast him and it was a very successful collaboration.

AUDITION FORM A

Your Name_____ Today's Date_____

Address_____ Phone_____

E-Mail address_____

Height_____ Hair Color_____ Eye Color_____

Role preference (if any) _____

Do you have any dance experience? _____List details on back.

Do you play a musical instrument?_____Which one?_____

Do you have any other special skills? (Juggling, gymnastics, etc.) List on back.

Do you have any interest in Technical and Production Staff Work?

Please indicate preference _____

_____

Cross out times below when you are not available for rehearsal due to classes, employment or other unbreakable commitments. If you are sometimes able to rehearse – on weekends, for example – indicate by putting an 'S' in the blank.

	Mon	Tues	Wed	Thur	Fri	Sat	Sun
11am							
12am							
1pm							
2pm							
3pm							
4pm							
5pm							
6pm							
7pm							
8pm							
9pm							
10pm							
11pm							

Are there any dates between now and the time of production when you know you will be **unavailable** for rehearsals? (Weddings, funerals, birthdays, Prior commitments, etc). If so please list them here.

Please list performance experience on the back of this sheet

AUDITION FORM B

Your Name _____ Today's Date _____

e-mail Address _____

Cell Phone _____

Other Phone _____

Height _____ Hair Color _____ Eye Color _____

Role preference (if any)

_____

Do you have any interest in Technical and Production Staff Work?

Please indicate preference _____

_____

Cross out times below when you are not available for rehearsal due to employment or other unbreakable commitments. If you are sometimes able to rehearse – on weekends, for example – indicate by putting an 'S' in the blank.

Are there any dates between now and the time of production when you know you will be unavailable for rehearsals? (Weddings, funerals, birthdays, prior commitments, etc.). If so please list them here.

Please list on the back of this sheet: Representative Acting Experience and Special Skills (Singing, Musical Instrument, Gymnastics, etc.)

Sample Audition Forms

	Sun	Mon	Tue	Wed	Thur	Fri	Sat
11am							
12am							
1pm							
2pm							
3pm							
4pm							
5pm							
6pm							
7pm							
8pm							
9pm							
10pm							
11pm							

Appendix 9

A Sample Prop List for *Dracula* by Steven Dietz

(*Note*: It's always best to make your own prop list. Do not rely on those printed at the back of some scripts. The best method is to do a skim-through of the script, making notes of props that come to your mind. If you do this ahead of meetings with prop people, then they will get an accurate idea of what you want. If you ignore this and let someone else do it, there will inevitably be something left out.)

Dracula by Bram Stoker

Adapted for the stage by Steven Dietz
   Director: Daniel Patterson

Proplist

(*Note: Set-props marked with an asterisk**)

No.	Description	Page
1.*	Small table with cloth	3
2.	"Elegant table setting"	3
3.*	Chair at table	3
4.	Napkin (cloth-fine)	3
5,	Bottle of red wine	3
6.	Wine glass	3
7.	Framed picture of Bram Stoker	3
8.	Covered silver platter	3
9.	Large edible rat	3
10.	Bed (Mina and Lucy)	3

11.	Chest at foot of bed	3
12.	Vanity w. chair (by bed)	3
13.	Bedside table (opposite side of bed)	3
14.	Large window seat (becomes large box w. sliding lid, stairs beneath)	3
15.	Business notebook (Mina)	3
16.	Traveling valise (largish) and briefcase (Harker)	5
17.	Rosary w. Crucifix (Harker)	6
18.	Small framed trio of connected photo frames (Lucy)	8
19.	Official papers (Harker)	9
20.	Silver goblet (Harker)	9
21.	Small hand mirror	11
22.	Crude notebook (Renfield)	11
23.	Ankle chains (Renfield)	11
24.	Crude birdcage (Renfield)	11
25.	Newspaper (Attendant)	11
26.*	Bench (Renfield)	11
27.*	Chair (Attendant)	11
28.	Billy clubs (2) (Attendants)	11
29.	Large ring of keys (Attendant)	11
30.	Straight jacket (attendant)	16
31.	Sparrow feather (Renfield)	17
32.*	Large wooden box (coffin-sized) (lid rigged to look like splintered boards pushed up from the inside). Should look like a packing crate with shipping labels	18
33.*	Large ship wheel	18
34.	Human skeleton or mummy (full sized) tied to the wheel w. rosary beads covered in "mud and seaweed"	18
35.	"Cloth across her forehead" (Lucy)	21
36.	Leather doctor's bag	21
37.	Stethoscope (Seward)	21

38.	Pocket Watch (Seward) (check's pulse)	21
39.	"Small pointed tool" (Seward)	23
40.	"Small glass container"	23
41.	"Small jar of ointment"	23
42.	"Small white cloth around Lucy's finger"	23
43.	Feather duster (Maid)	25
44.*	Simple white chair	26
45.	"Small bag" for traveling (carpetbag?) (Mina)	26
46.	"Leather-bound journal"	26
47.	Blue ribbon (to tie around the journal)	26
48.	Wolf's head????	27
49.	Wrist shackles (Renfield	27
50.	Letter (Van Helsing)	29
51.	Small valise (Van Helsing)	29
52.	Scarf (Lucy)	31
53.	Small bottle of liquid (from VH valise)	31
54.	Glass and pitcher (beside bed)	31
55.	Packet of powder (from VH valise)	31
56.	Spoon (beside bed)	31
57.	"Transfusion equipment" (from VH valise)	31
58.	Cloth (from VH valise)	31
59.	Alcohol bottle (from VH valise)	31
60.	Large hunting knife (Harker) (Dan has)	34
61.*	Small table w. candelabra (candles light on cue)	35
62.*	Table set for supper (elegant) (covered with black cloth)	36
63.	Roast chicken on covered silver platter (platter from earlier)	36
64.	Dusty wine bottle	36
65.	Wine glass	36
66.*	Small bed and night table (covered w. black cloth)	38

67.	"Pitcher, basin of water & towel" (on night table)	38
68.	"Mug of shaving cream"	39
69.	"Straight razor"	39
70.	Small shaving mirror	39
71.	A deed	39
72.	"Writing instrument"	42
73.	"Ties" (To tie Harker to the bed)	42
74.	Small cloth sack (bloody)	45
75.	"Small crying baby" (bloody)	45
76.*	"Coffin-sized wooden box" (same as earlier with solid lid, should look like a packing crate with shipping labels)	46
77.	Strings of garlic (six or seven)	47
78.*	Bars on windows???	47
79.*	Small table and chairs in bedroom????	47
80.	Large hatbox, wrapped w. colorful ribbon (Contains a beautiful wreath of garlic flowers)	48
81.	"Odd ornate chair made of golden bones bedecked w. jewels" (Renfield)	53
82.	Small curved knife (Renfield)	55
83.	"Tea service on a tray"	56
84.	Hand mirror (from earlier?)	58
85.	Large crucifix (Van Helsing)	59
86.	"Large steaming cup of liquid" (dry ice?) (Renfield)	62
87.	"Large rat, blood gushes from it when squeezed"	64
88.	Newspaper (Mina)	65
89.*	"Raised Stone Sepulchre"	66
90.	Lantern (Van Helsing)	66
91.	Large Cloth bag (Harker)	66
92.	A Bible (Harker)	66
93.	Large mallet/hammer and oak stakes	66
94.	"String of children's shoes" (Lucy)	68

A Sample Prop List for Dracula by Steven Dietz

95.	Flat silver case (Van Helsing)	70
96.	"Host", white holy communion wafer (Van Helsing)	70
97.	"Large wishbone" (Renfield) (he snaps it in two every night)	73
98.	"A wild red rose" (Van Helsing)	73
99.	Scarf (Mina)	74
100.	"A beautiful violin" (Renfield)	79
101.	Violin bow (Dracula cuts Renfield's throat with it)	79
102.	Pocket watch (Van Helsing)	87
103.	Binoculars (Van Helsing)	92
104.	Crow bars (2) (Seward and Harker)	93
105.*	The box again (ideally the sides would drop down to reveal the beautiful coffin beneath – Ha ha ha)	93
106.	Pistol (Seward – Dan has)	93
107.	Pistol (Harker – Dan has)	94
108.	Wild red rose	96
109.	Sword (Seward – Dan has)	98
110.	"Grey ash" (in box)	98
111.	"Dracula's severed head/skull (on a covered silver platter)	98

Appendix 10

Sample Character Sketches

Note: This is particularly good to post or send out prior to auditions. This gives actors an idea of what you are looking for.
Dracula by Bram Stoker
Adapted for the stage by Steven Dietz
Director: Daniel Patterson

Character Sketches

(5 men, 5 women, plus extras)

Mina

A woman in her early twenties. A "modern woman" in the sense that, though she is born to privilege, she desires to earn her way in the world. She is fascinated with the modern world and its new technology and insists on learning to use a new device called a "typewriter". All her letters are typed on this machine. She has gone to college and has taken her education seriously. She wants to teach school. She is virtuous and moral and a "proper" Victorian woman, with the exception that she does not see herself as "only" the wife and mother that women of her time were destined to be. She is a strong woman and must be attractive in ways that make Count Dracula desire her for his queen.

Harker

Mina's fiancé, a solicitor. In our world this means he is a lawyer and has finished his schooling and taken a position with a firm that trusts him enough to send him all the way to Europe to deal with a client, Count Dracula, who wishes to buy property in London and relocate there. It is a "test" of his abilities and his success may very well lead the way for promotion within the firm. He is a modern Victorian man and is also somewhat taken with modern technology, owning his own motorcar and learning enough modern "shorthand" to be able to send his letters to Mina coded in it. He is very much in love with Mina and will fight for her. To the death if necessary.

Lucy Westenra

Mina's friend. If Mina is born to privilege, then Lucy is born to nobility. Her family is vastly wealthy and she is being courted by no less than three suitors. She chooses a young man who will inherit the title of Lord Godalming. Lucy is a lot more sensuous and aware of her feminine powers and wiles than Mina. She is a little "naughty", although she would never violate her Victorian moral upbringing. She toys and teases though and Dracula finds her irresistible for a time, converting her to be one of his minions. After she is converted, she preys on young boys in the park. Her soul is finally put to rest by Van Helsing and Harker working with Seward.

Seward

Lucy's suitor, head of a lunatic asylum. Seward is a young doctor, whose area of major study are the ailments of the mind. His position as head of the lunatic asylum is a research position and might lead to much acclaim if he makes any discoveries and publishes his findings. He, too, had proposed to Lucy at one point and, when he is spurned, he vows to be her friend forever. His also has a life of privilege and his calling is a noble one.

Renfield

A madman. Renfield worked, at one time, for the same firm as Harker and was, in fact, also sent to make some preliminary arrangements with Count Dracula. However, his sanity was not as strong as Harkers and he has been forever damaged by his exposure to the Count. He served a useful function for the Count at one time, and the Count rewarded him by allowing him to remain human. His soul, however, is up for grabs, a fact that he recognizes in his moments of clarity. In fact, one might say that his main mental problem is the war within his mind between his desire to serve Count Dracula and his desire to preserve his own soul. Unfortunately, he loses.

Van Helsing

A professor. A brilliant man in his field, he is obviously somewhat familiar with vampirism. He alludes to having dealings before and even has a dispensation from the Pope to carry and use the Host in his dealings with the undead and the unholy. He is also a very modern man and, as a doctor, has learned about the mysteries of the blood and the art of transfusion. If ever there were a steam-punk character in this play, it would be him. He believes in many things supernatural and may even be capable of some magic of his own, along with his use of technology to fight Count Dracula.

Dracula

A Count from Transylvania. He is not a descendent of Vlad, the ruler of Transylvania in the time of the Ottoman Empire. He *is* Vlad. For he is immortal in the sense that he cannot die as long as he is able to replenish the vital energies of his body with the blood of other humans. His age makes him wily and cunning and he has wealth and power and strength that are far beyond those of mortal man. It cannot be an easy thing to defeat him, but the modern world may give those fighting against him a slight advantage. He is not used to being opposed by such intelligence and guile. When we first see him, he is an old man but he becomes younger with the increase of blood that becomes available to him as he arrives in London. One might say he has only one weakness: he is lonely. He seeks a bride and seems to finally choose Mina for that honor. He can become a wolf, a bat, and a mist at will and he has hypnotic power over those who gaze into his eyes. He is a tragic character in many ways, since he was essentially betrayed by Christendom during his wars with the Turks and apparently lost his one true love many ages ago in that conflict. But he would have had to make a pact with the unholy in order to claim the powers that he now has and his soul must surely be damned.

Three Vixens

These are past attempts by Dracula to find his soul-mate. One is a peasant girl, one is an aristocrat, and one is a gypsy. Apparently, it didn't work because now they are just bitter and vindictive, living off Dracula and whatever little "treats" he brings them.
  Waiters
  Attendants
  Maid

Appendix 11
Sample Photocall Lists

Note: It is *always* preferable to prepare this list well in advance of your photocall date. Having this list will save a lot of time as you can just move from shot to shot with a minimum of prep time. Also remember to frame your list from the *end* to the *beginning* as you will probably have just finished a performance and everyone will be in their last costumes as well as the last setting and lighting cues.

Send-Ups and Put-Ons PhotoCall
(From the end to the beginning)

Hamlet from The Compleat Shakespeare

1.		Final curtain call	All
2.	p. 47	"Queen the comes here, Yorick poor alas: (Matt spits the water into the cup)	Phil, Loring, Matt
3.	p. 46	"Thou Wilt not Murther me?"	Phil, Matt (Matt wearing everything)
4.	p. 43	"The Queen carouses to thy fortune, Hamlet"	Phil, Loring, Matt (Matt as reverse Gertrude)
5.	p. 42	"Sweets to the Sweet, Farewell"	Loring, Matt, Dummy
6.	p. 42	"Now Mother, What's the matter?"	Phil, Matt
7.	p. 38	"Speak the speech I pray you"	Phil, players, puppets
8.	p. 31	"My lord as I was sewing in your closet"	Loring, Matt
9.	p. 30	"Let not the the royal bed of Denmark become a couch for incest"	Phil, Loring, Matt
10.	p. 2	"Mark it, Horatio, It would be spoke to"	Phil, Loring, sock

"Last Call before Breakfast" from *The Coarse Acting Show*

1.	p. 22	"Last Call" curtain call	Shanna, Carla, Matt, Phil, Josh
2.	p. 21	"I'm Stuck"	Carla, Matt
3.	p. 19	"Savage Procreation"	Shanna
4.	p. 19	He and She on the cubes, with stagehands between	Matt, Carla, Josh, Phil

For Whom the Southern Belle Tolls by Christopher Durang

1.	p. 63	"Or the memory of some trick"	Josh, Kim, Matt
2.	p. 56	"Oh God, I feel sorry for their children"	Kim, Josh, Matt, Kate
3.	p. 55	"Come, Tom, to the kitchen and help me prepare the supper"	Kim, Josh, Matt, Kate
4.	p. 51	"Conversation is an Art, Lawrence"	Kim, Matt

Medea by Christopher Durang

1.	p. 28	"They're as nice as Dionysus" Chorus, Medea	Chorus, Medea
2.	p. 27	"I am eternally grateful to you"	Chorus, Medea, Angel
3.	p. 26	"Caesar is Dead"	Chorus, Medea, Matt
4.	p. 25	"I am in pain … Debbie kill for sure"	Chorus, Medea
5.	p. 24	"Hello, Medea"	Medea, Jason

Actor's Nightmare by Christopher Durang

1.	p. 18	"You send me to God" (Executioner raises sword)	Shanna, Carla, Erica, Loring, Josh
2.	p. 16	"That blade looks very real to me, I want to wake up now"	Shanna, Carla, Erica, Loring, Josh
3.	p. 13	"So we're really not waiting for anyone, are we?"	Loring, Erica
4.	p. 9	"He wore his beaver up!"	Loring, Phil
5.	p. 8	"You could never have a lasting relationship with a maid"	Loring, Kate, Shanna
6.	p. 5	"My, this balcony looks dusty"	Shanna, Carla, Loring
7.	p. 4	"Tell me about Sibyl"	Shanna, Loring

Appendix 12

Sample Sound Concept Themes and Bridges

Better Living by George Walker

The concept developed out of the discovery that a particular piece of music I was listening to and was very attracted to for the thematic tone of the play was written by Leonard Cohen, who is a Canadian, as is George Walker. I don't know why this particular serendipity tickled my fancy, but it did and the music had a lovely urban darkness of tone that I felt served the play well. As I explored, I found the entire soundtrack could very easily come from Leonard Cohen's music. I like to provide a connection with the music I use and often using multiple pieces by the same artist will help provide that connection. Here is the list of pieces used which I felt would easily communicate a theme.

Better Living Sound List

Cues

1. Theme: Don Henley – "Everybody Knows" by Leonard Cohen
2. Scene 1–2 Bridge: Leonard Cohen – "Anthem"
3. Scene 2–3 Bridge: Leonard Cohen – "Why Don't You Try"
4. Scene 3–4 Bridge: Leonard Cohen – "The Future"
5. Scene 4–5 Bridge: Leonard Cohen – "Waiting for the Miracle"
6. Scene 5–Intermission: Don Henley – "Everybody Knows"
7. Act II Theme: Leonard Cohen – "Everybody Knows"
8. Scene 6–7 Bridge: Leonard Cohen – "Be for Real"
9. Scene 7–8 Bridge: Leonard Cohen – "Democracy"
10. Scene 8–9 Bridge: Leonard Cohen – "First We Take Manhattan"
11. Scene 9–10 Bridge: Leonard Cohen – "A Singer Must Die"
12. Scene 10–end: Leonard Cohen – "Always"

Sample of a Sound Chart for *Dracula* by Brahm Stoker, Adapted for the Stage by Stephen Deitz

Note: Almost all of the music was selected from the copious works of a group called "Nox Arcana". Nox Arcana is the American dark neoclassical, dark ambient musical project of Joseph Vargo. The name in Latin translates to "mysteries of the night". Their music is generally classified as dark neoclassical or dark ambient, and aptly labeled "atmospheric gothic". The moods associated with Nox Arcana music describe it as ominous, romantic, lush, epic, otherworldly, menacing, spooky and eerie.

Act I *Dracula* Sound Chart

No.	Description	Cue	Page
1.	Theme	As house out (plays under Renfield)	3
2.	Manic Laughter w. Screaming	"Renfield lifts the cover"	3
3.	Door slam (cuts off all other sound)	Light shift to bedroom	3
4.	Clock ticking	Mina writes in notebook	5
5.	Bell tolling, trees rustling	Light shift to Harker	8
6.	Crashing waves	Maid opens window	9
7.	Wolves howling in distance	Light shift to Harker	9
8.	Thunder crash	"Renfield!"	11
9.	Bird (sparrow chirping)	Renfield looking in cage	11
10.	Thunder crash	"My master told me"	14
11.	Music (ominous)	Red eyes appear	14
12.	Bats shrieking/Doors slamming	Light on Harker	14
13.	Storm rages (runs under)	"I dare not think of …"	15
14.	Wolf howl	Lights up on Lucy asleep in the bed	15
15.	Wicked crack of thunder	Lucy writhes against the w	15
16.	Howl of wolf	Mina places the robe around Lucy's shoulders	15
17.	Huge thunder crack	"Bind him Now!"	17
18.	Eerie Laughter (in place of ringing)	Lights up on Harker	17
19.	Severe crack of thunder	"I am a prisoner!"	17

20.	Mix of storm/bats/wolves/laughter	Lights up on Harker	17
21.	Storm and sounds crescendo	"The master is at hand!"	18
22.	Sound snaps out	Lights up DC on box	18
23.	Music with wind (stormy sea)	After lights snap out on box	18
24.	Wind fades out	"Good day"	20
25.	Beautiful church bell	"And then …"	22
26.	Music Dracula theme (from cue 11)	Lights shift downstage	25
27.	Music fades	Dracula leaves	26
28.	Clock chiming midnight (grandfather)	Lights shift to bedroom	27
29.	Wolf howl (near)	After clock	27
30.	Wolf howl (very near)	Lucy opens window	27
31.	Music: Dracula theme	"I share his diagnosis"	27
32.	Music snaps out	As lights snap out	28
33.	Voice over: Dracula	"The attendant turns and looks at Renfield"	29
34.	Low musical rumble	After Harker is pulled from room	34
35.	large Wings flapping	Mina slumps to the floor	34
36.	Huge door opening	Mina opens the journal	35
37.	Music: castle theme	Auto-follows door slam	35
38.	Cock crow	"too precious to be spilt"	38
39.	Cock crow repeat	"You would better understand"	38
40.	Wolf howl long and plaintive	Harker prepares to shave	39
41.	Wolf howl	Harker holds up mirror	39
42.	Wolf howl	Dracula's eyes close	39
43.	Wolf howl	"Please allow me"	40
44.	Wolves howling	Dracula tilts Harker's head	40
45.	Huge door slamming	Dracula stumbles away	40
46.	Wolves howling volume increases	Dracula licks the razor	40

No.	Description	Cue	Page
47.	High ringing sound	"Do tell me the name again"	41
48.	Sound of distant digging	"And it's location?"	41
49.	Digging louder	"How can that be?"	41
50.	Tension building music	"Here is the deed"	42
51.	Bats shrieking	Holds pen out to Harker	42
52.	Wolves join the bats	"Finish what you started"	42
53.	Music ends	"rewarded ten-fold"	42
54.	Doors slamming shut, being bolted	"ALL the doors!"	43
55.	Ringing sound	Extends his fingers toward Harker's eyes	43
56.	Ringing ends	"Oh Mina"	44
57.	Pounding heart	"I must know it all!"	44
58.	Heartbeat ends	HOW DARE YOU!"	45
59.	Music: Dracula theme	"HE IS MINE!!!"	45
60.	Crying baby	"Are we to have nothing tonight?"	45
61.	Music: Dracula theme swells	Vixens pounce on baby	46
62.	Music: Dracula theme crescendos	"I AM BOUND FOR ENGLAND!"	46
63.	Box slams shut	Dracula lowers himself into box, black-out	46
64.	Large flapping wings	Mina, still crying, raises her head	46
65.	Storm sea wind and water sounds	Lights out (plays through intermission)	46

Act II *Dracula* Sound Chart

No.	Description	Cue	Page
66.	Wind out, crossfades with theme	House out	47
67.	Music – Renfield	"I don't know what I've become"	53
68.	Boys choir – funereal	"Remember that"	56
69.	Lucy – Vampire music	"Oh Johnny, don't cry"	58

70.	Lucy's music ends	"NOT FOR YOUR LIFE"	59
71.	Bell tolls mournfully	"I swear on it"	60
72.	Voice over – Dracula	Attendant leaves	63
73.	Dracula theme	"Rats"	63
74.	Whip strikes flesh	"What to eat the DOGS!"	63
75.	Pack of wolves howling	"THE WOLVES!"	64
76.	All sounds stop	"BID ME ENTER"	64
77.	Thunder crash	"ENTER!"	64
78.	Music – ominous and building	Harker leaves	66
79.	Large door opening/hissing rattling snakes	Mina closes the drapes	66
80.	Door slams shut, sounds stop	Mina disappears into the window seat	66
81.	Thunder clap	"IT SHALL NOT STAND"	66
82.	Low rumbling music	Auto-follow thunder	66
83.	In sequence, rustle of branches, child screams, howl of wolf	WHAT HAVE YOU DONE WITH HER!"	67
84.	Rumbling music stops	"I COULD KILL YOU MYSELF!"	69
85.	Burning and sizzling sounds	Van H. drops the host into the tomb	70
86.	Angelic choir	Harker lifts the Bible	70
87.	Anvil clang	"Father"	71
88.	Anvil clang	"And of the Son"	71
89.	Anvil clang	"And of the Holy Ghost"	71
90.	Bell tolling mournfully	Lucy cries out	71
91.	Thunder clap	"Mina"	72
92.	Strange, high-pitched sound	Renfield's eyes pop open	72
93.	Huge tree snapping in two	"Make a wish!"	73
94.	High pitched sound fades	"MASTER!"	73
95.	Music – ominous	"Professor?"	75
96.	Music out	"evil grows richest in a soul most pure"	75
97.	Glass window breaking	"She's no strength at all"	77

98.	Music – building tension	"Move her to the bed"	77
99.	Music builds	"YOU MUST GO!"	79
100.	Single violin note-sting	"someone come quickly"	79
101.	Violin sting again	"SERVE YOU THROUGH THE AGES!"	79
102.	Violin sting again	"MORE DEEPLY THAN SHE!"	80
103.	Manic violin segment	"a holy –"	80
104.	Sickening crack of bone (may be live)	Dracula twists Renfield's head	80
105.	Music – Dracula theme	Licks the spilt blood from her arm	82
106.	Wolf howl	Dracula bites her neck	82
107.	Music stops	"You will cross oceans of time"	82
108.	Music	"Your sanctuaries have been destroyed"	83
109.	Crack of thunder	Crucifix is thrown to the side	84
110.	Voice over – Dracula	Dracula disappears through the window seat	84
111.	Wolf pack howling	With the voice over	84
112.	Giant wings flapping	"he has not been heard"	84
113.	All sounds fade	"disappearing"	85
114.	Crack of thunder, then wind and rain – plays under for a long time	"The lair of the Count!"	87
115.	Train whistle	"aboard the orient express"	88
116.	Waves against a ship	"the sound of the waves"	88
117.	Ship creaking	"searching the ship"	89
118.	Rushing river	"a softer sound"	89
119.	Rushing river	"following the Count's ship"	91
120.	Horses galloping, pulling a wagon	"Professor and I by wagon"	91
121.	Ship boards creaking	"the Count's boat heading for shore"	91
122.	Horses galloping w. wagon	"no driver at its head"	92
123.	Horses galloping w/o wagon	"we give chase"	92
124.	Sounds cease	"the object of our chase"	92

125.	Strange music	"NOW MR. HARKER –"	93
126.	Hissing rattling, breathing	with the strange music	93
127.	Violent Music crash	"It will not stop them now!"	94
128.	Gigantic clang (anvil?)	"NNNNNNNNNNOOOOOOOO!!!!!!!!"	96
129.	Music fades	after the burst of red vapor	96
130.	Heavenly music	"Makes us better than we are."	97
131.	Voice over – Dracula	Mina lifts the knife	97
132.	Rush of wind with great musical sting	She plunges the knife	97
133.	Wind and music fades away	Mina steps back	97
134.	Church bell tolling – mournful	"rightfully joined in his name"	97
135.	Distant boys choir	"cycle of vengeance"	98
136.	Church bells (wedding)	"a living truth"	98
137.	Curtain call music	Joins wedding bells	98
138.	Music fades for Renfield's epilogue	Renfield asks for quiet	98
139.	Music returns for rest of curtain call	"Sweet Dreams!"	98

Appendix 13

A Sample Sound Concept

After the Fall by Arthur Miller

Note: This is a description of the beginning and ending sound concepts for Arthur Miller's *After the Fall*. The concept was so crucial to the thrust of this production and my vision of it, that I have reproduced the notes I made for the way the beginning and the ending musical cues frame the piece. I include this example here in order to attempt to communicate the power of interpretation that a director can wield with something so simple as a carefully envisioned soundtrack.

> At rise we hear the sound of an emergency room heart monitor with its distinctive rhythmic beeping. This continues for a minute and then begins to flatline with a steady tone. This tone segues into the tone of a single child's voice singing a single tone which then becomes liturgical choir music.
>
> A number of shadowy figures enter and take positions at almost random spots throughout the stage. These are: Dan, Father and Mother downstage left (Mother in center); Lou, Mickey and Elsie behind center wall platform; Louise down right; Felice under center overhang; Jill, Jaclyn, Paige, Shanna, Loring, Josh, Evan, and Dominic, up right in a "surgery tableau" dressed in ER scrubs with face masks. Backlit shadow of Maggie behind screen in a "glamour" pose.
>
> Quentin appears far up right, coming from behind the "surgery tableau" and slowly wends his way downstage, stopping to take in almost every one of the frozen figures on the stage before noticing the audience for the first time and coming downstage center to speak to them.
>
> QUENTIN: Hello! God it's good to see you again! I'm fine! I just wanted to say hello, really. Thanks. Actually, I called you on the spur of the moment this morning, I have a bit of a decision to make. (*Lights go out on the "surgical" team and they exit*)

Skip to end.

QUENTIN: But what will defend her? (*He points up at Holga*) That woman hopes! Or is that ... (*Turns to the audience again*) exactly why she hopes, because she knows? What burning cities taught her and the death of love taught me ... that we are ... all ... very... dangerous! And that, that's why I wake each morning like a boy ... even now, even now! I swear to you, I could love the world again! Is the knowing all? To know, and even happily, that we meet unblessed; not in some garden of wax fruit and painted trees, that lie of EDEN, but after ... after the fall, after many, many deaths. Is the knowing all? And the wish to kill is never killed, but with some gift of courage one may look into its face when it appears, and with a stroke of love ... as to an idiot child ... forgive it; again, and again ... forever? (*He is evidently interrupted by the listener*) No, it's not certainty, I don't feel that. But it does seem feasible ... not to be afraid. Perhaps it's all one has. I'll tell her that. Yes, she will, she'll know what I mean. (*He turns upstage and all his people face him. He walks toward Louise, the ex-wife, pausing, she stares him down defiantly. He goes toward Mother, Father and Dan, his brother, and waves and they all wave back, smiling as if seeing him off at the train station. He crosses center and the pretty girl is about to raise her hand in blessing but he catches it and embraces her instead. He crosses behind the bed and looks down sadly at Maggie (the Marilyn Monroe character), who lies there inert. He walks upstage out of sight as the people of his life close in, moving toward the high platform. As he disappears, we hear the heart monitor coming to life again with its single "flatline" tone, which then bumps up into a steady beeping. Quentin appears on the platform behind Holga who doesn't see him. He puts his hands over her eyes from behind in the classic "guess who" pose. She turns and delightedly says)*

HOLGA: Hello! (He holds her arms out and says)

QUENTIN: Hello. (They embrace, the music swells with something triumphant under the beeping, drowning it out as the lights fade)

The framing of the play with the heart monitor sound effect and music was an attempt to symbolically show the audience that Quentin had "died" on the operating table at the beginning of the play and that everything that transpired until the end was done in a state of "limbo" while he struggles with the question of whether or not to go on with his life. At the end, he decides that he can go on and the heart monitor returns with a rhythmic beating. I thought the whole thing was a bit melodramatic and was afraid the audience would find it so, but was pleasantly surprised when they reacted to it with understanding and emotion. I felt it helped to make sense of the play for the audience.

Appendix 14

A Sample Blocking Groundplan

Blocking Groundplans

A blocking groundplan simply shows the set as viewed from above and shows the location of all the pertinent set props, at least those that will be utilized in blocking. It's a good idea to keep the drawing fairly simple and small (to fit on a sheet of copy paper) as you may want to copy it on the facing page of each page of script, or at least keep it to hand while envisioning the blocking of the play. Here are a couple of blocking groundplans with blocking arrows showing movement by character. With large casts I don't try to use the arrows, just notations in the script and generally coins on the groundplan itself to give me a visual for who moves where. The notation in your script should be sufficient to allow you to give blocking to the actors. The stage manager should have a duplicate of this and should work in pencil to be able to make changes as they occur. Ideally, the stage manager is the one who is the ultimate authority on script changes and blocking changes. A good stage manager is the one you turn to when you can't remember what was done yesterday. If you don't have a stage manager, or have one who doesn't know the job, then you will have to do this yourself. There is a danger in having your nose buried in the script all the time, as it precludes your ability to see what's happening at any given moment onstage. A good stage manager is worth their weight in gold and if anyone gets paid it should be them. The same applies to a good technical director but that's a conversation for another day. The groundplan shown here is for an original one-act play called *Arf* by Jerri Kunz (unpublished) which was done as a Master's qualifying production at the University of Texas in 1974. The B stands for the character named "Bubbie", the D stands for the character named "Doris", and the F stands for the character named "Freddie".

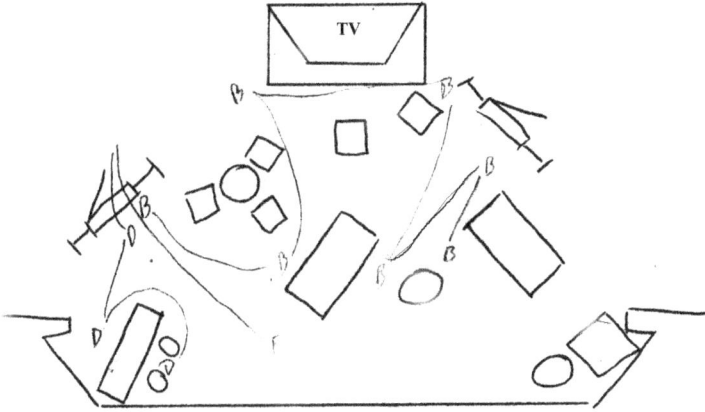

Figure A14.1 A Blocking Groundplan

Appendix 15

A Sample Blocking Script

A blocking script is simply a script with blocking notation entered into it. "C x's to DR" means that the character with the initial of "C" is "crossing" to the downstage right area. One can indicate how far by adding the number of steps involved or by giving a reference point such as "behind the armchair", or "to J", meaning the character with the initial "J". Often, to differentiate character initials, those are circled. Blocking notation should be easy to read and easy to give. Always note that stage directions are given to the actors from their point of view. If I tell an actor to move "left", I mean their left which would be my right. It can get confusing but it helps because you want to keep things as simple for the actors as possible. Not that they are stupid, but inexperienced people can get easily confused. I have seen actors' trip over painted lines. Speaking of which, when blocking on a stage where the set is not up, the groundplan should be laid down on the floor using tape. (If tape is not allowed, I have occasionally found it useful to use a groundcloth covering the available floor space upon which the groundplan has been marked.) The stage manager usually does this and should know how to translate the scale from paper to floor. I did a show set in Antarctica which had a large crevice in the very middle of it (*Terra Nova* by Ted Talley). We had to condition the actors to understand that, if they walked across a certain taped line on the floor, it meant they would fall 10 feet. We had them so tuned to this, that by the time we got onto the actual set, there were never any mishaps.

6

       Eric. *(E) x's to window L*
Sometime about mid-day I started to feel that something wasn't right and I went
looking for her. But of course, I had no place to even start looking. I didn't even
know her name. Over the next few days, I asked everyone I could if they had seen
her. No one had. - *sits chair L*
turns

       Manager. *M x's R w chair*
And so, after days of this, they brought you to me. *(He gets a funny look in his
eyes and pulls a chair closer to Eric.)* Now listen. I could lose my job for telling *sits*
you this. You're not the first one to see her. Over the years, we've had many
anguished young men just like you looking for her with much the same story. Sad,
gut-wrenching stories about how they had fallen in love with her and needed to
find her.

       Eric.
You mean?...

  stands   Manager.
Listen! There was a missing person case here about twenty years ago. A young
woman appeared in the lobby very early in the morning looking very lost and
(M x's to door R) distraught. The night man said he thought she left with another man but that it was
odd because she was only wearing her pajamas and a robe and was barefoot.
There was a search but it never turned up anything. We didn't even have a record
of her staying at the hotel. We figured she must have come in with a group. *(He is
getting choked up)* Ever since then she appears once in a while to some tortured *(M) x's to window L*
young man and spends some time with him and then... disappears.

     Eric. *stands*
My god! You've met her, haven't you?

  turns   Manager.
Yes..... Your story is my story. In fact, that's why I took the job here. I'm still
searching... searching. Night in and night out. Stories like yours do nothing but
remind me that she's still out there and she's searching for something too! I
want...need to get her back!   *(M) x's to (E) R*

     Eric. *puts hand*
There's one big difference between us. *on (M)'s shoulder*

Figure A15.1 A Blocking Script

Appendix 16

A Sample Master Movement Plan

This is a device that, as far as I know, was created by Dr. Francis Hodge, my directing teacher. After the paper blocking was done, he had us overlay *all* of the blocking groundplans and mark *all* of the stage movements on the same empty groundplan. This gave one an excellent idea of how much of the stage was being utilized and one could instantly see what areas were being under-used. His philosophy was that a show that is being done on a single set for two or three hours, needs fresh compositions and movement variations to hold an audience's interest. Obviously, shows involving multiple sets don't have this problem as much. Here is an example. The design was mine. It's a diagnostic tool.

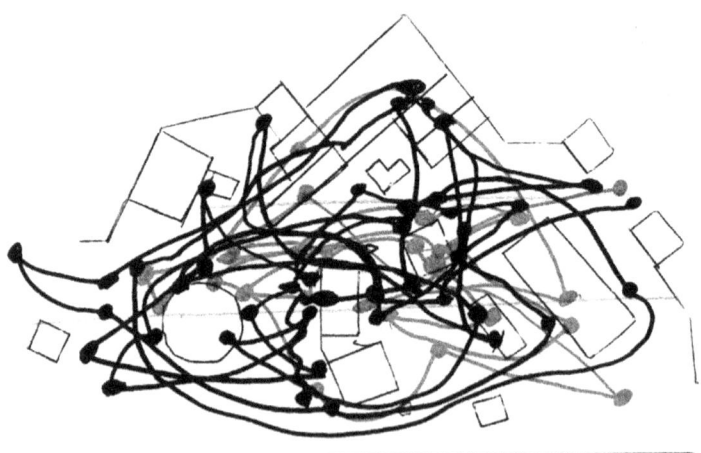

Figure A16.1 A Master Movement Plan

Appendix 17
A Sample Groundplan

A groundplan becomes the basis for all of the blocking which is the organic tool for the illustration of the action. There should never be any arbitrary or random movement. A groundplan should be an "obstacle course" for the characters of the play to overcome in their striving to confront each other. Many times, this means actual physical obstacles on the stage. In addition, this offers many variables for interesting and fresh compositions. However, I have found that there are also psychological obstacles as well, which can often be illustrated by the use of set pieces (fireplaces, bookshelves, windows, televisions, etc.). These are not things that a character has to physically move around, but are things that can occupy their attention, thus delaying their progress across the stage. It is always a good idea to keep many of the obstacles free of the walls, which enables movement completely around them. This is not what one does when arranging a realistic room, but it is what one does when arranging a stage setting. I once tried an experiment where I rearranged the living room in my house according to the "obstacle course" principle. At the subsequent party, I found that people were often uncomfortable with the flow of movement within this grouping. That's good, because a stage setting should help to illustrate the kind of conflict that the play represents. An interesting side note is that many objects placed off center and at unusual angles helps to create tension, while a very symmetrical arrangement of furniture helps to formulate the kind of precision timing necessary for comedy. If you are doing a serious play with lots of conflict, put things off-kilter. There are complex psychological reasons for this, but trust me, it works.

Note: The groundplan shown here is a pencil sketch for the design for the play *Light up the Sky* by Moss Hart. This production was done in a black-box theatre configured for a thrust stage. The design is mine. The interesting thing is that it is a comedy, which is why there is a lot of symmetry present, but within the comedy, there is a lot of conflict, which is why nothing is ever parallel or perpendicular to anything else. In other words, both compositional principles are at work in this groundplan.

188 A Sample Groundplan

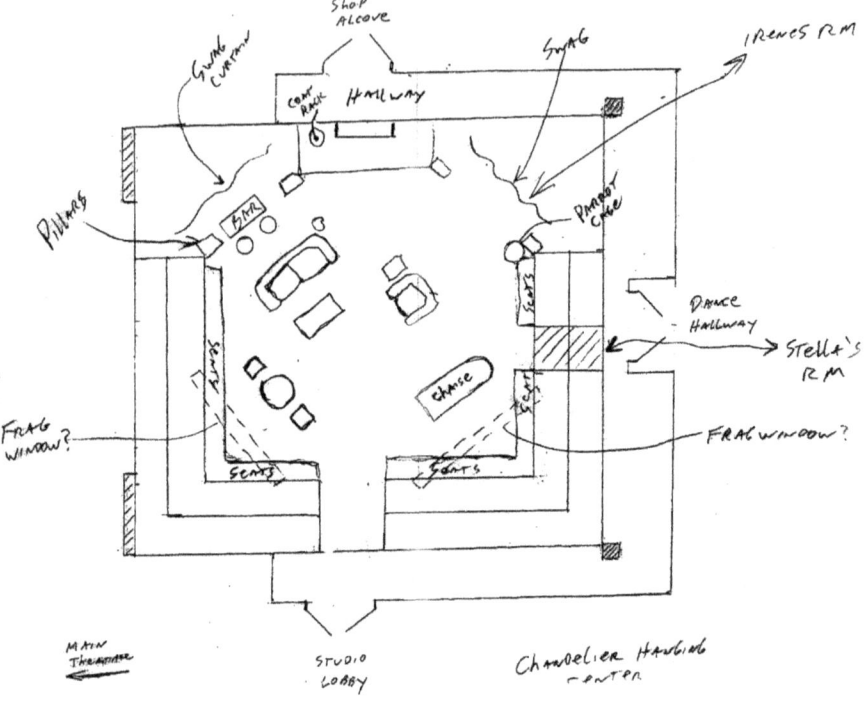

Figure A17.1 A Groundplan

Appendix 18
The Designer's Homework

Directors assume that designers have done their homework before they come to meet about the design. It certainly would not hurt for a designer to go through the entire "Environmental Facts" section of the play analysis as a key part of their homework. I have had initial conference with designers in which I strongly suspected that they hadn't read the play! One may not have the luxury of working with designers or at least not ones that have extensive training in that field. For that reason, I am including some basic information for designers to use in working with directors.

What follows is the kind of information and expectations that directors and designers may have for each other in their initial conferences concerning the play.

Basic Areas of Design

1. Choice of stage
    a. Proscenium
    b. Thrust
    c. Apron
    d. Arena
    e. Runway
    f. Unusual (odd configurations)
2. Scenery
3. Costumes
4. Lighting
5. Props
6. Sound
7. Make-up
8. Special effects
9. Projections. This is rapidly becoming a full-fledged area of design. With the development of LED projectors, many of the limitations of early projectors are being solved. One of these was the fact that even

rudimentary stage light tended to wash out projections so that they could not be seen well. Another development is the plethora of images available on the internet. This has led to new laws being drawn involving copyrights. One must be careful what one takes off the internet, even though it may be relatively easy to download. One of the first shows I did involving this new design area was a production of *Dracula*. I had a computer specialist and projection specialist working together and let them go. I would ask for things that I thought would be impossible, and they would give them to me. I wanted (as in one of the earliest movies of Dracula) the audience to see a bat flying past the windows of Mina's bedroom which then would appear to land on the balcony outside the windows and grow and morph into a human form. The windows would then open and Dracula would be revealed. Using the window curtains as projection screens, they gave me that very image. Another fun image they gave me was Dracula escaping by jumping out the window and turning into a giant bat which we then saw flying through the night sky, silhouetted against the moon. Another crucial moment was how the protagonists defeat Dracula when they find him at his castle at the end of the play. We staged a fight between Van Helsing, Dr. Seward, and the minions of Dracula. As Dracula himself appears, Dr. Seward appears to shoot the mullions out of the large skylight overhead that has been projecting its silhouette on the floor. As the mullions fly away, what is left is the shape of a large cross, whose shadow falls on Dracula, forcing him back to his coffin. It was, to say the least, spectacular.

Areas of Play Analysis (See Chapter #6)
1. Given circumstances, environmental facts, special world
2. Character
3. Action
4. Idea, themes
5. Moods, emotions.

First Concept Meeting

A. Everyone should have read the play before the meeting.
B. The rudimentary facts of the play as defined in the script:
   1. Number of characters in the play (number of costumes for each). Number of actors playing the characters.
   2. Entrances and exits. Only those actually called for by the script.
   3. Time and place of the play (including passage of time).
   4. Number of locations. Again, just what is called for in the script.
   5. Unusual props required.

6. Style of the play (comedy, tragedy, satire, farce, etc.).
7. Lighting indications (times of day mentioned, passages of time, general moods). *Note*: a close analysis of Macbeth reveals that a large portion of the play takes place at night.
8. Sound effects required (particularly unusual ones. *Heartbreak House* by George Bernard Shaw requires the sound of a zeppelin flying over).
9. Special make-up required.
10. Special effects indicated.

C. Discuss essences (possibly include visual material).
1. Themes
2. Characters
3. Dramatic action
4. Moods
5. Central metaphors.

Second Concept Meeting

A. Budgetary concerns.
B. Presentation of all visual ideas (sketches, photos, colors, paintings, etc.).
C. Preliminary decisions needed on:
1. Choice of stage
2. Scenic styles/concepts
3. Costume styles/concepts
4. Lighting styles/concepts
5. Sound style/concepts
   a. Effects
   b. Music
6. Make-up styles/concepts
7. Special effects.
D. Finalization of essences. By now, everyone should be on the same page regarding style/concepts, etc.

Final Concept Meeting: Formalize Decisions

Visual materials should be presented as well as developed sketches, drawings, groundplans, etc.

1. Groundplan
2. Scenery (nearly completed sketches/models)
3. Costumes (nearly completed sketches)
4. Lighting (mostly dealing with color and special needs at this point)
5. Sound concepts (theme music, scene bridges, stings, sound effects)

6. Make-up concepts (well-developed sketches, particularly if this is an area of special consideration – e.g. Aesop's *Fables* characters are almost all animals)
7. Special effects (this would include projections).

Final Design Meeting

All designs due. Finalized. Budgeted. Corrected. Finished visual material. Everyone should feel confident at this point about moving to the construction phase.

Note: These meetings are *very* important for getting everyone on the same page. I did a production of *A Midsummer Night's Dream* in which I brought the paintings of the illustrator Maxfield Parrish in for an early concept meeting. I was looking at the style of dress of the people in the paintings but somehow didn't manage to convey that to the scenic and costume designer. Later I kept getting the oddest stuff, all in pastel colors and then I came to the realization that they thought I was using the paintings as a color palette for the show. I distinctly remember saying that I thought Shakespeare had intended for the characters to be in Greek dress and there is much talk about "Athens". We finally did get together on our concepts. It definitely doesn't help that I am color blind and so color is not one of the things that I key on immediately.

Index

Note: *Italic* page numbers refer to figures.

8½ 49

acting exercises 95–100
action 102; as playwright's tool 104; unit 39–40; verbs 38, 39
actor–managers 25
Actors' Equity Association 122
Actor's Nightmare, The (Durang) 108
aesthetic distance 71
After the Fall (Miller) 3, 37, 41; sample of character analysis for 136–143; sample of dialogue analysis for 144–149; sample of given circumstances analysis for 127–131; sample of idea analysis for 132–135; sample of scene chart in 153; sample sound concept in 180–181
aggressive motion, as movement 88
Agnes of God (Pielmeier) 33
Albee, Edward 42
All My Sons (Miller) 25, 135
All That Jazz (Fosse) 11
American College Theatre Festival 85
Anderson, Lori 60
arena theatre 71, 90, 92–93
Arf (Kunz) 182
Aristotle 102
audition: forms 54–55, 158–162; notes, of actors 53–54; scenes 52–53; time, place, and schedule of 53

backstage rules, of behavior 116–118
balance and design 68
balance–wrestling exercise 97–98
Baltimore Waltz, The (Vogel) 22, 25
Barefoot in the Park (Simon) 41, 104
Barry Lyndon (Kubrick) 2, 59
Barton, Lucy 59

Becket, Samuel 25
Better Living 60, 173–178
Big Bang Theory, The 81
black box theatre 71
blank mind, onstage 109–110
blocking 7–8, 12–14, 30, 79; groundplan 57, 182, *183*; as means to communicate to audience 13; movement and 90, 91, 93; pre-planning of 23; script, sample of *184*, *185*; technique for 89; for thrust and arena stages 92–93; types of 13–14
body positions, for composition 82–83
box set 72
Bratter, Corrie 41
bridges and sound design 73
Brokaw, John 1

Camille (Dumas) 2
Cat and Mouse exercise 88–89, 100
catharsis, as essential for dramatic work 102–103
character: analysis of 43–44, 136–143; biography of 44–47; personal connection with 48; as playwright's tool 103–104; scene chart sample and 153; sketches, sample of 168–170; summary adjectives of 44, 142–143; synthesis of 48, 142
Chase, Mary 57
Christmas Carol, A (Dickens) 35, 61
cinematic style 105
cleaned scripts, use of 30–31
climactic composition 85
Clurman, Harold 41
Cohen, Leah Hager 6, 119
Cohen, Leonard 60, 173
color: design and 67; lighting design and 77
Coming to Terms with Acting (Moston) 116

composition, as visual tool 82; body positions for 82–83; climactic 85; diagonals for 84; focus types and 83–84; furniture use for 85–86; repetition and support for 84–85; space and mass for 84; stage areas for 85; triangles for 84
conflict, as essential for dramatic work 102
contextual structure 105
contract, on behavior 114–115
costumes: design 75–76; notes and production organization 58–59
Coward, Noel 56
crew view 55
Crucible, The 135
cues 16, 112, 117, 173; importance of 16–17; light 76; sound 74–75; technical 18
cummings, e. e. 60

decorum 86
Deitz, Stephen 174
design: conferences 22, 69–70; execution 70
designers, homework of 189–192; for basic areas 189–190; for play analysis areas 190–192
designers, process of 69–72
determinism, theory of 26
diagonal principle 81, 84
dialogue 36; analysis, sample of 144–149; images and metaphors for 38; pauses and silences for 37, 149; phrase choice for 37, 146–149; as playwright's tool 103; unusual characteristics for 38, 149; word choice for 36–37, 144–146
Dickens, Charles 35
directors 109; as authority on script 30; design and 65–77; duties of 21–25; ethics and behavior and 111–115, 117, 118; functions of 21; history of 25–26; importance of 21; play analysis and 31, 37, 38, 39, 43, 49, 50; production organization and 52, 55, 56, 58–61, 63; stage manager and 122–124; vision of 22; visual tools and 79, 82, 85, 86, 87, 92–93
distribution and lighting design 76
diversity 119–121
Doll's House, A (Ibsen) 121
Doubt (Shanley) 33
Dracula 190; character sketches of 168–170; sound chart of 174–179
dramatic action: analysis, sample of 150–152; significance of 39–40; unit divisions and 40–43
Dramatists Play Service 56

dress rehearsals 18–19, 24
Dumas, Alexandre 2
Durang, Christopher 108, 172

economic environment and facts 32, 128
emotion: and action, relationship between 39; as essential for dramatic work 102
emotional memory 26
emotional reinforcement 73–74
empathy, as essential for dramatic work 102
Endgame (Becket) 25
environmental theatre 71
ethics and behavior 111; honoring of responsibilities and 111–114; Internet suggestions and 114–118
extremes, acting exercise 99

facts, for play analysis: environment types and 32–33; environmental 31–32, 127–129; polar attitudes and 35, 130; previous action and 34–35, 130; special world and 131; spine and 35–36; summary and 34; time and 32
Fairy Tales (Grimms) 61
first reading 10–12
first time, concept of 42
focus: concept of 82; design and 68; sharing of 84; types of 83–84
Foley artist 74
Forbidden Broadway 74
forcing, concept of 40
Fosse, Bob 11
fourth wall 71
Frayn, Michael 2, 57
Frazier 81
"French Scene" 39
French, Samuel 56
Friends 81
furniture use, for composition 85–86

geographic analysis, for play analysis 31–32
Gielgud, John 95
Goldman, James 33, 39, 42, 66
Grebenshikov, Boris 60
Grimms 61
groundplan 79, 89, 90; blocking 57, 182, *183*; rules to create 80–82; sample of 187, *188*
Guare, John 12

hand props 56
hands on, acting exercise 97
Hart, Moss 73, 187
Harvey (Chase) 57
Heartbreak House (Shaw) 74, 191

Hedda Gabler (Ibsen) 32, 33, 41
Historic Costume for the Stage (Barton) 59
Hodge, Francis 1, 28, 79, 186
House of Blue Leaves, The (Guare) 12

Ibsen, Henrik 32, 33, 121
idea analysis, sample of 48–49; philosophical statements and 48, 134–135; quotations and 48, 132–133; title meaning and 48, 133–134
images and metaphors, for dialogue 38
Indians (Kopit) 59
Inherit the Wind (Lawrence and Lee) 29, 35
Inspecting (Sullivan) 2
intensity and lighting design 76
Ionesco, Eugene 58, 61

Kopit, Arthur 59
Kubrick, Stanley 2, 59
Kunz, Jerri 182

Lawrence, Jerome 29, 35
League of Resident Theatres 119
Lee, Robert E. 29, 35
Leno, Jay 5
levels and composition 83
life and death intensity, idea of 41, 42
Light Up the Sky 73, 187
lighting: design and 76–77; production organization and 59
line and design 67–68
Lion in Winter, The (Goldman) 33, 39, 42, 66, 86
Love Actually 105–106

magic If 44
make 'em laugh, acting exercise 99
make-up and production organization 60–61
mass and design 68
master movement plan 89, 186
Medoff, Mark 65
melodrama, acting exercise 98
memorization 16–17, 107–110
Mercury Theatre 74
Method of Physical Action 7, 26, 79
Midsummer Night's Dream, A 61
Miller, Arthur 3, 25, 37, 41
Mockba 60
modeling and lighting design 77
Moll, James 1
mood and lighting design 77
Moonchildren (Weller) 33
Moscow Art Theatre 10, 60, 73

Moston, Doug 116
movement 88–89; lighting design and 76; of playwright 89–90; significance of 7; speaking and 8; stillness and 8; types of 88; variables of 90–91
Mrs. Warren's Profession (Shaw) 58
multiple-scene plays 82

Nancarrow, David 1
Newman, Danny 61
Night Mother (Norman) 65
Night That Panicked America, The 74
Noises Off (Frayn) 2, 57
Norman, Marsha 65
Nox Arcana 174

obsession, significance of 5–6
obstacle course 80–81, 187
off book, being 112
Olivier, Laurence 95
open space theatre 72
opposites of chosen emotion, acting exercise 98
organic blocking 12, 13–14

Pace, Chelsea 119
page visualization 108
Parrish, Maxfield 192
pauses and silences, for dialogue 37, 149
phobias 108
photocall lists, sample of 171–172
phrase choice, for dialogue 37, 146–149
physicality 7
physicalization 7, 12, 13, 15, 43, 79
picturization, as visual tool 87–88
Pielmeier, John 33
Pinter, Harold 37
planes and composition 83
play analysis: character and 43–48; dialogue and 36–38; dramatic action and 38–43; facts for 31–36; homework for areas of 190–192; ideas with 48–49; prep and 28; reading of play and 28–29; script preparation and 29–31; synthesis of 50
Play Directing (Hodge) 28, 79
playwright 15, 36, 58, 95; history of 25; play analysis and 29, 34, 35; script requirements and 59; tools of 103–106; working methodologies of 104–105
playwriting: importance of 101; structure of 105
plots 69, 70, 103, 104; simple and complex 105; sound 74–75

ploys, shifting of 39
Poetics (Aristotle) 102
pointing 90
polar attitudes and play analysis 35
polishing, of rehearsals 17
political environment 33, 128–129
political theatre 72
Powell, Jerry Rollins 1
pre-blocking 79
presentational theatre 71
pre-show music and sound design 73–74
previous action and play analysis 34–35
production organization: auditions and 52–55; costume notes and 58–59; lighting and 59; make-up and 60–61; programs and 62–63; props and 56–57; publicity and 61–62; rehearsal schedules and 55, 154–157; scenery and 57–58; sound and 59–60
programs and production organization 62–63
projected scenery 72
promptbook 91–92
proportion and design 68
props 113; hand 56; sample of 163–167; set 56–57
proscenium arch theatre 70–71, 83, 92
publicity and production organization 61–62

reading, of play 28–29
Real Inspector Hound, The (Tom Stoppard) 34
realism 26
realistic exterior 72
realistic interior *see* box set
reciprocation 7
rehearsal 10; blocking of 12–14; dress 18–19, 24; first reading as 10–12; memorization of 16–17; performance and 19; polishing of 17; technical 18, 23; working of 14–16
rehearsal schedules: production organization and 55; samples of 154–157
Reinhardt, Paul 1
religious environment 33, 129
repetition and support, for composition 84–85
representational theatre 71
retreating motion, as movement 88
Rhinocerous, The (Ionesco) 58, 61
rhythm and design 68
Richardson, Ralph 95
Rikard, Laura 119
role switching, acting exercise 99
Romeo and Juliet 49

rote repetition 108
Rothgeb, John 1
running lines technique 108

sample sound concept themes and bridges 173–179
Savoy Theatre, London 76
Saxe-Meiningen, Duke of 25–26
scene objective 41–42
scenery and production organization 57–58
scenic design, choices in 72
script preparation 29–31
selective focus and lighting design 77
set props 56–57
Shanley, John Patrick 33
Shaw, George Bernard 37, 58, 59, 74, 191
silent running thorough the script, acting exercise 96–97
Simon, Neil 104
singing of lines, acting exercise 98
six-foot rule 80
sketches and design conferences 69
Smalley, Webster 1
social environment and 33, 129
sound: design 3, 73–75; effects 59–60, 73, 74, 181, 191; plot 74–75; and production organization 59–60; reinforcement 73
space and mass, for composition 84
Spinal Tap 69
spine 35–36; *see also* super objective
stage areas, for composition 85
stage directions, as playwright's tool 103
stage manager 16–17, 31, 112, 182; auditioning and 52–53; duties of 123–124; importance of 122–123; movement written by 89; production book checklist for 124–125; promptbook and 91–92; rehearsal kit inventory of 125–126
Staging Sex (Pace and Rikard) 119
Stanislavski, Constantin 7, 10, 26, 40–41, 79
Star Wars 74
stasis 88
Stewart, Michael 2
stillness, importance of 8
Stoppard, Tom 34
stream-of-consciousness technique 36, 127, 132, 138, 149
Streetcar Named Desire, A (Williams) 121
Stuff of Dreams, The (Cohen) 6, 119
Subscribe Now (Newman) 61
subtext speaking, acting exercise 99–100
Sullivan, Daniel 2

summary: adjectives, of character 44, 142–143; and play analysis 34
super objective 40–41; *see also* spine
synthesis 48, 50, 142

table read *see* first reading
Talley, Ted 184
technical rehearsals 18, 23
tension creation, on stage 81
Terra Nova (Talley) 184
textual evidence, for character 43, 138–142
texture and design 68
theatre space, choice of 70–72
theatrical design: costume design and 75–76; designer's process and 69–72; elements of 67–68; goals of 65–66; lighting design and 76–77; principles of 68–69; sound design and 73–75
thematic plays 106
themes and sound design 73
Think Twice Before You Think 60
Those That Play the Clowns (Stewart) 2
thrust theatre 71, 90, 92–93
time factor, for play analysis 32
triangles, for composition 84
two-dimensional painted scenery 72

underscoring and sound design 73
unit: divisions 40–43; set 72

unity and design 68–69
unusual characteristics, for dialogue 38, 149

Vargo, Joseph 174
visibility and lighting design 77
vision development, for production 2
visual tools 79–80; blocking for thrust and arena and 92–93; composition as 82–86; gesture as 86–87; groundplan as 80–82; movement as 88–91; picturization as 87–88; promptbook as 91–92; properties as 87
Vogel, Paula 22, 25
voice overs, acting exercise 96

Waiting For Godot 76
Walker, George F. 60, 173
War of the Worlds 74
Weller, Michael 33
Welles, Orson 74
When Ya Comin' Back Red Ryder (Medoff) 65
Who's Afraid of Virginia Woolf? (Albee) 42
Williams, Tennessee 103, 121
wing-and-drop scenery *see* two-dimensional painted scenery
word choice, for dialogue 36–37, 144–146
work-throughs 14–16

Taylor & Francis eBooks

www.taylorfrancis.com

A single destination for eBooks from Taylor & Francis with increased functionality and an improved user experience to meet the needs of our customers.

90,000+ eBooks of award-winning academic content in Humanities, Social Science, Science, Technology, Engineering, and Medical written by a global network of editors and authors.

TAYLOR & FRANCIS EBOOKS OFFERS:

- A streamlined experience for our library customers
- A single point of discovery for all of our eBook content
- Improved search and discovery of content at both book and chapter level

REQUEST A FREE TRIAL
support@taylorfrancis.com

For Product Safety Concerns and Information please contact our EU representative GPSR@taylorandfrancis.com
Taylor & Francis Verlag GmbH, Kaufingerstraße 24, 80331 München, Germany

www.ingramcontent.com/pod-product-compliance
Lightning Source LLC
Chambersburg PA
CBHW050535300426
44113CB00012B/2118